A Panorama of American Film Noir

1941–1953

D0802346

A Panorama of American Film Noir
1941–1953

Raymond Borde and Etienne Chaumeton

Introduction by James Naremore
Translated from the French by Paul Hammond

City Lights Books
San Francisco

10 9 8 7 6 5 4 3 2 1

Cover design and photo: Stefan Gutermuth/double-u-gee
Book design and typography: Small World Productions
Editor and indexer: James Brook
Special thanks to Nancy Goldman and Philippe Garnier for their expert assistance.

This work, published as part of the program of aid for publication, received support from the French Ministry of Foreign Affairs and the Cultural Service of the French Embassy in the United States. Cet ouvrage publié dans le cadre du programme d'aide à la publication bénéficie du soutien du Ministère des Affaires Etrangères et du Service Culturel de l'Ambassade de France représenté aux Etats-Unis.

Borde, Raymond.
   [Panorama du film noir américain. English]
   A panorama of American film noir (1941-1953) / by Raymond Borde and Etienne Chaumeton ; translated from the French by Paul Hammond.
      p. cm.
   ISBN 0-87286-412-X (pbk.)
   1. Film noir--United States--History and criticism. I. Chaumeton, Étienne. II. Hammond, Paul, 1947 July 19- III. Title.
   PN1995.9.F54 B67 2002
   791.43'.655--dc21
                              2002073843

CITY LIGHTS BOOKS are edited by Lawrence Ferlinghetti and Nancy J. Peters and published at the City Lights Bookstore, 261 Columbus Avenue, San Francisco, CA 94133. Visit us on the Web at www.citylights.com.

Contents

A Season in Hell or the Snows of Yesteryear?

James Naremore

In the long history of French commentary on American culture, Raymond Borde and Etienne Chaumeton's *A Panorama of American Film Noir* occupies a special place. The first book ever written about a type of film for which Hollywood itself had no name, *Panorama* influenced cineastes of the late twentieth century in almost the same way as Charles Baudelaire's essays on Edgar Allan Poe influenced the literary world of the late nineteenth century. It gave identity and cachet to scores of pictures that might otherwise have been forgotten and in the process helped to establish what today's movie industry regards as a fully fledged genre. None of the many writers on film noir after Borde and Chaumeton has not been indebted to their book in some fashion (even if she or he hasn't read *Panorama*, which until now has never been completely translated into English), and few works of criticism in any field have had such a seminal effect on both scholars and artists.

Not the least of the reasons why *Panorama* remains an important book is the fact that it was written by a pair of intelligent, discerning viewers who were contemporary with the films under discussion. The first two editions were published in the 1950s, in direct response to a series of hard-boiled thrillers and bloody melodramas—beginning with John Huston's somewhat campy but sinister *The Maltese Falcon* (1941) and culminating with Robert Aldrich's jagged, apocalyptic *Kiss Me Deadly* (1955)— that Hollywood had been producing with some regularity for about fifteen years. Although many of these the films were redolent of pre–Second World War European cinema, Borde and

Chaumeton regarded them almost entirely as products of their country of origin, shaped by the Hollywood system of production and expressive of the quotidian violence and criminality of American life. A handful of commentators in America had already agreed with this idea, at least to a degree. In 1946, the German cultural critic Siegfried Kracauer, who had moved to the United States because of the war, wrote a think piece for *Commentary* magazine on the question of "Hollywood's Terror Films: Do They Reflect a State of Mind?" Having recently completed *From Caligari to Hitler,* a celebrated book about Weimar cinema, Kracauer argued that recent Hollywood pictures such as *Shadow of a Doubt* (1942), *The Lost Weekend* (1945), *The Stranger* (1946), and *The Spiral Staircase* (1946) were similar to certain German films of the 1920s and were symptomatic of a growing, American-style decadence.[1] Not long afterward, John Houseman offered his own version of the same argument in *Vogue,* implicitly criticizing one of his former collaborators, Raymond Chandler (*The Blue Dahlia* [1946]), for pandering to the American zeitgeist by means of "tough" movies about "a land of enervated, frightened people with spasms of vitality but a low moral sense."[2] What made Borde and Chaumeton different from Kracauer and Houseman was that, in common with most of their French colleagues, they didn't react in a tone of moral panic. On the contrary, they were fascinated by the perverse eroticism of postwar Hollywood thrillers. In their view, such pictures functioned as a critique of savage capitalism and a realistic, or at any rate fairly truthful, antidote to the social uplift in the average studio-manufactured daydream.

Because they were French, Borde and Chaumeton also had a good term to apply to the films they admired. The adjective "noir" had long been used in France to describe the Gothic novel, and in the 1930s it was sometimes employed in descriptions of French "poetic realist" films such as *Pépé le Moko* (1937) and *Le Jour se lève* (1939). It was best known in relation to the "Série noire," a series of crime novels that Gallimard (from 1945 until now) issued in paperback editions as *littérature de la gare,* or "train-station literature." The black-and-yellow-covered

Gallimard books appealed to a wide range of readers, and under the astute editorship of Marcel Duhamel they offered lively French translations of the new wave of crime writers who had emerged in America and England in the wake of Dashiell Hammett. ("I get all the latest *romans policiers* sent to me from Paris," Colonel Haki says in Eric Ambler's classic thriller *A Coffin for Dimitrios* [1937], "All the best of them are translated into French.") Thus in 1946, with the war ended and Hollywood movies once again appearing on Paris movie screens, several French critics were immediately attracted to *The Maltese Falcon, Double Indemnity* (1944), *Murder, My Sweet* (1944), and *Laura* (1944), and they knew what to name them. According to Nino Frank, who was writing that year in the socialist film journal *L'Ecran français*, something new had developed during the war: here were excellent American productions dealing with "criminal adventure," all of them grounded in "the social fantastic" and the "dynamism of violent death," which could truly be called film noir.[3]

In an important sense, the French invented the American film noir, and they did so because local conditions predisposed them to view movies in a certain way. Unlike America, France had a thriving film culture made up of journals and ciné clubs that treated film as art rather than commercial entertainment. France was also emerging from what it called *les années noires*— the dark years of the Occupation—and its younger generation was especially attracted to American jazz clubs and the smoky, world-weary ambience of the average Bogart thriller. Among literary intellectuals, this was of course the period of existentialism, when American crime writers like Hammett, Raymond Chandler, and James M. Cain, along with prewar American novelists such as Ernest Hemingway, John Dos Passos, William Faulkner, and Richard Wright, who had also written about crime and violence, were regarded as existentialists *avant la lettre*. No wonder the French admired the 1946 production of *The Killers*, which was elaborated from a Hemingway short story of the 1920s. The opening of that film, in which a couple of hired gunmen walk into a small-town diner on the road to nowhere and complain about the menu, seems to prefigure the dark absurdism of existentialist playwrights like Samuel Beckett and the early Harold Pinter.

It was not the existentialists, however, who wrote the most interesting commentaries on film noir. That honor belongs to the Surrealists, who were a residual force in French intellectual life, especially where movies were concerned. Many art historians have claimed Surrealism ended with the 1930s, but its influence on the general culture persisted a good deal longer, affecting the way certain films were viewed in the period between 1945 and 1970, and in some ways inflecting the style of theorists such as Roland Barthes, Jacques Lacan, and Jacques Derrida. Notice as well that Surrealism provided a model for avant-garde provocateur Guy Debord, who named one of the Situationist International's most famous manifestations of the 1960s after a volume of Weegee photographs and a Hollywood film noir: *The Naked City*. Surrealism, in fact, had always been crucial to the reception of any art described as "noir." In 1940, for instance, André Breton had published his *Anthologie de l'humour noir,* a collection of subversively dark humor that celebrated what Breton called a "superior revolt of the mind" against bourgeois sentimentality.[4] Marcel Duhamel, the editor of the "Série noire," was himself a member of the original French Surrealist group, and in the brief introduction he provided for a French edition of Borde and Chaumeton's *Panorama* (included in this volume), he reminisces about the period 1923–26, when he and his fellow Surrealists watched American crime films that were "curious, nonconformist, and as noir as you could wish."

The best account of the Surrealist fascination with cinema as a whole can be found in Paul Hammond's witty, perceptive introduction to *The Shadow and Its Shadow: Surrealist Writings on the Cinema*, a revised edition of which was published by City Lights Books in 2000.[5] Hammond, who is also the translator of this edition of *Panorama,* reminds us that during the years immediately after the First World War, the original Surrealists used movies as an instrument for the overthrow of bourgeois taste and the desublimation of everyday life. Engaging in what

Hammond describes as "an extremely Romantic project" and an "inspired salvage operation," Breton and his associates would randomly pop in and out of fleapit theaters for brief periods of time, sampling the imagery and writing lyrical essays about their experiences. Like everyone in the historical avant-garde, they were captivated by modernity, but they particularly relished the cinema because it was so productive of the "marvelous" and so like a waking dream. Willfully disrupting narrative continuities, they savored the cinematic mise-en-scène, which functioned as a springboard for their poetic imagination; and out of the practice they developed what Louis Aragon called a "synthetic" criticism designed to emphasize the latent, often libidinal implications of individual shots or short scenes. Even when cinema became too expensive for Breton's style of serial viewing, it remained the fetishistic medium par excellence. At certain moments, even in ordinary genre films or grade-B productions, it could involuntarily throw off bizarre images, strange juxtapositions, and erotic plays of light and shadow on human bodies, thus providing an opportunity for the audience to break free of repressive plot conventions and indulge in private fantasies.

Some films were especially conducive to such uses: Buster Keaton's crazy comedies, horror films like *King Kong,* and, in the years after the Second World War, Chandleresque detective pictures, which sometimes lost control of their plots and became a series of hallucinatory adventures in the criminal underworld. Then again, the Surrealists had always loved crime movies, beginning with Louis Feuillade's *Fantômas* and *Les Vampires* (1913–16), which jumped from one fantastic adventure to another and seemed to transform the wartime streets of Paris into a playground of anarchic rebellion and erotic imagination. Early crime pictures from America were equally satisfying, in part because they depicted violent, antisocial behavior, and in part because they made ordinary modern decor seem marvelous. In 1918, Aragon had written that Hollywood gangster movies "speak of daily life and manage to raise to a dramatic level a banknote on which our attention is riveted, a table with a revolver on it, a bottle that on occasion becomes a weapon, a handkerchief that reveals a crime, a typewriter that's the horizon of a desk."[6] He might as well have been describing crime films of the 1940s and 50s, many of which were confined to interiors and photographed in a deep-focus style that seemed to reveal the secret life of things. To anyone with a Surrealist's temperament, these films had still other attractions: they often told stories about doomed erotic love, they sometimes had Sadean titles like *Murder, My Sweet* and *Kiss Me Deadly*, and they tended to be derived from the literature of drugs and alcohol. A film such as Huston's *The Maltese Falcon* is perfect on all counts. Filled with hints of sexual perversity, spiced by touches of sadistic violence, driven by seduction, *Falcon* offers a field day for fetishistic pleasure. Throughout, Arthur Edeson's photography draws attention to small but fascinating details, such as the texture of Bogart's suit, the little gizmo on his desk with which he lights his cigarettes, or the blinking neon signs on the buildings outside his window ("KLVW," "DRINK"). The most important object in the mise-en-scène is of course the falcon itself—a sexual and commodity fetish, a fake, and what Bogart calls "the stuff that dreams are made of."

Although *Panorama* grew out of the cultural atmosphere and aesthetic taste I've been describing, its two authors were based not in Paris but in Toulouse. Raymond Borde, born in 1920, is the founder of the Cinémathèque de Toulouse, a major film archive that houses over 22,000 titles. In addition to his extensive writings about film, he has authored a critique of consumer society, *L'Extricable* (1964), and a novel, *Le 24 août 1939; suivi de 41–42* (1995). Borde was involved in the Surrealist Exhibition of 1965 ("L'Ecart absolu") and has also directed several films— among them a short study of Surrealist artist Pierre Molinier (1964) and, with Robert Benayoun and Jacques Brunius, an incomplete documentary about the Surrealist Group, *Le Surréalisme* (1964). Regarding Etienne Chaumeton I know less, except that until his death a few years ago he was the film critic for the Toulouse newspaper *La Dépêche*.[7] The major point to emphasize is that between them, Borde and Chaumeton not only synthesized a decade of French commentary on American film noir, but also constructed a full-scale history of the form. In succinct and pungent fashion, *Panorama* offers a definition of film noir, speculates about its immediate sources, charts its rise and fall during the 1940s and 50s, describes its influence on both French cinema and other types of Hollywood film, and constructs a "balance sheet" of its relative strengths and weaknesses. One could hardly ask for more.

At the beginning of *Panorama,* Borde and Chaumeton propose that the history of cinema can be written in terms of cycles or series—that is, in terms of successful films that produce a string of imitations. (In recent years, for example, *Pulp Fiction* [1994] and *There's Something About Mary* [1998] have each created a distinct film cycle.) The American film noir, they argue, is best understood as a series, a term they favor because they want to remind us of Duhamel's "Série noire," but also because they are speaking about a relatively short-lived phenomenon belonging to a specific period in the larger history of crime fiction. In order to distinguish the noir series from ordinary detective stories or other film cycles, Borde and Chaumeton take a different approach from subsequent writers on the topic, placing less emphasis on narrative structure or visual style than on the emotional or affective qualities of the films, which they describe with five adjectives typical of Surrealism: "oneiric, strange, erotic, ambivalent, and cruel." The second adjective—*insolite* in the original French—is especially important, but difficult to render in English. "Kafkaesque" might be one translation, but Paul Hammond wisely chooses "strange," in part because the word has something in common with Freud's "uncanny" and in part because it has a distant relationship to other modernist concepts that Borde and Chaumeton probably weren't much concerned with, such as the Russian Formalists' "defamiliarization" and Brecht's "estrangement" or "alienation effect."

How many of the five attributes does a film need, and in what proportion, in order to be called noir? Borde and Chaumeton don't say, and at the end of their book they make a somewhat unconvincing attempt to avoid difficulties by cataloging titles according to a variety of subcategories. (*The Maltese Falcon* is placed under "film noir," *Double Indemnity* under "criminal psychology," *The Big Heat* [1952] under "gangsters," etc.) In their introduction, they try to solve the problem of definition by announcing that their book refers to "productions the critics have most often deemed to be 'film noirs.'" This is probably as good a solution as any. (Film theorist Peter Wollen once remarked to me in conversation, not altogether facetiously, that the best way to define a film noir is to say that it is any movie described as noir by Borde and Chaumeton.) In fact, people never form complex categories in positivist fashion, by rounding up objects with identical characteristics and putting them in boxes. Categories are formed discursively, through a process of metaphoric association that creates networks of relationship; the result is nearly always what Mark Johnson describes as a "radial structure," with "prototypical members clustered in the center" and "less prototypical members at various distances from the central members."[8] Thus for Borde and Chaumeton, film noir is made up of a central core of influential crime films that have been dubbed noir by other critics and an array of other types (period films, psychological melodramas, Westerns, even cartoons) that can be more or less related to the central core by virtue of a certain noirishness. In the last analysis, therefore, *Panorama* defines noir with a *list* (a favorite tactic of the avant-garde, later adopted by the New Wave critics at *Cahiers du cinéma* and by American auteurists such as Andrew Sarris). In this way, they are able to establish a table of priorities and allow for open-ended revision or supplement. A great many later writers have followed a similar procedure, so that noir has become what French critic Mark Vernet calls a "collector's cinema," one of the charms of which is that "there is always an unknown film to be added to the list."[9]

At other junctures in *Panorama*, however, Borde and Chaumeton treat film noir as if it could be defined as an artistic style or a sociological phenomenon. Sometimes they make it seem less like a loosely connected series than like an antigenre representing the flip side of the average Hollywood feature. They

point out, for example, that unlike the typical police procedural, noir is usually told from the point of view of the criminal, who sometimes elicits our sympathy. Even when the central
character is on the right side of the law, he's often a corrupt
cop, a morally ambiguous private eye, or a "wrong man" accused of a crime. (Alfred Hitchcock specialized in the last of
these devices, until his more overtly noir-like television show
of the 1950s paved the way for *Psycho* [1960].) At almost every
level, as Borde and Chaumeton demonstrate, film noir inverts
Hollywood formulas: in place of straightforward narratives with
clearly motivated characters, it gives us convoluted actions popu-
lated by ambiguous figures whose psychology can be enigmatic;
in place of stalwart heroes, it offers middle-aged and "not particularly handsome" protagonists who undergo, before the
obligatory happy ending, "appalling beatings"; and in place of
virginal or domesticated heroines, it presents an array of femmes
fatales, modern-day descendants of Sade's Juliette, who contribute to an overwhelming "eroticization of violence."

Borde and Chaumeton are especially intrigued by the quality of violence in the noir series. The films in question replace
Hollywood's chivalric sword fights and melodramatic shoot-outs
with a richly elaborated "ceremony of killing" that has sadomasochistic overtones. Noir director Anthony Mann was adept
at such effects (Borde and Chaumeton mention two of his films,
T-Men [1947] and *Border Incident* [1949]), but there are plenty of
examples to be found in films by other directors of the same
period. In *The Killers,* gas-station attendant Burt Lancaster dies
under a fusillade of bullets as he lies in bed mourning Ava
Gardner, who has used and deserted him. In *Brute Force* (1947),
fascistic prison guard Hume Cronyn ritually tortures inmates
to the sound of classical music. In *The Set-Up* (1949), small-time
boxer Robert Ryan is cornered in an alley by gangsters who beat
him to death for failing to throw a fight. In *The Glass Key* (1942),
William Bendix pounds Alan Ladd's face into hamburger while
calling him "sweetheart." In *The Dark Corner* (1946), Bendix
(again) steps on the unconscious Mark Stevens's thumb and
crushes it. And in *Kiss of Death* (1947), Richard Widmark laughs

gleefully as he pushes a little old lady in a wheelchair down a flight of stairs. When the sadism isn't physical, it's psychological, as in *Rebecca* (1940), *Gilda* (1946), and *The Lady from Shanghai* (1948).

For Borde and Chaumeton, all this "incoherent brutality" creates something "dreamlike." Indeed, the films tend to be devoted to dreams, nowhere more so than in *The Woman in the Window* (1944), or situated at the margins of dreams, in a liminal area of darkness, memory, and desire often rendered through flashbacks and first-person narration. A classic instance of the latter technique is *Laura,* a crucial scene in which Borde and Chaumeton nicely describe: "A musical theme, which will accompany us everywhere, evokes the shadowy figure of a doubtless delightful young woman, and we submit to the most compelling of spells. The detective wanders like a sleepwalker through the deserted apartment, he opens and closes drawers, moves ornaments and underclothes around, sniffs at bottles of perfume. And while, dead beat, he slumbers in an armchair, the door opens. . . ."

According to Borde and Chaumeton, *Laura* and other examples of American film noir were shaped by a new realism about violence, a rise in the American crime rate, and the widespread institution and popularization of psychoanalysis after the Second World War. Among the artistic predecessors of the noir series were the hard-boiled novel, certain European films of the 1930s, plus horror films at Universal, gangster pictures at Warner, and detective movies at Fox. During the 1940s, Hollywood's Breen Office still exercised strong control over the sexual and social content of movies, but Borde and Chaumeton argue that censorship actually heightened the effectiveness of certain films by forcing directors to rely on the power of suggestion; sexuality was displaced onto a shadowy and seductive mise-en-scène, which drew attention to the curve of Veronica Lake's hair or the silken glitter of Rita Hayworth's glove. Few subsequent historians would quarrel with these assertions. In listing the productions that were crucial to the formation of noir, however, Borde and Chaumeton are sometimes unorthodox. For example, when they name the movies that inaugurated a noir "style" during the war years (1941–45), they emphasize not only *The Maltese Falcon* and *This Gun for Hire* (1942), but also Josef von Sternberg's *The Shanghai Gesture* (1941), which for most critics today seems like a throwback to the Dietrich films of the 1930s. (Significantly, *The Shanghai Gesture* was a special favorite of the Surrealists, who in 1951 had submitted it to an experiment in the "irrational enlargement" of a film.[10]) Elsewhere, Borde and Chaumeton place *Double Indemnity* outside the central core of the form, and they have relatively little to say about *Out of the Past* (1947), which has often been treated as the quintessential example of film noir. They are especially fond of two masterpieces of noir eroticism, *Gilda* and *The Lady from Shanghai,* both starring Hayworth, but they give almost as much praise to *Chicago Deadline* (1948), a largely forgotten Alan Ladd vehicle, and to *The Enforcer* (1951), a Bogart picture attributed to the virtually unknown Bretaigne Windust (historians later discovered that the actual director was Raoul Walsh). They are quite good at discussing marginal pictures, showing how a variety of Hollywood formulas became "noirified" during the 1940s and 50s, including "costume" films (*Dr. Jekyll and Mr. Hyde* [1941], *Gaslight* [1944], *The Spiral Staircase*), Shakespeare adaptations (Welles's *Macbeth* [1948]), and Westerns (*Ramrod* [1947]). They also write briefly but effectively about numerous low-budget movies, at the same time leaving many titles for aficionados of noir to discover and nominate.

"Film noir is noir *for us,*" Borde and Chaumeton declare at the opening of their first chapter; "that's to say, for Western and American audiences of the 1950s." But times were changing even as they wrote that sentence. The private-detective myth was already growing stale, the strange was becoming familiar, and a season in hell was beginning to look like the snows of yesteryear. At a revival of *Murder, My Sweet* at the cine club of Toulouse in 1953, people laughed whenever Philip Marlowe lost consciousness and disappeared into a black pool. (Exceptions to the rule included the films of Orson Welles, which have remained "strange" by any standard.) In response to television and the growing leisure industry, Hollywood was turning to wide-screen epics and biblical pictures. Although Borde and Chaumeton don't say so, this was also the McCarthy era, when several of the key writers and directors associated with film noir were blacklisted or imprisoned. At the beginning of the 1950s, important examples of film noir continued to appear, including John Huston's *The Asphalt Jungle* (1950), which influenced Jules Dassin's French production of *Rififi* (1954) and gave renewed life to the theme of organized criminal gangs; Alfred Hitchcock's *Strangers on a Train* (1951), which they describe as a "cocktail" of black humor and suspense; and above all Joseph H. Lewis's *Gun Crazy* (1950), which Borde and Chaumeton view as the "*L'Age d'or* of American film noir." Even so, noir seemed to be entering a predictable and decadent phase, leading up to its demise.

An apparent coup de grace was administered by two films that were made in response to Mickey Spillane, a right-wing author of pulp fiction who, in the early 1950s, had become the most popular writer in America and a lightning rod for cultural commentary on the dangers of mass culture. In the MGM musical *The Band Wagon* (1953), director Vincente Minnelli ("the most refined man in Hollywood") staged a balletic Technicolor parody of both Spillane and the classic film noir, transforming the clichés of dark thrillers into "a final concession to our past." "Sure," Borde and Chaumeton admit, "Fred Astaire doesn't have the weighty presence of a tough guy. Sure, Minnelli has been inspired by a facile and banalized Surrealism." For all that, they regard the climactic number in *The Band Wagon* as a brilliantly poetic success: "Never," they write, "had the noir series been grasped 'in its very essence' with such a lucid complicity." Not long afterward came Robert Aldrich's ideologically incoherent but in many ways subversive adaptation of Spillane's *Kiss Me Deadly* (1955), which Borde and Chaumeton describe in the Postface to the 1979 edition of *Panorama* as the despairing opposite of *The Maltese Falcon*: "between 1941 and 1955, between the eve of war and the advent of consumer society, the tone has changed. A savage lyricism hurls us into a world in manifest

decomposition . . . to these intrigues of wild men and weaklings, Aldrich offers the most radical of solutions: nuclear apocalypse."

At its best, classic or historical film noir had represented for
Borde and Chaumeton an intermingling of social realism and
oneirism, an erotic treatment of violence, and a feeling of psychological disorientation, as if capitalist and puritan values were
being systematically inverted. Despite its contradictions and
compromises (and despite the fact that it was almost exclusively
a white male phenomenon), film noir seemed to offer a romantic and approximately Surrealist "morality," which was expressed
through a marked propensity for *amour fou,* a sort of left-wing
anarchy, and a sympathy with loners, outcasts, and criminals.
Borde and Chaumeton were probably correct to say that the
"glory days" of this phenomenon were the late 1940s; and yet,
when they revisited the cinematic landscape in the Postface to
the 1979 edition of *Panorama,* they found that noir was enjoy-
ing a "renaissance." In commenting on the years that had passed
since 1955, they fail to mention the fact that the French New
Wave had emerged out of a kind of dialogue with the American
film noir, most notably in Jean-Luc Godard's *Breathless* (1959)
and François Truffaut's *Shoot the Piano Player* (1960). They also
say little about the parodies and pastiches of classic noir during
the 1970s, and nothing about the best of the retro-styled films
in that period, Roman Polanski's *Chinatown* (1974). On the other
hand, they list a broad range of new films about crime and violence in a modern setting, including *Point Blank* (1967), *Dirty
Harry* (1972), *The Godfather* (1972) *Badlands* (1973), and *The
Conversation* (1974). They even have good things to say about
Dr. No (1962), the first of the James Bond films, in which
"[v]iolence and sadism were rehabilitated." The old censorship
restrictions have now been modified, so that "a spade is called
a spade," and although Borde and Chaumeton miss the charms
of black-and-white photography, they praise certain uses of color,
which is able to create "a new kind of morbid toughness" and a
"standardized world in which people already have the look of
the condemned."

The 1970s were in fact an important period for America's dark cinema. During those years, the British critic Raymond Durgnat and the American Paul Schrader each wrote important essays in English on film noir, and each drew heavily on Borde and Chaumeton.[11] An American version of the New Wave soon emerged in Hollywood, fueled by Schrader, Martin Scorsese, Brian DePalma, and Peter Bogdanovich, who grounded their earliest work in a noir tradition and a neo-expressionist use of color. By the middle of the decade the word "noir" (along with "auteur") had fully entered the English language. Meanwhile, the social revolutions and antiwar movements of the 1960s had given way to the Nixon era, and a mood of despair and apocalypse was infiltrating the work of younger directors. As Paul Schrader wrote in 1972, "The Forties may be to the Seventies what the Thirties were to the Sixties." The result was a series of films such as *The French Connection* (1971) and *Taxi Driver* (1976), in which the urban environment seemed increasingly anarchistic and bombed out, as if modernity had come to the end of its tether. Viewers today will probably not agree with Borde and Chaumeton that Richard Fleischer's dystopian sci-fi thriller *Soylent Green* (1973) is "the most terrifying film in the history of cinema," but that picture could serve as well as any to represent the mood of certain filmmakers in the period.

It would take another book to chronicle all the social and industrial changes since the 1970s and to connect them with all the films since then about burned-out detectives, crooked cops, charming con men, bands of thieves, duplicitous lovers, and violent death in urban settings. Far from dying out, film noir has become a standard feature of popular memory in the postmodern age, and it continues to produce new cycles. As I write this introduction, I'm reminded that during the years 2001–02 American audiences could see Hollywood pictures such as *Shaft* and *Training Day*, which are distantly related to classic film noirs about rogue cops, alongside several "independent" or quasi-art films such as *Memento, Mulholland Drive, The Deep End*, and *The Man Who Wasn't There*, which were clearly made with the idea of film noir in mind. Borde and Chaumeton helped to create that idea. What they wrote still resonates in the contemporary imagination and is still the best place to begin reading about the intriguing, always recurring manifestations of Hollywood's dark side.

References

1 Siegfried Kracauer, "Hollywood's Terror Films: Do They Reflect an American State of Mind?" *Commentary* (August 1946): 132–36.

2 John Houseman quoted in Richard Maltby, "The Politics of the Maladjusted Text," in *The Book of Film Noir,* ed. Ian Cameron (New York: Continuum, 1993), 41.

3 Nino Frank, "Un Nouveau genre 'policier': L'Aventure criminelle," *L'Ecran français* 61 (28 August 1946): 14. My translation.

4 Andre Breton, ed. *Anthology of Black Humor,* trans. Mark Polizzotti (San Francisco: City Lights Books, 1997), xvi.

5 Paul Hammond, "Available Light," in *The Shadow and Its Shadow: Surrealist Writings on the Cinema*, ed. Paul Hammond (San Francisco: City Lights Books, 2000), 1–43.

6 Louis Aragon, "On Decor," in Hammond, 51.

7 I am grateful to Paul Hammond for supplying me with biographical information about Borde and Chaumeton.

8 Mark Johnson, *The Body and the Mind: The Bodily Basis of Meaning, Imagination, and Reason* (Chicago: University of Chicago Press, 1987).

9 Marc Vernet, "Film Noir on the Edge of Doom," in *Shades of Noir,* ed. Joan Copjec (London: Verso, 1993), 26.

10 The Surrealist Group, "Data Toward the Irrational Enlargement of a Film: *The Shanghai Gesture,*" in Hammond, 121–29.

11 See Raymond Durgnat, "Paint It Black: The Family Tree of Film Noir," in *Film Noir Reader,* ed. Alain Silver and James Ursini (New York: Limelight Editions, 1996), 37–52; and Paul Schrader, "Notes on Film Noir," also in Silver and Ursini, 53–64.

Preface

Marcel Duhamel

Dearly beloved brethren,
I will die,
You will die,
We will all die. . . .

The country priest who voiced these revelations from his pulpit on high in the church I strayed into one day at the age of six is perhaps the real person responsible for the "Série noire" and the inspiration for these lines. What is certain is that the phrases "noir novel" and "film noir" always sound like pleonasms to me and that the latent presence of the idea of death in a person's mind, far from appearing symptomatic of a morbid condition, seems, on the contrary, to be eminently healthy and suited to engendering skepticism, therefore humor, therefore a certain optimism. The moral of the story is that noir is, at base, pink or at least yellow and vice versa. And as, in any event and whatever you do, it's always the good that's exalted, nothing could be more edifying and decidedly moral than *Un aller simple* (Série noire) or, at the cinema, *Night Must Fall,* for example.[1]

Reading *A Panorama of American Film Noir* (and I take my hat off, in passing, to the enormous work of compilation and close study accomplished by its authors) has stirred many a memory in me. And particularly of the 1923–26 period when, like faithful followers celebrating some magic rite, we spent our nights, Jacques Prévert, Yves Tanguy, and I, in the basement of the Erka-Prodisko Company. Pierre Prévert, already a cameraman at the time, used to secretly show us mile upon mile of movie film. Solely the noir kind. Loads of William Wellman, notably. I could be wrong, but his *Chinatown Nights* has stayed in my memory as the masterpiece of silent noir gangster film. Along with *Club 73* (I don't know who by anymore), years before *Underworld. . . .*[2] At daybreak, we emerged onto the pavement of Avenue de la République, replete, satiated, besotted, and happy. . . .

And two or three times a week we were back again in Rue de la Gaîté at the Thousand Columns cinema, of odoriferous memory, where a George O'Brien movie was billed. This astonishing actor suddenly disappeared from the screen one day, only to make his comeback twenty years later as a lead in Westerns. During the period I'm referring to, he appeared in a series of features about which I unfortunately remember little, except that they were curious, nonconformist, and as noir as you could wish. And neither André Breton, nor Raymond Queneau, nor Benjamin Péret will contradict me here.

Let's shed a tear in passing for the silent period, the blissful era of the double bill. . . . Almost every day, after having seen a first feature in Montparnasse, we crossed Paris by taxi during the intermission to see a second film on Boulevard de Clichy. . . . I reckon that if we'd had to suffer, then, the first halves you have to put up with now—an insipid documentary, ice cream, a newsreel (already seen three times during the week), intermission, ice cream, ads, second intermission—we'd have set the damn place on fire. At present, I foam gently at the mouth and chew my nails. They've ended up putting one over on us. . . .

That said, and since the problem is posed about film noir's origins, let's observe that it goes back in fact to the birth of the cinema. From *L'Assassinat du Duc de Guise* to *Night Must Fall* and taking in *Les Vampires,* cinema has always mirrored literature, which (may I be forgiven this truism) draws its inspiration from life and from the news event. The German Expressionist noir cinema of 1924 depicted the extraordinary atmosphere reigning in that country after the 1914–18 war. The debut of the gangster film around 1923 exactly coincides with the voting-in of Prohibition, and ever since then American cinema has merely expressed a point of fact: the persistence of racketeering in a more or less disguised form. And we won't see the end of this as long as society isn't considerably changed. All of which promises us quite a few eventful evenings.

For ten years now, they've been predicting the end of the thriller in the USA. Well, record attendances have been announced for last year. Every now and then the "Série noire" is interred, but this is wishful thinking. And as 75 percent of the 250 or so published volumes have been filmed; and since the latter represent only a small part of noir movie output, one sees how wide of the mark such lists and statistics are. Ought this to be deplored? Surely not, since, taken together, good books and good film noirs keep very close to current events and constitute an excellent testimony of our times. And to those who have no interest in history, I advise them to meditate on this Chinese proverb: "It is better to dream of fish than to have one's wife dipped in boiling oil."

In conclusion, read masses of noir novels and see film noirs in abundance. As long as you only do your killing in your imagination, we'll be able to sleep in peace. It's the blessing I wish for us all.

References

1 *Un aller simple,* published in 1950 in Duhamel's "Série noire" collection for Gallimard, is the French version of Henry Edward Helseth's noir novel, *The Chair for Martin Rome* (1948). —*Trans.*

2 *Club 73* is untraceable. Perhaps Duhamel is thinking of Tod Browning's *The Unholy Three* (1925), released in France as *Le Club des trois.* The three memorable villains of the title are a ventriloquist, a dwarf, and a giant. . . . —*Trans.*

1

Introduction[1]

It was during the summer of 1946 that the French public experienced the revelation of a new kind of American film. In the course of a few weeks, from mid-July to the end of August, five films followed one another on the cinema screens of Paris, films which had an unusual and cruel atmosphere in common, one tinted by a very particular eroticism: John Huston's *The Maltese Falcon*, Otto Preminger's *Laura*, Edward Dmytryk's *Murder, My Sweet*, Billy Wilder's *Double Indemnity*, and Fritz Lang's *The Woman in the Window.*

Long cut off from America, ill-informed about Hollywood's output during the war, living in thrall to Wyler, Ford, and Capra, not even knowing who the new big names in directing were, French critics didn't register the true extent of this revelation. Nino Frank, one of the first to speak of "film noir," and who subsequently managed to diagnose some of the basic traits of the series, nevertheless wrote, apropos of *The Maltese Falcon* and *Murder, My Sweet*: "[these movies] belong to what used to be known as the detective genre, and that from now on we'd do better to call 'crime adventure stories' or, better still, 'criminal psychology.'"[2] This was also the opinion of a certain specialized criticism, one that lacked, it has to be said, the necessary distance.

A few months later, however, Frank Tuttle's *This Gun for Hire,* Robert Siodmak's *The Killers,* Robert Montgomery's *The Lady in the Lake,* Charles Vidor's *Gilda,* and Howard Hawks's *The Big Sleep* obliged the public to accept the idea of film noir. A new "series" was emerging in the history of the cinema.

A series could be defined as a group of nationally identifiable films sharing certain common features (style, atmosphere, subject), features sufficiently strong to mark them unequivocally and to give them, with time, an inimitable quality. Such series have a variable life: now two years, now ten. Up to a point it's the viewer who decides this. From the "filmological" point of view, series have their origins in a few old movies, a few scattered titles. Afterward, they reach a climax; that's to say, a moment of exceptional purity. Following that, they fade and die, their aftereffects being felt in other genres.

To a large extent the history of the cinema is a history of series. Unclassifiable films exist, of course: Orson Welles's *Citizen Kane* or Clifford Odets's *None But the Lonely Heart* are two such. But often a great film is unclassifiable only because it's the first in a new series and the necessary time lag is lacking. *Caligari* was unclassifiable before giving rise to "Caligarism."

Since the advent of sound we would cite, in the USA, for example, the social series, the gangster film, and the so-called "period" film; in Germany, the light comedy of the years 1930 to 1933, an immediate prelude to American comedy; in the USSR, films devoted to the October Revolution; in France, the realism of Carné, Renoir, and Duvivier.

Nearer to our own time: English comedy, the French epic escape film (from *L'Eternel retour* to *Singoalla* and *Juliette ou La Clé des songes*), the social documentary of Daquin, Rouquier, Nicole Védrès. In the USSR, works to the glory of collective work (from *Three Encounters* to *It Happened in the Donbas*) and the kolkhoz cycle. In the USA, the police documentary (Hathaway, Kazan, Dassin), the psychoanalytic film, the new Western school. All series with their own laws, their own traditions, and often their own public.

That for years there might have been a noir series[3] within Hollywood production is seemingly beyond question. It's another thing to define its essential traits.

We'd be oversimplifying things in calling film noir oneiric, strange, erotic, ambivalent, and cruel. . . .[4] All these qualities are present in the series, but sometimes it's the oneiric quality that predominates—and we get *The Shanghai Gesture;* sometimes eroticism—and we get *Gilda;* sometimes the cruelty of a strange act. Often a film's noir side has to do with a single character, a single scene, a single decor. *The Set-Up* is an excellent documentary on boxing: it becomes film noir in the sequence of the final showdown, that terrible beating at the end of a blind alley. The spellbinding sadism of a psychological film like *Rope* links it per se to the noir series. On the other hand, *The Big Sleep, This Gun for Hire,* and *The Lady in the Lake* seem to be typical thrillers. This problem of definition will be evoked first, by referring to productions the critics have most often deemed to be "film noirs."

One final comment. We will constantly use a convention; we will hypothetically concede the paternity of films to their directors. It's a convention because one never knows, where American films are concerned, if the director is really the key figure. Sternberg himself recently said: "I work on assignment; namely, to order. And this order is exactly the same as those the cabinetmaker, bookbinder, or shoemaker commissioned to do a particular job receive."[5] What is the producer's contribution, the scriptwriter's, the editor's? Is it pure chance that the late Mark Hellinger produced three such unmistakable films as *The Killers, Brute Force,* and *The Naked City?* Who can say, apart from the people concerned, if Hellinger really put his stamp on these works or if he let Siodmak and Dassin work with a free hand?

Actually, if there's not much genuine freedom for a director in Hollywood, it seems he's occasionally granted something other than a merely subaltern role: his degree of independence varies to a very great extent in relation to his commercial "efficiency." The persistence of a common style in the works of a particular director would thus be explained: the themes of failure and adventure in John Huston, the theme of cruelty in Raoul Walsh, the theme of urban realism in Jules Dassin. And even Sternberg has hardly ever quit the confines of a sensual exoticism. All in all, this prior convention is acceptable, then.

References

1 Our thanks are due to Freddy Buache, General Secretary of the Cinémathèque de Lausanne, who agreed to publish this introduction in the magazine *Carreau*.

2 *L'Ecran français* 61 (28 August 1946).

3 The French here is *série noire,* but since the authors speak of other series—the crime series and the psychoanalytic series, for instance—this phrase has been Englished. It is hoped, however, that when readers comes across "noir series" they will bear the French term in mind, since this resonates with the hard-boiled novels edited by Marcel Duhamel, Gallimard's famous "Série noire," which popularized such names as W.R. Burnett, James M. Cain, Raymond Chandler, David Goodis, Dashiell Hammett, Horace McCoy, Jim Thompson, and Charles Williams. —*Trans.*

4 The second of these adjectives—*insolite*—is difficult to translate. It can mean strange, unusual, peculiar, unaccustomed, odd; even uncanny, at a pinch. If the word "strange" appears, well, strange to readers, they are asked to recall these other meanings. —*Trans.*

5 *Le Figaro* (8 May 1951).

2

Toward a definition of film noir

The bloody channels through which logic at bay is obliged to pass.
—Lautréamont[1]

Film noir is noir *for us;* that's to say, for Western and American audiences of the 1950s. It responds to a certain kind of emotional resonance as singular in time as it is in space. It's on the basis of a response to possibly ephemeral reactions that the roots of this "style" must be sought, therefore: this is what forges a link between productions as different as *The Shanghai Gesture* and *The Asphalt Jungle*.

As a result, the method is imposed by and of itself: while remaining on as technical and objective a terrain as possible, it consists in studying the most typical characteristics of films the critics have generally deemed to be noir; then, by comparing these qualities, in seeking a common denominator and defining the single emotional attitude all the works in the series tend to bring into play.

It's the presence of crime that gives film noir its most distinctive stamp. "The dynamism of violent death," as Nino Frank put it, and the expression is excellent. Blackmail, informing, theft, or drug trafficking weave the plot of an adventure whose final stake is death. Few series in the history of cinema have, in just seven or eight years, accumulated so many hideous acts of brutality and murder. Sordid or strange, death always emerges at the end of a tortuous journey. Film noir is a film of death, in all senses of the word.

Yet it doesn't have a monopoly here, and an essential distinction is called for. In principle, a film noir is not a "police documentary."[2] We know that since 1946 Hollywood has exported a dozen or so movies to France that have the common characteristic of describing a criminal investigation by following the documents in the police file page by page. Furthermore, at the start of the film a title or commentary advises the public that this is a true story, occurring at such and such a time, in New York or some other place. And the images on the screen faithfully describe the investigation: a call to headquarters, the discovery of the body; from time to time some seemingly minor incident, a local precinct report that will start the ball rolling. Then the "thankless" task of the police department: detailed and futile inquiries, useless leads, abortive roundups. At last a glimmer of light, a bit of cross-checking, a testimony, and then the final chase that unmasks a bunch of killers. This series, which has given us some interesting works—Henry Hathaway's *Call Northside 777* and *The House on 92nd Street,* Elia Kazan's *Boomerang!* and *Panic in the Streets,* László Benedek's *Port of New York,* Jules Dassin's *The Naked City,* and, on the fringes of the genre, Bretaigne Windust's *The Enforcer*—has several features in common with film noir: realistic locations, carefully crafted supporting roles, extremely brutal scenes, and bits of bravura in the final chase sequences. On top of that, these police documentaries often have more typically noir features: it will be a long time before we forget the unusual figure of the killers' boss in *The Enforcer* or the impassive gangster in *Panic in the Streets.* It may even be that during his career a director alternates between the two genres. Jules Dassin has put his name to *The Naked City* but also to *Night and the City.* In 1950, Joseph H. Lewis gave us an incontestably noir opus in *Gun Crazy,* yet the year before he'd described the work of some tax officials in *The Undercover Man.*

There are some differences between the two series, for all that. And first and foremost a different angle of vision. The documentary considers the murder from without, from the official police viewpoint; the film noir from within, from the criminals'. In movies of *The Naked City* type, the action begins after the crime, and the murderers, heavies, and their accomplices traverse the screen solely in order to be tailed, spied on, interrogated, hunted down, or killed. If a flashback evokes a scene between gangsters, it's to illustrate a confession or a testimony, the transcript of which figures in the report. The police are omnipresent, so as to intervene or to lend an ear. There's none of this in the film noir, which is set in the criminal milieu itself and describes the latter, now through simple touches (*The Big Sleep* or *Dark Passage*), now in depth and with obliging subtlety (*The Asphalt Jungle*). In any event, it proposes a psychology of crime that isn't without its echoes, in another domain, of that worldly psychology so appreciated at the end of the nineteenth century: both shed light on forbidden worlds.

The second difference is of a moral, and maybe even more essential, kind. It's part of the tradition of the police documentary to present the investigators as upright, incorruptible, and courageous men. The ship's doctor in *Panic in the Streets* is a hero. A hero, too, albeit more complex, is the short Irish detective of *The Naked City* who believes in God and consecrates his nights to the triumph of justice. An edifying film, the American police documentary is, in fact, a documentary to the glory of the police and belongs in the same bag as such productions, in France, as *Identité judiciaire* or, in England, *The Blue Lamp*.

None of this exists in the noir series. If there are policemen, they're of dubious character—like the inspector in *The Asphalt Jungle* or that evil-looking, corrupt brute played by Lloyd Nolan in *The Lady in the Lake*—even murderers at times (Otto Preminger's *Fallen Angel* and *Where the Sidewalk Ends*). Or at least they allow themselves to get caught up in the machinery of crime, like the attorney in *The File on Thelma Jordan*. It's no accident, then, if scriptwriters have frequently had recourse to the character of the private detective. Casting too many aspersions on the official U.S. police force was a ticklish problem. The private detective, midway between order and crime, running with the hare and hunting with the hounds, not overly scrupulous and responsible for himself alone, satisfied both the exigencies of morality and those of the criminal adventure story. As if by way of compensation, the lawbreakers themselves are rather personable. Of course, the old motto of MGM's prewar short films, "Crime Doesn't Pay," remains the order of the day, and the ending witnesses the chastisement of the guilty. But then the action is so adroitly handled that at certain moments the public sympathizes and identifies with the gangsters. Think back to that breathtaking scene in *The Asphalt Jungle,* the raid on the jewelers. What spectator isn't instinctively on the side of the crooks? And *Gun Crazy* depicted a couple of killers of an exemplary beauty, if we may say so.

Few films have shown the instability of the relations between underworld types as well as *The Big Sleep* and, in its noir sequence (Rico's testimony), *The Enforcer.* In this gallery of suspects and criminals one glimpses the complex and shifting patterns of domination based on money, blackmail, vice, and informing. Who'll do the killing, and who'll get killed? Here is all the ambiguity of a criminal milieu in which the power relationships ceaselessly change.

This equivocation extends to the ambivalence of the characters themselves. The rough-hewn hero, the Scarface-type thug, has disappeared from film noir, making way for a whole host of angelic killers, neurotic gangsters, megalomaniac gang bosses, and disturbing or depraved stooges. Here is the solitary, scientific assassin of *He Walked by Night,* here the self-punishing failure of *Night and the City,* here the awesomely mother-fixated fanatic of *White Heat.* Here are the henchmen of *The Enforcer*—vicious, venomous, or spineless.

Ambiguity, too, as to the victims, forever suspect, at least partly. The relationships they maintain with the mob makes them first cousins to their torturers. If they're often victims, it's because they haven't managed to be executioners. Like the dubious partner in *The Lady from Shanghai* who meets his death while simulating his own murder and who will long remain the finest example of an equivocal victim. One also thinks of the terrorized heroine of Jacques Tourneur's *Out of the Past,* whom one expects to see done in before the film is over and who sees her executioner off in a carefully prepared trap. A lamb to the slaughter, this heavy secretly marked out for execution.

Contradictions on the hero's side: often he's a man who's already middle-aged, old almost, and not particularly handsome. Humphrey Bogart is the model here. He's also an inglorious victim who undergoes, before the happy end, some appalling beatings. Added to which, he's often the masochistic type, his own executioner, someone hoist by his own petard, someone who gets tangled up in dangerous situations, not so much through a concern for justice or through cupidity as through a sort of morbid curiosity. Sometimes he's a passive hero who is willingly taken to the frontier between lawfulness and crime, like Orson Welles in *The Lady from Shanghai*. We're a long way, then, from the adventure film superman.

Contradictions, finally, on the woman's side: the femme fatale is also fatal unto herself. Frustrated and guilty, half man-eater, half man-eaten, blasé and cornered, she falls victim to her own wiles. While the ambiguous behavior of Lauren Bacall in *The Big Sleep* doesn't cost her her life, Barbara Stanwyck will not survive her own murderous schemes in *The File on Thelma Jordan*. This new kind of woman, rubbing shoulders with and masterminding crime, tough as the milieu surrounding her, as expert in blackmail and "vice" as in the use of firearms—and probably frigid—has left her mark on a noir eroticism that is at times merely an eroticization of violence. We're a long way from the chaste heroines of the classic Western or the historical film.

In terms of the history of the cinema, film noir has given a new lease of life to the theme of violence. First of all, by abandoning one of the conventions of the adventure film: the combat with equal weapons. The fair fight gives way to the settling of scores, to the working over, to the cold-blooded execution. Bodyguards bounce a powerless victim between them like a ball, a victim they then leave bleeding on a public square (*Ride the Pink Horse*), in a blind alley (*The Set-Up*), or in a yard, among the trash cans (*I Walk Alone*). Crime itself becomes mechanical, professional, and it's the hired killer who now performs this duty "without anger and without hatred." The first sequence of the Robert

Siodmak film, *The Killers,* that famous scene in the diner in which two men in search of their victim terrify the clients with contemptible self-confidence, will abide as one of the most striking moments in American cinema, an unforgettable slice of documentary: a hitherto unknown race looms up before us with its tics, its stigmata. This race has its artistes, exceedingly gentle on the whole (Alan Ladd in *This Gun for Hire*), its unreasoning brutes (William Bendix), and its lucid and fearsome organization men (Everett Sloane in *The Enforcer*). It also has its mental defectives, its overweight killers, oozing cowardice, humiliated by their accomplices, and suddenly let loose (Laird Cregar or Raymond Burr).

As for the ceremony of killing, this remains one of the richest in the entire history of the cinema. Let us cite at random: that un-self-conscious gesture of the wealthy publisher who sends a potentially embarrassing witness, busy washing the tiles, hurtling down the lift shaft; all he need do is nudge the man's stepladder with the knob of his cane while shooting the breeze (*High Wall;* the gruesome razor killing in *The Enforcer;* a tap of the foot given to a hydraulic jack (*Red Light*). Elsewhere, a paralyzed victim is pushed down a flight of stairs after being tied to her wheelchair (*Kiss of Death*); a stool pigeon is locked inside a Turkish bath, then the steam turned up; a prisoner is gradually driven under a power hammer by threatening him with blazing blow torches (*Brute Force*); someone is crushed beneath a tractor, someone else sinks into the quicksand (*Border Incident*). . . . An unprecedented panoply of cruelties and sufferings unfolds in film noir.

But then more than with the violence, the anguish has to do, perhaps, with the strange unfolding of the action. A private detective accepts the vaguest of missions: to find a woman, to halt a blackmail attempt, to deter someone—and straightaway his path is littered with corpses. He's tailed, hit over the head, arrested. Let him ask for information, and he finds himself tied up, bleeding, in some deep cellar. Various men, questioned at night, shoot and then run off. There is, in this incoherent brutality, something dreamlike, and yet this is the atmosphere common to most film noirs: *The Big Sleep, Ride the Pink Horse, The Lady in the Lake, Chicago Deadline*. On this score, Georges Sadoul suggests that "the story remains opaque, like a nightmare, or the ramblings of a drunk."[3] This is so manifestly true that one of the rare parodies of the genre, Elliott Nugent's *My Favorite Brunette,* begins in just this way. Bob Hope has elected to play at being a detective, and Dorothy Lamour entrusts him with one of those confused investigations the Americans possess the secret of—like, for instance, "Find my brother" or "Find my sister"—by handing him a check. Instantly, the knives are out, corpses bar his way, and the inexorable wheels of fate lead him to the electric chair via a hospital that's a gangster hideout.

At times, the mystery is more convincing: a man who's lost his memory sets off in search of the past, only for crime to rear its ugly head. This theme has been exploited by Robert Florey in *The Crooked Way* and by Joseph Mankiewicz in *Somewhere in the Night.* But here the stated facts of the problem are such that the public expects a certain amount of confusion in advance. In genuine film noir, strangeness is inseparable from what could be called the *uncertainty of the motives*. What, for instance, are Bannister or his associate seeking through their sinister doings in *The Lady from Shanghai?* The very strangeness of the oeuvre lies in these spineless, mysterious creatures who lay their cards on the table only in death. Elsewhere, will a figure glimpsed in some nondescript nightclub finger an accomplice or an enemy? This enigmatic killer, is he to be executioner or victim? The complexity of criminal relationships, the multifarious intermeshings of blackmail, the mystery as to motives—all this converges in incoherence.

In our opinion, this note of confusion is at the very heart of the oneiric quality specific to the series. A number of titles could readily be found in which the action is deliberately situated at the level of the dream; for example, Fritz Lang's *The Woman in the Window*. There are also works in which the artificial setting relates to symbol and fiction alone; Sternberg's *The Shanghai Gesture* is a case in point. As a general rule, however, the point of departure is realistic and, taken on its own, each scene could pass for a fragment of documentary. It's the accumulation of these realistic shots on a bizarre theme that creates a nightmarish atmosphere.

One gets the feeling that all the components of noir style lead to the same result: to disorient the spectators, who no longer encounter their customary frames of reference. The cinema public was habituated to certain conventions: a logic to the action, a clear distinction between good and evil, well-defined characters, clear motives, scenes more spectacular than genuinely brutal, an exquisitely feminine heroine, and an upright hero. These at least were the postulates of the American adventure film before the war.

As things stand, though, the public is offered a highly sympathetic image of the criminal milieu, of attractive killers, dubious policemen. Good and evil often rub shoulders to the point of merging into one another. The thieves are average guys; they have kids, love their young wives, and aspire to return to the rural haunts of their childhood (*The Asphalt Jungle*). The victim is as suspect as the executioner, while the latter remains likeable. The first of those frames of reference, moral fictions, is blurred.

The heroine is vicious, deadly, venomous, or alcoholic. The hero lets himself be led astray, gets to "take a lot of punishment," as they say in boxing, during ruthless settlings of scores. And the second frame of reference, the myth of superman and his chaste fiancée, goes by the board.

The action is confused, the motives uncertain. This is a far cry from classical drama or the moral tale of the realist era: many of the hoods have murky relationships with each other (*The Big Sleep*); a policeman arrives unexpectedly, proves to be a crook, and his presence only adds to the tension of the viewer (*The Lady in the Lake*); proceedings in which a man's life is at stake turn into the craziest of stories (*The Lady from Shanghai*). The film takes on the quality of a dream, and the audience searches in vain for the good old logic of yore.

In the end, the violence "oversteps the mark." This gratuitous cruelty and this one-upmanship in murder add to the strangeness. The sense of dread is dissipated only in the very last images.

It is easy to come to a conclusion: the moral ambivalence, criminal violence, and contradictory complexity of the situations and motives all combine to give the public a shared feeling of anguish or insecurity, which is the identifying sign of film noir at this time. All the works in this series exhibit a consistency of an emotional sort; *namely, the state of tension created in the spectators by the disappearance of their psychological bearings*. The vocation of film noir has been to create *a specific sense of malaise*.

References

1 Since this citation is not, in fact, from Lautréamont's *Les Chants de Maldoror,* but from *Poésies,* it would be more correct to sign it "Isidore Ducasse." —*Trans.*

2 What the authors call a "police documentary" we'd now call a "police procedural." —*Trans.*

3 A review of *The Big Sleep* in *Les Lettres françaises.*

3

The sources of film noir

The immediate source of film noir is obviously the hard-boiled detective novel of American or English origin. Dashiell Hammett, whose earliest writings go back to around 1925, is both the creator of this new American literary current and an author whose talent largely transcends the framework of the genre (as does Georges Simenon in French). The latent homosexuality of his characters has almost always disappeared when their adventures have been transferred to the screen (*The Glass Key*). But then the fact that the first great film noir is precisely *The Maltese Falcon*, adapted from one of his finest tales, underlines Dashiell Hammett's importance.

W.R. Burnett was the source for *Little Caesar* (1930) as well as *The Asphalt Jungle* (1950). Scripts inspired by James M. Cain, another founder, were long victim to the censor due to their violent sexuality (*Double Indemnity, The Postman Always Rings Twice*).

Commercial exploitation began much later in Raymond Chandler's case (*The Lady in the Lake, The Big Sleep*). He is nevertheless the group's most important author. He was to write original screenplays (*The Blue Dahlia*) and to sign adaptations like *Double Indemnity* and *Strangers on a Train*. The depictions, at which he excels, of a world in complete decomposition, his corrupt millionaires or men of the law, have attracted the attention of producers, and a certain poetry of bars, rain-swept streets, or cold lights even more so. Jonathan Latimer, author of the popular *Lady in the Morgue,* has also frequently worked in Hollywood.

The metaphysical aspect of Graham Greene's oeuvre was infinitely more perceptible to the French Catholic elite than to the Anglo-Saxon general public, who immediately took these novels to be simple thrillers. Greene has played a certain role in the birth of the noir series (*This Gun for Hire*), its acclimatization in England (*Brighton Rock*), and its international development (*The Third Man*). Peter Cheyney and James Hadley Chase represent a profitable and hardly worthwhile vulgarization of the American "manner"; they have adroitly plagiarized all those authors and popularized the genre in England and in France. Their greatest, and maybe only, quality is humor, above all when Chase uses the pen name Raymond Marshall.

It must be said that the first few movies are not the product of original screenplays. From 1941 to 1945 the series is not yet a constituted genre, with its rules and stereotypes, its professional writers or its public: over a period of four years the titles are few. It may be assumed, then, that Hollywood producers have proceeded as per usual. A new kind of detective novel began having a certain success, so they tried to adapt the same themes to the screen. This they did with extreme prudence, however. Commercially, the operation was risky and might have ended in failure. Backing was extremely limited: a mere handful of low-budget films was the result.

The Maltese Falcon suffers from this lack of means: there are a lot of apartment scenes, few characters, no extras, a dearth of technical innovation. A star is called in, Humphrey Bogart, who appears to be over the hill (but who will in fact carve out a new career in the series), and a director, John Huston, whose first film this is. The same thing goes for *Murder, My Sweet* or *This Gun for Hire,* which is entrusted to a Hollywood journeyman director, Frank Tuttle, and acted in by two unknowns, Alan Ladd and Veronica Lake. As yet, no major director ventures into film noir. One waits for audiences to become habituated to this new series.

In short, there is at first, and for seemingly financial reasons, a total submission of the cinema to literature. Later, the noir-inflected film will free itself from this tutelage by becoming, around 1946, one of the richest seams of the American market.

On top of that, film and novel are not identical. The boldness of the latter is all the greater since censorship plays less of a role and the theme of sexuality, for instance, is expressed more freely. Just think of the scenes of prostitution in James Hadley Chase's novel *Miss Callaghan Comes to Grief* or the extremely audacious episodes in an excellent remake of Faulkner's *Sanctuary*, *No Orchids for Miss Blandish*. The cinema has had to proceed by allusion more than by direct description. It would have been absolutely contrary to good manners to say, in the film, that "the lady from Shanghai" was a former resident of the brothels of that city. Besides, Rita Hayworth would perhaps have turned the part down. Nevertheless, censorship has had a paradoxically positive effect: where sensuality is concerned, the implied meaning can only add to the turbid atmosphere, to the images' power of suggestion.

It also happens that the adaptation does not retain all the details of a particularly complex plot. Certain episodes are cut, and the film becomes even more disjointed than the novel. It's often been said that to fully understand *The Big Sleep* or *The Lady from Shanghai* (in which Welles has jocularly claimed to understand nothing of the plot himself) it's necessary to refer back to the original works. But at times these rushed adaptations only add to the strangeness of the film. An example is the shot showing some Chinese people listening to the radio in *The Lady from Shanghai*, a shot bearing no relation to the rest of the action.

Finally, the novel can go much further in the gratuitousness of the violence and the piling up of bodies. But then this is a freedom that has its reverse side: one ends up losing contact with the real, and everything is reduced to a simple exercise in style. After the shock of the first works, the ever-increasing amount of murder has become a convention neither better nor worse than that of the tales of pure deduction appearing before the war. In part, the cinema has been sheltered from this excess. It has almost always kept to a realistic style, with genuine locations and a certain documentary look. It's easier to describe a series of ten murders by pen than it is to film them. Added to which, the screen is a magnifying mirror, and a single act of violence, artfully suggested, has more impact than a text in which the crimes mount up. Just think of the striking image of the killer honing his razor in a barber's salon (*The Enforcer*). In a few years, all those hard-boiled novels will be mixed up or blurred in our memory, but we'll still remember the close-up of that criminal hand and its professional ways.

Psychoanalysis, which has not, furthermore, been without its impact on all this literature, was to exercise an even greater influence on the scriptwriters, dialogue writers, producers, and their public. It's striking how the main wave of popularization of "dynamic psychology" in the USA comes about during the years immediately before the birth of film noir. This is worth thinking about. In 1929, a statistic on the various activities of the 893 professional psychologists belonging to the American Psychological Association bore, under the heading "psycho-analysis," the figure of 0.5. (Each psychologist questioned counted as 1, but the basic unit of measurement was divided according to the number of scientific activities indicated.) Whence the ironical commentary of a specialist called Cattell: "Among American academics, there's only half a psychologist who dares admit his interest in psychoanalysis."

In fact, it's the psychiatrists and not the psychologists who gradually introduced the new methods to the United States. Their wide therapeutic diffusion, which dates from around 1935, was soon prolonged, around the early forties and especially after 1945, in an enormous publicity campaign among the general public on the part of the press and radio. Tests applied systematically during the war to recruits in the U.S. Army had detected a significant percentage of neuropaths and psychopaths, and, after the end of hostilities, the increase in admissions to psychiatric hospitals and clinics focused general attention on the social problem of psychological maladjustment and the mental health measures suitable for remedying this.

As it is, after 1939 many Hollywood producers' names were to be found on the list of subscribers to *The Psychoanalytical Review*.[1] And the cinema didn't take long in taking advantage of this, whether in an explicit manner or in the more discreet form of an implicit theme.

Let's understand as explicitly psychoanalytical films those

works devoted to the description and final explication of a case history, with or without intervention from a practitioner. One of the most typical examples is Anatole Litvak's *The Snake Pit*, but Mark Robson's *Home of the Brave* or Alfred Hitchcock's *Spellbound* could also be cited. As for films of an implicit psychoanalysis, they simply restitute a psychological atmosphere whose coloring is borrowed from this theory of affectivity: the characters obviously have "complexes," but the author doesn't at all seek to give us the key to these: this is the case with Charles Vidor's *Gilda,* John Stahl's *Leave Her to Heaven,* and Raoul Walsh's *White Heat.*

In any event, psychoanalysis has furnished the detective film with many features of a noir psychology. To begin with, it has underlined the irrational character of criminal motivation: the gangster is a neurotic whose behavior can be fully understood only in utilitarian terms; aggressiveness, sadism, and masochism are self-serving; the interest in, or love of, money is often only a cover for libidinal fixation or infantile conflict. This, moreover, is the argument of the first explicitly psychoanalytic film, *Blind Alley,* adeptly directed by Charles Vidor: a gang boss hunted by the police hides out with his mistress and some of his men in a psychiatrist's house in the country. A hideous nightmare (depicted in negative in the film) prevents him from relaxing. The doctor gains his confidence and manages, despite the usual resistances, to link the dream to a secret from his childhood. The gangster, freed from his complex, has no more need to kill and will be gunned down by a policeman. Under the title *The Dark Past,* Rudolph Maté directed a remake of the film in 1948.

Let's think back to the dramatic motif of the ambivalence of feelings: in such an individual, sadism is openly twinned with masochism, sympathy masks hostility, etc. The importance of this trait in the definition of film noir has often been remarked.

In the end, there's a certain cynicism in the views of Freud that accords well with the moral decor of the series. Psychiatry no longer believes in traditionally defined good or evil. It knows that criminal behavior patterns often hide self-destructive reactions or guilt complexes, while moral conscience (the super-ego) is linked to the instincts it represses by means of an entire network of complicity.

Thus the ambience of this "depth psychology," as the Germans put it, with its ambiguous or secret meanings, its infantile background, is transposed in the enigmatic situations of film noir, in imbroglios of intentions and of traps whose ultimate meaning remains remote and appears to recede indefinitely.

Yet its influence didn't end there. It seems, indeed, to have simultaneously prepared the public itself for the strangeness and ambivalence of the noir series. Up to a point, it prepared the organisms of censorship for this, too: the psychoanalytic explanation, acting as a scientific guarantee, was able to push back the limits of what it is permissible to show.

These remarks on the intellectual and literary atmosphere that, at the time, attracted producers and directors do not exhaust the issue, obviously. Film noir is linked to a much wider social context, and the depiction of the criminal milieu derives from the everyday reality of the USA. Local police corruption, the connections between the underworld and politics, large-scale drug trafficking, widespread prostitution, and the all-powerfulness of organized gangs have often been denounced in the American press. All that was needed was to transpose these themes to the cinema.

A few months ago the France-Presse Agency reported the following: "Washington, 20 September – In his weekly report Mr. J. Edgar Hoover, Director of the FBI, states that 1,047,290 crimes and serious offenses have been committed in the United States between 1 January and 30 June 1953. The number of crimes and offenses reached 2,036,000 in 1952, a record figure. This record will be beaten in 1953 if the current trend continues. Statistics show that a crime or serious offense is committed every 14 seconds, a murder every 40 minutes, a rape every 29 minutes, a burglary every 72 seconds, a theft every 25 seconds, an armed robbery every 8 minutes, and a car theft every 2 minutes. 6,470 individuals have died as a result of criminal acts, and there are more than 54,000 injured or rape victims."

Furthermore, it is rare in the production of different countries for crime films situated in a national setting to have a fictional basis. Realism is almost obligatory here. The London criminal fraternity has never been better evoked than in the English works *The Blue Lamp* and *Brighton Rock*. French films like *Un flic* or *Dupont-Barbès* make reference to the existence of a typical underworld, that of Greater Paris. *M,* which Lang directed in Germany, has become an authentic description of 1930s German lowlife.

The main issue is to ascertain why crime has suddenly assumed such importance in the Hollywood output of the last ten years. Because in itself the existence of a given phenomenon doesn't explain its artistic exploitation: artists and public alike may disregard it, deliberately reject it, or consider it unaesthetic. Why have American audiences become sensitized to films of violence and murder? In the absence of truly rigorous empirical studies (questionnaires, "content analyses," etc.), the most plausible explanation seems, indeed, to be the following. A systematic review of prewar American output reveals the preponderance of comedies (of the *Merrily We Live* kind), films about a couple's romance (the *Love Affair* genre), historical films (*Robin Hood* style), and melodramas (the *Dark Victory* type). It is inevitable that such series sooner or later fall out of favor with audiences. It may reasonably be assumed that the public of 1941 or 1942 was tired of comedies and melodramas.

Now, this is precisely the date that war affects the nation. Instantly, the documentary in all its forms (propaganda films or newsreels) assumes much greater importance in cinema programming, and the public acquires a taste for them. In the United States and England, as in the USSR, and later in Italy or France, the hostilities trigger the prodigious rise of cinematic realism. In the case of America, this realism engenders three new genres: the war film, the police documentary, and, from a certain angle at least, film noir.

But then events themselves also habituated people to violence and prepared the way for a crueler kind of cinema. The description of German and Japanese atrocities, widely disseminated after the victory, did the rest. Let us add that the American public has not experienced certain of the horrors of war as directly as European audiences. The tortures of the Gestapo unfolded on the other side of the ocean and retained an exotic, unreal aspect. It would scarcely be tolerated, in a French or Italian film, for a local gangster to behave like a henchman of the Gestapo. There's a sort of taboo, we believe, in this. In America, things were easier, and film noir was able, there, to create a synthesis between realism and cruelty.

Furthermore, it undoubtedly polarized all the dark desires of the average spectator. Weren't the acts of violence committed on children (*The Window*), on the disabled and the sick (*Panic in the Streets, Kiss of Death*), on Jews or black people, a means of inexpensively assuaging, on an imaginary plane, certain secret wishes, conscious or not?

It suffices, at present, to reinsert this nascent genre within the professional milieu entrusted with "thinking it through" in technical terms: Hollywood, with its own way of looking at things, its own procedures, its own traditions.

Because this series is typically American in atmosphere. The action rarely occurs outside the borders of the USA. At very most one could cite, in the setting of Mexico, Robert Montgomery's *Ride the Pink Horse* and Anthony Mann's *Border Incident;* in the context of Central America, John Huston's *Across the Pacific;* and, in a China more "Chinese" than it really is, the famous *Shanghai Gesture* by Sternberg, a great inventor of American eroticism. Even abroad, the drama unfolds among Americans. It's to Hollywood that this pilgrimage to the source must be made.

Furthermore, in the best of cases the influence of Europe seems to be feeble. Prewar Italian output was split between amiable comedies, high-society dramas, epic films, and a number of war documentaries. In England, there'd hardly be anything worth retaining, from our angle, apart from Hitchcock's oeuvre, with its mysterious and fascinating atmosphere (*The*

Thirty-Nine Steps, Sabotage) and its unforgettable villains (*Jamaica Inn*). Germany specialized in historical frescos and national flights of lyricism. There remained France, where the "three greats" (Duvivier and, above all, Renoir and Carné) had created a certain noir realism. Did *Pépé le Moko, Quai des brumes,* and *La Bête humaine* announce American film noir? We think not. In the first instance, oneirism and strangeness are completely lacking in these films from the years 1936–38. Right from the start, the action is located in a well-defined social milieu. There's no trace, either, of any gratuitous violence, if it isn't from time to time in the dialogue of Jacques Prévert who, let's not forget, participated in the Surrealist movement until 1930: Jean Gabin kills, but he's a sentimental criminal, a decent guy who sees red. The drama of passion and fate: that's all there is in these county-court murders. Perhaps the *Quai des brumes* character played by Michel Simon, that sexually repressed amateur organ player, is an exception to the rule. In the end, eroticism is rare, and the more complex figure of Simone Simon in *La Bête humaine* will be insufficient to make a deep mark on French realism. Among possible influences let's not forget, though, the poetry of wet cobblestones, suburban nights, and pallid dawns. The distribution of European films has always been excessively weak on the American market, however, and there's no evidence that a John Huston or a Howard Hawks may have attended the showing of a single French movie from that period.

On the other hand, this is clearly not the case as far as producers are concerned: during the war or immediately afterward various remakes of the best French noir works—which were barely shown in their country of origin—have been made in Hollywood. *Pépé le Moko* was treated to two versions; Jean Renoir's *La Chienne* was brought to the screen a second time by Fritz Lang; Anatole Litvak remade *Le Jour se lève* by flagrantly plagiarizing Carné; and Otto Preminger tackled Clouzot's *Le Corbeau. Quai des brumes* and *Remorques* were destined for the same end. One can, in these conditions, argue that the style of French film noirs has influenced American producers in the creation of an atmosphere bearing on the unfolding and the verisimilitude of the narrative as well as on a choice of subjects in which sordidness, audacity, and violence rub shoulders with an incontestable Romanticism. Let's note in passing that certain producers like Hughes or Hellinger, and scriptwriters like Faulkner and Furthman, have undoubtedly played an important role in the development of this series.

As for Surrealism, its real expansion in the United States is contemporaneous with the development of film noir: it dates from the war and is due to the presence of André Breton, Salvador Dalí, Max Ernst, and Marcel Duchamp. After a timid incursion in cinema around 1934 (Robert Florey's "avant-garde" works), Surrealism has barely manifested itself except in a few young enthusiasts working in 16mm, in the collective feature *Dreams That Money Can Buy,* and in certain musical and vaudeville-type films by the highly discerning Vincente Minnelli, seduced by the movement from 1930 onward (*Ziegfeld Follies,* etc.). In the noir series the only notable manifestation of Surrealism is the dream sequence designed by Dalí in *Spellbound.* In fact, Hollywood, and perhaps censorship too, has preferred analysis of the unconscious (psychoanalysis) to its expression (Surrealism).

The most marked and persistent influence, however, is surely that of German Expressionism. American horror films owe a huge amount to Caligarism (Robert Florey's *The Face Behind the Mask* is proof of this), and films like *The Last Warning,* by the newly arrived Paul Leni, announce the noir series in many ways. Furthermore, Robert Siodmak and Curtis Bernhardt are Germans who've directed in America only since 1940. Both left their country in 1933 to work in French studios until the war. They've introduced a twin tradition into American cinema: that of the Expressionism already implanted by Leni and Murnau and, in all probability, that of 1930s Surrealist cruelty. Fritz Lang met with a similar fate and crossed the Atlantic in 1935. Once again, Europe will have exerted its influence by sending, in the absence of films, directors of talent.

We will be on much firmer ground in looking for sources in the American film, 1932 to 1940. The noir series has created a synthesis of three kinds of film, films that were evolving during the period with such a degree of autonomy that the Hollywood studios themselves had specialized in one or another of them: the gangster film, brutal and intense, which lent style to the dramatic output of Warner Brothers; the horror film, on which Universal had acquired a quasimonopoly; and the classic deduction-based detective film, which, in principle, Fox and MGM divided between them.

On the gangster film's credit side, a wonderful virtuosity in the fight scenes and the brutal, criminal atmosphere will both be recalled. This extraordinary series, from which come George Hill's *The Big House* (1930), Howard Hawks's *Scarface* (1932), William Keighley's *G-Men* (1931), *Bullets or Ballots* (1936), and *Each Dawn I Die* (1939), J. Walter Ruben's *Riffraff* (1936), Lewis Seiler's *Crime School* (1938) and *You Can't Get Away with Murder* (1939), Michael Curtiz's *Angels with Dirty Faces* (1939), and, above all, William Wyler's *Dead End* (1937), has long marked American output. The underworld, with its smoke-filled haunts, Italian killers, poker games, and the wan look of its informers, has been rediscovered by the noir genre, but not the ultraprimitive simplicity of the action, or the stereotyped character of gang leaders and policemen, or "that summary, sporting testing of good and evil," of which Brasillach speaks.[2] Today, the detectives are more suspect, the killers more neurotic, and the intrigue much stranger. For all that, two titles mark the transition to the new series, and they each bear the signature of Lloyd Bacon: *Marked Woman* (1937), more devious in its violence, more desolate in its conclusion, and *Invisible Stripes* (1938 [1939]), a story of the rackets in the markets of New York, with impressive outbursts of brutality, which directly announces Jules Dassin's *Thieves' Highway*.

Before the war, the horror film (the *Frankenstein* and *Dracula* series, *The Werewolf of London*, *The Crime of Dr. Crespi*, *The Devil-Doll*) undoubtedly played an emotional role akin to film noir's. The horror today is more rational, yet responds to the same need to experience shudders of fear. It's no mere accident that Hitchcock himself declares, "In order to shake us from our torpor and to put a stop to our inertia, you can still artificially provoke these shudders; and to me the cinema remains the best way of doing this."[3] It's no mere accident if in France the great lovers of noir (the critics of *St-Cinéma des Prés* and *L'Age du cinéma*) are also the faithful keepers of the horror flame. It's no mere accident, finally, if Robert Wise and Mark Robson made their debuts in the direction of fantasy films.[4]

As for the "deductive" detective film, it has brought a solid tradition of crime mystery and, above all, an audience.

The cinema has followed the same development as literature. A similar phenomenon of saturation has operated in both instances: pure logic has been imperceptibly substituted by adventure, eroticism, and violence. In that respect, a little-known detail is significant: in 1937, Charles Vidor signed *The Great Gambini*, a movie that pushed pure deduction to its furthermost limit. It included, in the final sequence, a sort of challenge to the spectators: they were invited to find the solution in two minutes, during which time the hands of a clock appeared on the screen and, in an inset, a run-through of the main scenes. Ten years later Vidor was to direct one of the foremost noir productions, *Gilda*.

But the detective series contributed yet one more thing: the meticulously described murder, with its extremely horrible details. B-movies were often involved. And yet think back to the reconstruction of the crime in George B. Seitz's *The Thirteenth Chair*. A murder has been committed during a spiritualist séance. The corpse was put back on its chair and the light turned off. After interminable seconds, a piercing cry rent the darkness. The light was turned on. And—we'll long remember it with a shiver of delight—the corpse itself was pointing to the murder weapon embedded in the ceiling. Think back, too, to the subtle crimes of the *Charlie Chan* series (*Charlie Chan in Egypt, Charlie Chan's Secret*) and those supporting movies with their all-but forgotten titles (*Sinner Take All, Night Club Scandal*, etc.), in which then little-known but always picturesque actors like Ricardo Cortez, Joseph Calleia, Bruce Cabot, Brian Donlevy, and Lloyd Nolan prefigured film noir's gallery of suspects.

In the animated cartoon, whole series masked, as humor, an inexhaustible sadistic imagination: the animal fights in *Mickey*

Mouse and, above all, the Fleischer Brothers' *Popeye the Sailor* series, which always centered on a knockabout fight between Popeye and his giant opposite number.

The American comedy, however, has had a more certain influence, albeit one of a very different kind. First, because of a certain absurdity to the action and a pleasant cynicism it sufficed to give a darker tinge to. But mainly because of the faces chosen for the minor roles. More often than not these bit-part players were old troupers from classical rep (Frank Morgan, Walter Connolly, Eugene Pallette, Edward Everett Horton). It just so happened, though, that a hotel porter, a detective, a bureaucrat, or a tax official had a striking or marked presence. All that was needed was to transfer these figures to film noir to give it the realistic look that is its trademark.

Because this series is also a realist series. Whence the importance of all the documentary forms, fictional or not, of American production: MGM's "Crime Doesn't Pay" short films, the first war films from the years 1943–44, Lewis Milestone's excellent transfer to the screen of John Steinbeck's *Of Mice and Men* (1939), and, above all, the whole group of social films extending from the major works of Mervyn LeRoy (*I Am a Fugitive from a Chain Gang* in 1932, *They Won't Forget* in 1937) to the crucial works of John Ford (*The Grapes of Wrath* in 1940, *Tobacco Road* in 1941). The noir sequence in Preston Sturges's *Sullivan's Travels,* in which, as in a nightmare, the hero bangs against the strange walls of the prison—isn't this lifted from *I Am a Fugitive?* The cynical attorney magnificently portrayed by Claude Rains in *They Won't Forget*—doesn't he announce certain film noir figures? And *Tobacco Road*—aside from being a documentary, isn't it a noir poem on the fate of agriculture in the Deep South?

Lastly, two titles would have to be pinpointed from the 1932–41 period of American output, titles that, for their time, avoid all classification and that prove to be *hors série* (in the sense the word "series" has been given in the introduction). Noir works *avant la lettre,* they indeed seem to be. First, there's Ernest Schoedsack's *The Most Dangerous Game* (1932), in which two of the world's finest marksmen confront each other in a hunt to the death: the survivor will win the woman they both covet. The setting is a jungle in the Pacific, a remote island dominated by a medieval-style manor house. Next comes Anatole Litvak's *The Amazing Dr. Clitterhouse* (1938), an unusual mélange of medicine and crime.

References

1 Zazzo, *Psychologues et psychologies d'Amérique,* p. 148.
2 *Histoire du cinéma,* p. 314.
3 *St-Cinéma des Prés* 3.
4 *L'Age du cinéma* 3.

4

The war years and the formation of a style (1941–1945)

Something very odd occurs in the history of American film noir. The first typical work seems to be John Huston's *The Maltese Falcon,* which dates from 1941. In fact, from 1941 to 1945 the productions fitting our criteria are very rare: *The Shanghai Gesture, This Gun for Hire, The Glass Key*, and maybe *Journey into Fear*. The real advent of the series dates to 1946. It's only then that *The Lady in the Lake, Gilda, The Big Sleep, The Dark Corner*, etc., appear on the screen.

Why this false start, followed by this long silence interspersed with a few rare stabs at the new style? It's necessary, we believe, to consider the war here.

It's only at the end of 1941 that the war overtakes the United States, and the war effort quickly mobilizes all the nation's energies. Now, film noir is to a large degree "antisocial." Even if he has a moral aim, its hero remains ambivalent in the face of Evil; he's sometimes a killer pure and simple; the action is confined to a venal, debased milieu; one hides neither the existence of the gangs, nor the corruption of the police, nor the all-powerfulness of money. This was out of place in a world under fire, in which American soldiers were defending a certain kind of order and set of values. There was an obvious discrepancy with official ideology. Whence this laying dormant for five years.

Nevertheless, after 1941 many indicators suggested that Hollywood production was at a turning point in its history: it was evolving toward a more authentic and often more brutal art.

The noir series responded to this need for renewal. Its time having come, yet halted in its development, it was to influence a number of neighboring series.

One can indeed speak of alibis here. After the immense Allied war effort of 1943, the victory that was in sight leads to a détente, and cinema production was liberated from certain constraints. The noir atmosphere and style reclaim their rights, on condition that they find a cover, insinuate themselves in a different genre. For this reason, a twin current takes shape in the years 1944–45: a "noirified" criminal psychology centered on a particularly neurotic or corrupt individual, and the noirified period film in which murder cloaks itself in nostalgia for a remote era.[1] By means of these often unexpected, sometimes contradictory, experiments directors like Siodmak, Bernhardt, Preminger, Brahm, and Dmytryk cut their teeth. They will create a style that will later influence all forms of national output. Finally, following his arrival in Hollywood in 1940, Alfred Hitchcock gets into his stride with *Rebecca,* in which the theme of the tormented young woman is already present; then he makes *Foreign Correspondent,* which contains some typical "bits of bravura": an escape across the rooftops, a torture scene in a Dutch windmill, and a murder attempt on the dome of St. Paul's Cathedral.

A pivotal year in a world at war, 1941 is equally so for Hollywood. In *Citizen Kane* Orson Welles creates one of the great sound films. John Ford completes *Tobacco Road,* which draws its inspiration, like *The Grapes of Wrath* (1940), from the farm crisis, but goes much further in the social fantastic, the downfall of a group of people, and eroticism. Eroticism once more with *The Outlaw,* which will permit Howard Hughes, influenced by Josef von Sternberg, to inaugurate the neo-Western series. Preston Sturges transforms American comedy and gives it a few years' grace by orienting it toward social issues (*Sullivan's Travels*).

The same year also marks a decisive change in a genre almost as old as cinema itself, criminal psychology. Four titles— *Rage in Heaven, Suspicion, King's Row,* and *Dr. Jekyll and Mr.*

Hyde—use, in the presentation of the killers and the unfolding of the plot, a number of devices the noir series will later turn to its advantage.

Rage in Heaven is the work of W.S. (Woody) Van Dyke, an old Hollywood hand who had hitherto managed to adapt to differing styles: exoticism (*White Shadows of the South Seas, Eskimo*), American comedy (*Personal Property*), the epic (*San Francisco*), the historical film (*Marie Antoinette*), social drama (*They Gave Him a Gun*), and the comic detective story (*The Thin Man* and *After the Thin Man,* two works drawn, let us note in passing, from Dashiell Hammett). *Rage in Heaven,* based on a novel by James Hilton, remains within the tradition of the psychological film, since it involves the description of a case history: the jealousy of an unbalanced, doubtless paranoiac, individual. The mystery is imperceptibly created, however, through little touches. The first murder attempt seems so ambiguous that at first we ask ourselves, as does the victim herself, if it wasn't an accident. Then the tension mounts, up until that meticulous suicide dressed up as a crime, one of the most fiendish in the history of the cinema. In fact, the ambivalence of the central figure, the jealous man, appears to be an essential trait here. Is this merely by chance? Is it intentional? An until-then likeable actor, Robert Montgomery, was chosen to play the murderer.[2] For five or six years audiences had been used to seeing this charming and distinguished young man playing in comedy, bringing his humor and his phlegm to it. Whence the aura of saintliness that helps give the film a disturbing edge.

There's the same tension, the same heavily nuanced atmosphere of anxiety, in Alfred Hitchcock's *Suspicion.* And, above all, the same ambiguity in the hero. Here it's Cary Grant, another of American comedy's familiar faces, one of the public's best-loved actors, who plays a charming killer. We say killer, even though in the final sequence there's a sudden shift, leading to a happy ending. Yet this ending didn't exist in Frances Iles's novel, which had until then been meticulously followed. It's been tacked on to a rigorous crime story, and we persist in classifying *Suspicion* as a murder film.

King's Row is the work of a fine, and very prolific, series director, Sam Wood, who a year earlier had made an extremely saccharine movie about American small-town life, *Our Town* (1940). This ultraconventional depiction of provincial life is also found in *King's Row,* which is nonetheless remarkable for one typically noir figure: a doctor who delights in his patients' sufferings and amputates, for no justifiable reason, the legs of the penniless young man his daughter is in love with. Once again an ambiguous character is involved: on the outside, a diamond in the rough, one of those slightly anachronistic, yet "so devoted" country practitioners one has seen a thousand times in the cinema; in reality, a maniacal devotee of pain who sets himself up as both judge and executioner. Here, too, the saintly effect comes from the choice of actor, Charles Coburn, who had made a career for himself as an old trouper in American comedy.

This same year Victor Fleming brings Robert Louis Stevenson's novella, *The Strange Case of Dr. Jekyll and Mr. Hyde,* to the screen. This is a remake, yet it appears at just the right time because it pushes the theme of ambivalence to its furthest—its most absurd, it could be argued—extremes. And the actor designated for the Jekyll role is none other than Spencer Tracy, the man who for ten years had symbolized rectitude and camaraderie. When he's transformed into Mr. Hyde, a chaos of images describes his sensations. One of these is suggestive: Tracy, standing on the buckboard of a wagon drawn by his fiancée, Lana Turner, and his mistress, Ingrid Bergman, horsewhips his ravishing mares. Another sequence describes the relationship between Hyde and his lover, become a slave: her body bears the marks of it. He forces her to play the piano while spitting grape skins at her from time to time. Ingrid Bergman accepts her martyrdom with such good grace, her paroxysms of fright clothe a carnal aspect so attractive, that it is permissible to think of certain pages by Restif de la Bretonne. One will recall the night sequence of Hyde's flight through a fog that the diffuse halo of the gas lamps pierces at regular intervals. A top hat perched on his head, his black cape swirling around him, he runs desperately along the silent, empty streets, leaping any fences at a single bound, with all the agility of a dream.

A 1942 film must be added to this list, one very close, given the disturbing penumbra reigning within it, to *Rage in Heaven* or *Suspicion*: *The Shadow of a Doubt*. This is a major Hitchcock opus, an almost total success, with an admirable exordium on the motif of the hunted man. Of this man nothing is known, however. Who is hunting him? Gangsters or policemen? Given their suspect look, killers, one would reckon. The man returns to his family. Generous, a charmer, irresistible, he spreads happiness all about him. What comes next, however, will reveal him to be a ruthless killer specializing in the murder of rich widows.

Around the same time Hitchcock makes *Saboteur*, an unjustly scorned chase film that contained, as well as a pursuit atop the Statue of Liberty, a very beautiful and strange sequence: a man on the run takes refuge in a cinema during the showing of a detective film. His derisory shadow glides along at the bottom of the screen at the instant the detectives in the film surround some gangsters. The voice of an actor, magnified by the sound system, invites someone to give himself up, and gunshots echo simultaneously on the screen and in the cinema.

Let's sum up. Around 1941 ambiguity and ambivalence penetrated the psychological drama, bringing with them a new accent. The way was open for the noir series. An essential difference exists, however: women rarely have a criminal role. With the exception of one or two vicious types (William Morgan's *Mr. District Attorney*[3] and Richard Wallace's *She Knew All the Answers*, both 1941), they remain affectionate fiancées or loving wives. In *Rage in Heaven* and *Dr. Jekyll*, Ingrid Bergman begins a career as the *ideal victim,* tormented by sadistic males or bewildering dilemmas, that was one day to fatally lead to *Joan of Arc*. Likewise, the doctor in *King's Row* and the killer in *The Shadow of a Doubt* are one-offs. There's nothing degenerate in their entourage; in these families so worthy, so credulous, that one would think them drawn from a textbook on morality.

It's in 1941 that the first typically noir titles appear: *The Maltese*

Falcon by John Huston, the former coscriptwriter of Wyler's *Jezebel*, and Josef von Sternberg's *The Shanghai Gesture*. *The Maltese Falcon*, the third adaptation of a Dashiell Hammett novel, has been rightly described by Georges Sadoul as the first in a series: "John Huston . . . created a new genre, the noir detective film. At the level of sociology, if not of art, this genre could well have an importance similar to that of *Underworld* in introducing a then-new figure, the gangster. *The Maltese Falcon* creates, in one fell swoop, the conventions of film noir."[4]

The story involves a gold statuette, saved from a sinking ship, and sought after by an outlandish bunch of crooks who eagerly fight over it. The film is first of all striking for its astounding gallery of suspects. Like the boss, the enormous Sydney Greenstreet, a fanatical collector with a huge potbelly, who constantly plays with his heavy watch chain. He will stop at nothing to satisfy his passion. His accomplices are no less odd, and their uncommon ways as far as baseness and extravagance go will soon spawn many imitations. The professional killer is a nasty piece of work; his sole pleasure is murder. Yet all through the film this executioner-cum-victim will let himself be slapped around by the detective like some snot-nosed kid. Here once more is an edgy Greek, forever ready to switch sides, sporting weird bangs that tumble over his forehead, giving him an ambiguous air; among this crowd he will display a sneaky cynicism on a par with his cupidity. The heroine, in the shape of Mary Astor, getting on in years but ever beautiful, knows perfectly well how to make the most of her curves in tight dresses and in the forsaken attitudes of a poor defenseless woman. She will turn out to be the instigator of many a heinous crime and the female big boss. Finally, the private detective negotiates the no-man's-land between felony and the law. He is barely distinguishable from the classic gangster: greedy, contemptuous, ferociously misogynist, and ready to take on any job, yet simultaneously driven by a deep-seated curiosity. It's in this sucker detective role that Humphrey Bogart, extraordinary in his forcefulness and sobriety, commences a new career, one that will make him a key film noir figure. And *The Maltese Falcon* inaugurates the series of his "doomed love affairs": violently romantic, fleeting feelings of love for women who will betray and try to kill him (*Dead Reckoning*). A happy end has always been somewhat ridiculous in the case of Bogart, whose sad, desperate look it is essential to vindicate.

The film is shot almost entirely in interiors. In the stifling atmosphere of this closed world the imprecise nature of the motives plays an essential role. Unsure of their objectives, each one ready to sell the other out, the suspects pose themselves questions of which the least that can be said is that they are far from being trite. Then on whom can such a murder be pinned? All eyes turn toward the boss's diminutive protégé, who takes part in the haggling over his own sacrifice, mad with impotent rage. Sydney Greenstreet oversees the bidding with a fine paternal smile for the victim.

The ending has a surprise in store: the Maltese falcon, for which so much blood has been spilt, is an imitation. The absurdity of a derisory destiny—such is the conclusion of this work by John Huston, his first. All the films he will subsequently make end in failures like this one, failures that are relative or total, far-reaching or insignificant. The fundamental meaning of his "universe" doesn't reside in this, however. Added to which, this trait grows weaker as Huston develops. French journalists who've interviewed him in Paris have encountered in him an apologist of action, one not without optimism.

The Shanghai Gesture is a film apart. Noir in many respects, it nevertheless remains a Sternberg work above all else. In it one rediscovers the sensual exoticism of a world of depraved morals, festivities peopled by voluptuous, bedizened women, the obscure magic of which its creator delights in. And this film is a sort of frenetic adieu on the threshold of a ten-year exile, since Sternberg will not direct again until 1951.

The story is straightforward: it's about female revenge in the unlikely setting of a Shanghai gambling den. An opium-rich vapor, a sickly smell of lechery and ecstasy emanate from the pallid faces of these weary, wanton women and these terribly lonely men, a cosmopolitan group drawn to the game of roulette. One appreciates, in passing, the suggestive stylization of the decor and the playing of the actors, the tastefulness of the elaborate female disguises, the bizarre ostentation, replete with dragons and flames, of the Chinese New Year. We will reencounter a milder prolongation of all this in *Gilda*.

The film ends in a sumptuous, sinister repast in which the secrets of the dinner guests are laid bare and resentments are assuaged. A giant figure draws back the curtains, opens a window: one glimpses beautiful, half-naked girls shut up in cages swinging above a voracious, howling crowd. Then Mother Gin Sling, the hostess, announces that in the past she, too, was suspended in a cage, one New Year's Day, and sold to the highest bidder. A man abducted and betrayed her, he has changed his name, he is present (of course) at the dinner party: he's a rich financier, Sir Guy Charteris. Mother Gin Sling, however, has met Sir Guy's daughter, Poppy, and has had her revenge by thrusting Poppy into the arms of Dr. Omar, a poet of Shanghai and Gomorrah, "Doctor of nothing." . . . A few weeks' debauchery and drug abuse have turned her into a limp rag. A door opens and Poppy enters, her dress undone, her hair disordered. This dinner party can end only in bloodshed. Sir Guy, one guesses, will learn from Gin Sling that she is Poppy's mother. Poppy launches into a series of jibes, however, and Gin Sling kills her.

Gene Tierney, whose first big role this is, makes an unforgettable Poppy. She has to be seen sobbing, raging before the obstinately closed door of Omar, pretending to make off, then returning and collapsing against the wall. Omar, lying back comfortably in an armchair, feet on the table, listens with attentive indifference to Poppy's entreaties while smoking a long cigarette. Finally, when he senses that she is completely crushed, he slowly gets up, opens the door, and, without saying a word, offers his arms.

As an *homme fatal*, Victor Mature is the worthy male counterpart of Marlene Dietrich. Elegant, libertine, phlegmatic, he attains, in the lubricity of his ways, the well-studied fulsomeness of certain mature women. As a fallen young woman indifferent to her fate, Phyllis Brooks is absolutely extraordinary.

The following year, 1942, the same series gives us a new work of great merit, Frank Tuttle's *This Gun for Hire,* based on a Graham Greene novel.

It involves a thug whose name recalls, symbolically perhaps, a poem by Edgar Allan Poe: Philip Raven. He's been paid in marked bills by agents of the fifth column to carry out a murder. He turns against his employers and, a victim to duty, falls in the service of the just cause, not without having met and loved (hopelessly so) Veronica Lake.

This fact, it must be added, is a mere pretext. The film scores through the breathless rhythm of a chase that takes us from a miserable shack shrouded in fog and surrounded by the police to a sensational manhunt inside a gas plant. Ensconced in an imperial palace setting, funereal and grandiose, the spy master, a paralytic mummy hauled along in a wheelchair, transmits his murderous orders to his second-in-command, a gross and dangerous, angst-stricken oaf. Their presence is not intended to lessen the feeling of malaise.

The central character, just for once, is the most disturbing. In his role as the solitary hit man, Alan Ladd is a truly remarkable creation. His slight frame and his overly docile baby face, with its limpid eyes, its gentle, unobtrusive features, appear to have come from some other planet, after all the huge and brutal killers who peopled prewar gangster films. Only his expressionless features in situations of great tension reveal a fearsome, inhuman frigidity in this fallen angel. Baudelaire's lines seem written for him: "I will strike you without anger / And without hate, like a butcher."

We will not easily forget the opening sequence of the film: in a seedy, barely furnished attic Philip Raven has just got up. He checks his gun one last time and gives a bit of milk to his cat. Before going off to do his killing, he icily entrusts the creature to the cleaning woman. As soon as his back is turned, she wreaks her revenge by driving the animal away. He returns, however, and catches her at it. Without a word, he slaps her twice, sending her sobbing at his feet. He pours more milk for the kitten, strokes it for a moment, and again leaves, ever silent, ever unfeeling, toward his destiny. Alan Ladd, "angelic killer," has become part of noir mythology.

The Maltese Falcon had contributed one basic theme to the series: the instability of the relationships within a criminal group; in *The Shanghai Gesture,* Sternberg introduced oneirism and eroticism; *This Gun for Hire* described a new kind of murderer and inaugurated the manhunt in an unexpected location. These will all become genre conventions.

The Glass Key has other qualities. It's an uneven film, signed by a generally mediocre director, Stuart Heisler, and often inferior to the Dashiell Hammett novel on which it's based. But then during these apprenticeship years each production contributes an original something that will subsequently be integrated into the definitive style.

Here the contribution is twofold. First, the dramatic motif of the uneven struggle, of the settling of accounts. As the anonymous critic of an exhibitors' guide says: "In boxing terms, Alan Ladd takes much more than he gives."[30] In fact, this is one of the most sensational beatings the cinema has seen. The man's been captured by the rival political gang. Periodically, with machine-like regularity, his captors give him a good going-over. He no longer has a human face; he's a rag doll, crushed and dirty. He essays a movement. He's bashed over the head and thrown into a tank full of water. A torturer observes, "Hey, he floats." He's put back on a broken-down bed, and the henchmen resume their card game. Ladd has pretended to be unconscious; when their backs are turned, he creeps toward the window. He breaks the pane with a chair, launches himself into space, crashes through a glass roof, and lands in the middle of a kitchen.

The Glass Key was also important for its description of political mores in the United States, one that shed new light on the electoral "machine." This theme was to be picked up on in other films heavily influenced by the crime series, such as Michael

Curtiz's *Flamingo Road* or Robert Rossen's *All the King's Men.*

Nineteen forty-three was a year of intense war effort in the USA. Industrial production reached a figure it wouldn't match again until 1951. The war marked all civic activity. The cinema, of course, could not remain aloof, and Hollywood produced patriotic comedies, movies about espionage and resistance movements, propaganda films, and documentaries. During this transition period only two works merit attention: *Journey into Fear* and *Flesh and Fantasy.*

Journey into Fear, or "how fear makes people heroic," bears the signature of Norman Foster, to be sure. But then Orson Welles collaborated on the scenario, and the exceptional breeziness and subtlety of his style emerge in the precision of the shooting script and the plastic beauty of the photography. Basing the film on a spy case that's only a pretext and visibly turns into a hoax, Foster and Welles have rediscovered the chief laws of the noir genre: an oneiric plot; strange suspects; a silent killer in thick glasses, a genuine tub of lard buttoned up in a raincoat, who before each murder plays an old, scratched record on a antique phonograph; and the final bit of bravura, which takes place on the façade of the grand hotel of Batum. We may admire Orson Welles, with graying hair and mustache, in one of those minor, easy-going roles in which he excels: the Turkish Colonel Haki, head of the intelligence service and a womanizer.

Julien Duvivier's *Flesh and Fantasy* is a compilation film placed under the sign of the supernatural. The second tale, though, with Edward G. Robinson, contains some beautiful and atmospheric images of crime and demonstrates that from now on a number of renowned directors working in Hollywood will begin showing an interest in the new style.

In France we've seen very few works of a specifically noir kind dating from 1944–45. Jean Negulesco's *The Mask of Dimitrios* (1944) is an investigation in the *Citizen Kane* mold into the personality of a redoubtable adventurer, Dimitrios Makropoulus, whose body has just been fished out of the Bosphorus. His personality is partially revealed by his victims, and, during the course of a sinister journey to Sofia, Belgrade, and Paris, it's finally learned that he's still alive. Not for long, though. . . . Served by a carefully constructed screenplay, Jean Negulesco succeeds in intriguing us with his irreproachable technique, using the flashback with supple ease and lending originality to his camera angles. As a prying, world-weary novelist in search of the unexpected, Peter Lorre is already introduced as first cousin to the private detective Philip Marlowe who, that same year, makes his appearance on screen in Edward Dmytryk's *Murder, My Sweet.*

Shown in France under the titles of *Adieu ma belle* and *Le Crime vient à la fin,* this film dominated the period. It's the uneven work of a capable director, one that more often than not attains an indisputable visual perfection. Scriptwriter John Paxton has been accused of a lack of rigor that makes the plot, drawn from a Raymond Chandler novel, all but incomprehensible. The writer's text has nonetheless been very closely followed, but a scrupulous adaptation proved difficult due to the complexity of both the facts and the motives. What's more, there's every indication that the filmmakers deliberately omitted certain details in order to reinforce the strangeness of the situations.

As in *The Maltese Falcon,* private detective Philip Marlowe is involved in events whose meaning he is *absolutely* unaware of. He undertakes two different investigations at once, which will connect up after the discovery of secret links between his two clients. The accent has been placed on the highly pernicious character of the heroine, Claire Trevor, in her provocative negligees. A married woman, she's committed a murder to elude a blackmail attempt relating to her past, a past that one has the feeling was turbulent. She resolutely throws herself into Marlowe's arms in order to make him her accomplice in a new stab at murder.

As for the direction, visually of great interest, it occasionally suffers from an internal lack of balance due to the shooting script and the editing: extremely long sequences in static medium shots and shorter, angle/reverse-angle close-ups impair the film's rhythmic unity. Elaborate framings are rare, but the sobriety of the lighting and the interiors must be underlined as well as the infighting between the characters and the camera that's a constant in Dmytryk's style.

During the beatings to which Philip Marlowe is regularly subjected, the camera attempts to render some of the visual impressions the detective must be feeling. These images make one think of researches into pure cinema from the 1923–1930 period: Dmytryk uses fast cutting, fixed or tracking superimpositions, multiple masks permitting the juxtaposition of characters at varying scales, big and very big close-ups (the doctor's hypodermic), and astonishing sound effects. A blurred sheet of glass set in front of the lens restitutes the vision of a drugged and beaten Marlowe. Finally, and this is exceedingly rare in the history of sound cinema, on three occasions Dmytryk utilizes a system of masks each time Marlowe loses consciousness.

This slovenly and somewhat obtuse detective hero is played by the one-time "crooner" in prewar sentimental comedies, Dick Powell, who seeks here to carve out a new career for himself, but will never attain the class of Humphrey Bogart or Alan Ladd.

If film noir's big takeoff is delayed until 1946, the 1944–45 period will at least produce an important "criminal" series linked formally to classic psychology, but tending toward the somber. This series will bring a number of quality directors to the fore—Preminger, Wilder, Bernhardt—while also confirming the ability of some old Hollywood hands: Lang, Curtiz, Stahl. The majority of these directors are German in origin, and the "Hollywood German school" was sometimes spoken of at the time.

The Viennese Otto Preminger, who will later put his name to often commercial productions (*A Royal Scandal, Forever Amber*), had a hit with *Laura* (1944), one of those works that marks an era, a success as unexpected as Henry Hathaway's *Peter Ibbetson* or Tay Garnett's *One Way Passage*. Developing a banal schema (a killer mistakes his victim, attempts a new murder, and gets caught), *Laura* is in fact situated somewhere between film noir and detective-style intrigue.

Yet from the very first image a style asserts itself. From the darkened screen a voice from beyond the grave intones: "I shall never forget the weekend Laura died." A musical theme, which will accompany us everywhere, evokes the shadowy figure of a doubtless delightful young woman, and we submit to the most compelling of spells. The detective wanders like a sleepwalker through the deserted apartment, he opens and closes drawers, moves ornaments and underclothes around, sniffs at bottles of perfume. And while he slumbers dead beat in an armchair, the door opens. Laura—a miracle of triumphant desire—appears, surprised at finding a stranger in her home. We've just lived one of the great moments of postwar American cinema.

The investigation will take us through the crowd Laura was knocking around with: a spineless, fake gigolo; a hard, middle-aged woman on the prowl for handsome young men; and a sensation-seeking man of letters (magnificently played by Clifton Webb), who has a certain renown in literary and moral-izing criticism somewhat analogous to Maurois's in France. Ugly, curt, yet refined and cynical, he nourishes a pride as unrestrained as his unavowed love for Laura. Because he's always loved her from a distance, being content with seeing off potential rivals by all possible means. For all that, she would certainly have accepted to marry him, and this absurd situation could only be resolved by a murder.

A fastidious and doughty manipulator, haughty custodian of the key to the mystery, Clifton Webb sometimes leaves ob-jects carelessly scattered about, objects which through their very insignificance become curious symbols: an old shotgun, a Ba-roque clock. His death is remarkable. He gently subsides in the arms of Laura, murmuring, "Goodbye, my love," at the mo-ment the radio broadcasts a recording of his last talk, which invited listeners to mistrust the idea of eternal love.

Thanks be to Otto Preminger and Gene Tierney for our en-chantment before one of the most adorable creatures in the movies. Pretty, flawless, confident in her power over men, Laura is simplicity made woman. She single-mindedly follows a path she seems to have traced out in advance. She goes for the rug-ged type and does little to hide the fact. If her dear murderer, whose homicidal intentions she has doubtless guessed, hadn't discouraged her three suitors, she'd have been married long ago. Laura will remain a model of voluptuous grace and poise.

Dana Andrews, the police detective, is not unworthy of her. His direct, somewhat rough ways are not displeasing, even when he makes the heroine submit, in the beam of a spotlight, to a cruel interrogation about her past, a scene that already bespeaks jealousy.

Following this remarkable success, Preminger made, in 1945, *Fallen Angel,* a very uneven film that, after a guileless start, rapidly got bogged down in the most inane concessions to morality.

Getting off the bus, a young ne'er-do-well falls madly in love with a waitress in a bar, who's a prostitute on the side. Having no money, he marries an honest and rich young woman, the idea being to fleece her and remarry the waitress. The body of the girl is discovered, however, and all the signs point to him. He goes on the run with his lover, only to reappear a few days later and thwart the real culprit, a police detective thrown off the force for his brutality.

Fallen Angel was saved by the lively depiction of American small-town mores and by the truthfulness of the setting: a provincial bar and its clientele; the spiritualist séance in a charlatan's tent; a seedy rooming house in a big city. . . . Some scenes, such as the bludgeoning, in which the rubber-gloved murderer attempts to extort a confession from an innocent man, possess all the intensity of great film noir.

The very smooth acting was dominated by Charles Bickford, Dana Andrews, and, in one of her first big roles, Linda Darnell. She was able, through suggestive lip movements, a drawling accent, and a strange way of exhibiting her long legs, to express the extremely vulgar sensuality of a corrupt waitress. There's an adroit use of music in the last sequence: before being taken away by the police, the murderer inserts a coin into the bar's jukebox. The waitress's favorite melody starts up, restituting her invisible presence for an instant.

Billy Wilder had made a career for himself as a scriptwriter before tackling direction. In fact, *Double Indemnity,* adapted by Wilder and Raymond Chandler in 1944 from a short James M. Cain novel, scores through its tremendous narrative sureness and through a conclusion that, while moral, is no less logical, for all that. Like *Laura,* this is a film about criminal psychology that assumes its place in the noir series through the intervention of a generic character. In *Laura* it was an aristocratic murderer consumed by neurosis. Here it's a greedy, exciting woman avid for sexual kicks but almost certainly frigid. The myth of the blonde murderess has just been born. One will not forget the first image of Barbara Stanwyck and the upward glide of the camera from her ankles to her face. She was to die as she'd lived, in passion and in blood. She's attempted to kill her lover, Fred MacMurray, but the shot merely clips his shoulder; MacMurray goes over to her, takes her revolver, gently clasps it, and fires a bullet into her heart while murmuring, "Goodbye, baby." In the meantime, it's been learned that she'd also seen off her husband's first wife and that she was sleeping with her stepdaughter's fiancé.

In 1945 Curtis Bernhardt, another émigré of German origin, directed *Conflict,* a film Hitchcock might not have disowned: there's the same air of mystery created by little touches, the same sureness in the shooting script, the same dramatic tension. In it, Humphrey Bogart remained true to character as an impassive murderer, and Sydney Greenstreet placed his atrocious bonhomie at the service of morality. Once again Bernhardt visibly hesitated between the noir series and the psychoanalytic or psychiatric series. He was soon to elect the second and give us *Possessed* and *High Wall.*

The Unseen (1945), unimaginatively directed by Lewis Allen and based on a detective-story script by Hagar Wilde and Raymond Chandler, drew its main interest from the oppressive atmosphere of an old uninhabited house and the mysterious figure of a little boy.

Fritz Lang has never, during the course of his American career, been a director of the strange. A specialist, just before the war, in well-crafted social drama (*Fury, You Only Live Once*), he was and still is extremely foreign to the new atmosphere. Nevertheless, *Man Hunt,* which dates from 1941, contains an astonishing chase in the Underground. *Ministry of Fear,* based on the Graham Greene novel of the same name, is a genuine thriller. The action takes place in the charged atmosphere of London during the Blitz. In the first few images, Ray Milland is released from the mental asylum where he's been incarcerated for poisoning his wife, suffering from an incurable illness. By accident he comes across a Nazi spy ring and, in trying to get to the bottom of the mystery, plunges headlong into the direst adventures. If certain sequences, like the charity ball and the exteriors in the London countryside, smack (agreeably so) of the studio, the spiritualist séance, the night of the bombing alert in the tunnels of the Underground, and the final showdown on the roof of an apartment block are masterfully handled. The stark, cold, high-contrast photography harmonizes perfectly with the implacable unfolding of the action. Fritz Lang is not one to forget the Expressionist lessons of his youth.

The following year he made *The Woman in the Window,* a film with two sides to it. As in *Ministry of Fear,* he again picks up on the theme dearest to his heart, which might be called the motif of the spider web: a man, led despite himself into a crime, struggles against his fate, but sinks deeper into the mire with every step. Here the spider web is stretched tighter by a witness who blackmails him, and by the DA himself. In *M* it was the underworld and the police, momentarily joining forces in order to capture the ripper. In *Fury* it was public opinion, thirsting for blood. In *You Only Live Once* it was the social order, its administration, its laws, and its guardians. *The Woman in the Window,* though, relates to the noir series in its chiaroscuro technique and in different night scenes—such as the discovery of the chief blackmailer's body, huddled at the foot of a brick stairway leading to a cellar—and also because of an increasing tension that gives the work, notwithstanding its implacable logic, a nightmarish rhythm.

Scarlet Street, which dates from 1945, is certainly less successful. This is a remake of the Renoir movie *La Chienne,* which had blazed the trail in 1931 for French realism. Never uninteresting, although more might have been expected of its creator, the work is mainly memorable for its fascinating orchestration of remorse. The murderer of a woman who'd rejected him, Edward G. Robinson wanders through the town, haunted by the voice of his victim, who endlessly repeats the name of the man she loved and who Robinson has just let be condemned in his place. Censorship has been at work and we haven't seen the best scene: the killer, perched on a post carrying electric cables, listening with delight to the buzzing of the current that's going to electrocute the innocent lover. We've been deprived of an exemplary sequence here.

As far as other minor productions from 1945 go, let's note, in addition, Herman Shumlin's *Confidential Agent.* Following the success of *This Gun for Hire,* the producers set themselves to mining the seam of Graham Greene's novels, their cohort of doomed men on the run. The best of *Confidential Agent,* its anguishing and pitiless rigor, was in fact due to Greene and not to Shumlin.

It is significant that Michael Curtiz and John Stahl have also tried to grapple in one way or another with the series that concerns us. This is the rallying of academicism, and it involved two journeymen directors who are customarily undemanding as to the quality of the subject and who lovingly employed the most banal psychology, the most puerile conformism. And yet *Mildred Pierce,* which Curtiz made in 1945, is more than just a slice of life. The ruthlessness of the passions involved, the figure of the second husband, a wanton gigolo, and, above all, that of the cynical and twisted daughter, clearly show the influences at work.

A curious work by John Stahl, *Leave Her to Heaven,* which also dates from 1945, is adapted from the American bestseller by Ben Ames Williams. This is an often audacious film of implicit psychoanalysis centered on the mad doings of a passionate but troubled love affair. The chief character is a woman,

Ellen, who recalls, in her behavior, an Emily Brontë heroine. Afflicted with a formidable Oedipus complex, she meets a novelist in a train, Richard, with whom she instantly falls in love, in a sort of frenzy. We find out why later: he resembles her father. And Richard lets himself be invited, courted, seduced. Almost without realizing it, he finds himself married. Then tragedy takes over. Ellen, who vows a ferociously exclusive love to her husband, spends all her energy chaining him to her for all time, yet unconsciously does all she can to lose him. Richard has, in fact, a half-paralyzed younger brother, egotistical and mediocre, to whom he's deeply attached. This maudlin intrusion disturbs their moments of intimacy. During a swimming excursion, Ellen encourages the brother to attempt a distance that's too much for him. He drowns. From her rowboat, impassable, she watches him foundering in the lake. Richard is overcome with grief, but she becomes jealous of even this feeling. She thinks it opportune to have a child. In vain: she's ordered to rest, and Richard starts going out with his sister-in-law, the charming Ruth. Ellen then throws herself down the stairs (as we know, Hollywood knows of no other abortion technique). Too late. A ditch has been dug between her and her husband, and she launches into the craziest of revenges: she poisons herself in such a way that her suicide passes for a crime and Ruth gets charged with it. Here the worthwhile bit of the story ends, since the climax is as moralizing as can be.

Ellen, a typical film noir figure, converts this opus into something more than a psychological essay: self-assured, strikingly feminine, ready to commit any excess in order to preserve her love. The camera has contrived to film her long supple body, inanimate at the foot of the stairs, in a high-angle shot. Magnificently played by Gene Tierney, she is worthy of figuring in the glittering gallery of deadly seductresses.

One detail must be noted. This is the first time Technicolor has been used in a crime film. Up to this moment it had been reserved for exoticism, adventure films, and musicals. But then "the landscape is a state of soul," and John Stahl has contrived to accentuate the tragic aspect of the story by utilizing scenes of dawn and dusk, the rolling landscape, the color of dried blood, of the deserts of New Mexico, the oppressive solitude of a cabin lost in the verdure of the pine forests, and the glaucous waters of a high mountain lake.

Love Letters (1945) is one of the two or three good films by the prolific William Dieterle. This classic melodrama, flirting with noir, possesses the ardent and melancholy charm of those works by English novelists in which, between the lines, the pendulum swing of passing time is heard. A country setting with its gentle horizons, an old house that's charmed, a ravishing and accommodating female amnesiac in search of a past veiled in blood are sufficient to provoke mystery and enchantment. And William Dieterle has used, with much skill, all the procedures suited to the particular ambience of the screenplay: depth of field, low-angle shots up at the ceilings, chiaroscuro, experiments in framing.

A few years before the war, American cinema had launched a new formula: the costume drama situated between 1830 and 1910. This was the fashion for the "period film." The phenomenon was to reproduce itself in Europe, and French output would experience a similar craze with the films of Claude Autant-Lara and the insipid Jacqueline Audry. In the United States, most of the new ground had been broken by George Cukor: witness the virginal period film (*Little Women*, 1933), the bustling period film à la Dickens (*David Copperfield*, 1935), the melodramatic period film à la Dumas (*Camille*, 1935 [1937]), the pseudo-picturesqueness of the early 1900s (*Zaza*, 1939). In the end, however, all these films displayed only the meagerest of resources, and on the eve of the war the genre seemed to have already given its best.

The years 1944–45 witnessed the conjunction of this style with the noir series. A twofold explanation for this could easily be found: *the noir atmosphere signified renewal for the period film model, and the faded charm of the setting provided an alibi for film noir.*

There again, the great pioneer was George Cukor, with *Gas-*

light, which he made in 1944. This was a remake of the English work by Thorold Dickinson, but a quality remake all the same. The story took place in that London of the early 1900s in which the memorable affair of *Dr. Jekyll and Mr. Hyde* had recently unfolded. The fogbound nights, the silhouettes of bobbies melting into the mist, the muffled sound of hansom cabs, the vast wooden staircases with creaking treads, and the rooms encumbered with Victorian furniture made for a singular decor, at once conventional and disturbing. From time to time, bizarre footsteps in the attic made the chandeliers flicker, and the light lowered in intensity. There was, furthermore, something of Hitchcock in *Gaslight:* an atmosphere created by little touches of suspicion and coincidence. There was also an excellent noir figure: a charming and sadistic murderer. In this role, Charles Boyer, with his smile, his elegant, international playboy looks, heightened the ambivalence and malaise still more. Ingrid Bergman was the victim, a willing victim who recalled Joan Fontaine in *Suspicion.* Through her resolutely edgy acting, from the first alarums to the final hallucinations, she lent a genuine physical presence to the mounting terror.

Other directors took the same path. In 1944 John Brahm made, in *The Lodger,* an engaging film in which atmosphere was created by the lighting, by the London background of highly sinister furnished rooms, by the pallid face of a killer with limpid eyes, Laird Cregar, by a judicious use of water and the river, and by immense discretion in the violence. We weren't present at Jack the Ripper's murders. They were suggested. But then that woman's expression at the approach of the killer, that body quaking with fear, were more gripping than the killing itself.

On a similar theme of criminal madness in the London of the early 1900s and with two of the actors from *The Lodger,* Laird Cregar and George Sanders, John Brahm was to make a less convincing work a year later, *Hangover Square.* Linda Darnell did display a laudable sensuality in it, for all that.

The interesting early titles from Robert Siodmak's American career would have to be related to the noir period style. In Europe, the skillful touch of this German director had long been known. To him we owed a number of realist films (*Autour d'une enquête* in 1931 and *Tumultes* in 1932), various comedies, one of the first films of implicit psychoanalysis (*Pièges*, in 1939), and, above all, a psychological drama of great acuity (*Mollenard*, in 1938). With their customary contempt for European directors, Hollywood producers first of all bestowed on Siodmak subjects that were unworthy of him. He signed that awesome potboiler, *Cobra Woman*. Another early film, *Phantom Lady* (1944), was a brilliant thriller with clever lighting. It bore the acid charm of its heroine, Ella Raines, and contained five ear-splitting minutes of jazz. Nevertheless, it's the noirified period style that helped Siodmak make a name for himself, first with *The Suspect* (1944), the story of a double crime, again with a London atmosphere, haunted here by a murderer, played by Charles Laughton, with a good-natured way to him.

Happily, a year later, *The Spiral Staircase* made the most of a story about criminal madness in a period setting: an English manor house in the middle of a great park; a bedridden old woman who senses danger beckoning; a perfectionist who does away with young female invalids; Helen, a touching aphasiac. Robert Siodmak managed to lend a purely visual efficacy of expression to his style. He even attempted to recreate the hallucinations of the madman, possessed of the desire to kill: whence the enormously enlarged view of his eye, in which the victim is reflected, elongated as in a deforming mirror; whence Helen's face, the mouth effaced. The girl looks in the mirror at that instant and suddenly brings her hand to her mouth. Siodmak's reputation was henceforth secure.

Lastly, Jacques Tourneur has also contributed to the vogue for period crime. Nearer to our own time—1930—yet conserving all the charms of the past, *Experiment Perilous* (1944) described a series of murders in which jealousy and madness went hand in hand. Fast-moving, elliptical, forever sure in its little touches, the mise-en-scène admirably rendered the often odd tinge of those old crimes.

Cukor, Brahm, Siodmak, and Tourneur, then, appeared to have come across a fecund source, to have inaugurated a new series. It was not to be. After 1946 criminal works in an old-fashioned setting were to become more and more rare. Resolutely turning his back on the past, Siodmak made ready to direct *The Killers*. This change of direction was significant. During the war, the period film had served as a pretext, as did the recourse to classical psychology. With the hostilities over, nothing prevented the unleashing of crime in the contemporary setting of the American city. Nothing stood in the way of the flowering of film noir.

References

1 The adjective is *noirci;* literally, "darkened" or "blackened." The neologism "noirified" has the virtue of retaining the root and sustaining the idea. —*Trans.*

2 Excepting the role he played in 1937 in Richard Thorpe's *Night Must Fall.*

3 The 1941 *Mr. District Attorney* was directed by William Morgan, not by Robert B. Sinclair, as cited in the original; he directed the 1947 version. —*Trans.*

4 In his weekly critical column in *Les Lettres françaises.*

5 *Index de la cinématographie française 1948–1949.*

5

The glory days (1946–1948)

The years 1946–48 mark both the ascension and the apogee of film noir in the United States. Criminal psychology and the classic gangster type are relegated to the background. From *Gilda* to *Dark Passage,* the new style produces its most striking and accomplished works.

It's always easy to explain the formation of an artistic tendency after the event. Let's observe, though, that a particularly favorable set of conditions was produced simultaneously.

The war had just ended and rearmament hadn't begun. This transitional period guaranteed a maximum amount of freedom. If it's true that there is a certain audacity in the noir style, this audacity was confronted by the absolute minimum of constraints.

On the technical side, the technical hardware of the American studios was, in 1946, the finest in the world. Hollywood's facilities hadn't been affected by the hostilities, and its equipment, renewed or improved, provided the least photographer, the most minor director, with resources that none of their European colleagues as yet had access to. In any event, inventiveness had its own technical requirements here: urban locations, night shooting, chase scenes, etc.

The acting personnel had been renewed. Most of the familiar faces from before the war had disappeared from the screen. Now, in movies that were seeking to be both strange and realistic, it was important for faces not to be recognized, for the shock effect not to be lessened by any feeling of déjà vu. Obviously, for economic reasons the major roles remained the prerogative of the stars, but often the killers or minor suspects were unknown to us. In its infancy, film noir tended to approximate to the ideal conditions of cinema: an art without big stars, in which an actor or actress would be used in one film alone.

Directing itself had also sloughed off its old skin: William Wyler, King Vidor, John Ford, Frank Capra—all the prewar "greats" appeared to be running out of steam. And men formerly condemned to menial commercial tasks, the émigrés or newcomers, put their personal stamp on things: Welles, Montgomery, Wilder, Siodmak, Rossen, Daves. . . .

Lastly, as was only to be expected with this type of economy, the postwar period posed a number of disturbing problems: unemployment relating to the redeployment of workers, the déclassé status of certain veterans, the rise in crime. . . . As a statement on a society, the new series came at just the right moment.

Film noirs

Among the major productions of 1946 Charles Vidor's *Gilda* immediately stands out, albeit the film was condemned by the critics and misunderstood by the public, who turned it into a success for reasons at odds with its true qualities. Entirely bathed in a specifically noir atmosphere, this opus remains, with John Stahl's *Leave Her to Heaven,* perhaps the most magisterial lesson of applied psychoanalysis on the screen.

Here is a brief summary of the scenario: a young American hooked on gambling, Johnny Farrell, is saved from certain death by a gentleman night owl, Ballin Mundson, the owner of a redoubtable sword stick and an aficionado of handsome young men. He offers Johnny a lucrative job in the wealthy circle he controls, advising him not to forget that women and business are two essentially different things. After a brief absence, he returns, married to Gilda, a magnificent young woman who is none other than Johnny's former mistress. Desirous of renewing the affair and forsaken by her husband, Gilda attempts to sow discord between the two men, since Johnny doesn't want her, and she begins flirting outrageously. But Mundson, mixed up in a dark tale of tungsten dealing and Nazi espionage, spectacularly disappears, while faking suicide—by airplane! Johnny takes the place of the dead man in his business affairs as well as in his private life and weds Gilda. But his marriage remains unconsummated because he can't rid himself of the obscure hold Mundson had on him in life. Perhaps Johnny also believes that his suicide is due to his wife's unfaithfulness. And he doesn't hesitate to persecute Gilda, to lock her up, assuaging his own hatred and gaining revenge on his benefactor at one and the same time. At the end of her tether, the unsatisfied belle flaunts herself in public in a compensatory, intensely erotic display. Faced with this spectacle, Johnny finally becomes conscious of his virility. He gives the alluring Gilda a resounding slap and hands Mundson's secret papers over to the police. The pseudo–dead man's final, brief apparition ("phantasm" might be the word here), come to settle accounts and claim what's his (using the threat of his maleficent stick), a no less rapid dispatching of this now inoffensive ghost to the nether regions, and Johnny will at last be able to find happiness with Gilda. . . .

This apparently disconcerting plot is often, for the person who knows how to look, studied in the extreme. It concretizes and "dramatizes," as in a dream, a series of affective automatisms. Whence its extremely agreeable mechanical side, accentuated still further by the icy elegance of the characters, the Baroque sumptuousness of the sets (in the grand opera or 1920s cinema style), and Rudolph Maté's ostentatious framing of the image.

Charles Vidor has managed to excellently limn in the umpteen wrangles of Johnny Farrell, torn between Gilda and her husband, who's clearly a father substitute for him. In this impressive illustration of the Oedipus complex, the director has laid bare the obscure ties that bind the two men, thus evoking, perhaps without realizing it, the complex behavior of children in relation to their own father, something which remains, whatever one says, one of the least popularized aspects of psychoanalysis.

Choice tableaux are not lacking during the course of the film. One sequence describes Johnny's fitful sleep as he tosses and turns in his bed. All of a sudden, like the very emanation of his semi-nightmare, a woman's voice is heard in the dark. . . . For a moment he believes it's a hallucination. Then he hastily gets dressed and discovers, in the half-light of the big, empty room of the gambling joint, in the midst of the stacked chairs, with a member of the kitchen staff for audience, the insomniac Gilda seated on the edge of a table, her long legs crossed at the thigh, who is singing a lullaby while accompanying herself on the guitar.

Another justly acclaimed scene: to the rhythm of an evocative swaying of the hips, Gilda peels off, with studied slowness, the black stockings that serve her as gloves,[1] revealing the dazzling whiteness of her arms to the spectator. And her voice, the extremely inviting voice of a sensual woman ready to surrender herself, marking her phrasing with the disordered shaking of her magnificent head of hair, sings the henceforth famous "Put the Blame on Mame."

The sculptural shoulders of Rita Hayworth effortlessly bear the whole weight of the film. The new Lola-Lola of the "atomic age," she is the worthy representative of a certain American eroticism. Her extravagant clothes have been conceived with an intention that Alexandre Astruc has perfectly captured: "the black silk sheath dresses, the gloves stretching up to the elbows and the *cuir-bouilli* boots have a precise function: they strip the woman of all human character and turn her into an object."[2] A statue of flesh escaped from some luxuriant dream, Gilda moves around behind the grilles, imposts, and heavy curtains of casinos more closed off than harems.

One sequence, as symbolic as you'd wish, has as its backdrop the carnival that floods the nocturnal streets of Buenos Aires, and in which one divines, beneath the masks, the paroxysm of passions contained too long, passions that clash and meld.

Within the noir series *Gilda* was a film apart, an almost unclassifiable movie in which eroticism triumphed over violence and strangeness. Howard Hawks's *The Big Sleep* is, on the other hand, a veritable classic of the genre, the essential laws of which it encapsulates.

Up to that point Howard Hawks had done good things and bad things. Good in *Scarface* (1932) and *Only Angels Have Wings* (1939), bad in *Sergeant York* (1941). But then *The Big Sleep* doubtless owes a lot to the original novel by Raymond Chandler and to the adaptation by William Faulkner.

The plot involves an investigation by Chandler's favorite hero, Philip Marlowe, hired to get General Sherwood's two daughters out of a tight spot. One of these, Carmen, an ether addict and nymphomaniac, is prone to outbreaks of destructive rage toward her lovers, outbreaks that can stretch as far as murder. The other, Vivian, divorced and blasé, assiduously frequents the baccarat tables and loves the big thrill.

There again, it's impossible to describe in detail the jungle these women frequent: our anxious curiosity is aroused by this world of torturers and victims, each bound to the other by unavowable ties.

The sordid settings and their bizarre details, the brief but merciless fistfights, the furtive murders, the sudden reversal of roles, the "objects," in the Surrealist sense of the word (such as the Khmer statue hiding a camera which takes pictures of the orgy scenes), the eroticism of blood and pain (Vivian kissing Marlowe's bruised lips), the killer who lets himself be poisoned in order to go on concealing his accomplice's name, the armed prowlers who watch over the nocturnal rendezvous and the environs of secret gambling joints, and lastly the wild dancing of the women: all this makes *The Big Sleep* a major event in the history of American cinema. Never will film noir go further in the description of a cynical, sensual, and ferocious world.

Howard Hawks, a great specialist in violence, has lost none of his touch. He's obtained a peerless performance from all his actors, from Humphrey Bogart, who takes over from Dick Powell in the role of Marlowe, as well as from Lauren Bacall, a cat woman with an attractive, jutting jaw, with moist, full lips. These celebrated lovers fire off remarks of a surprising eroticism, remarks the censors have let pass because they used metaphors from horse racing. And the mise-en-scène possesses all the necessary brilliance and toughness.

The Lady in the Lake, made in 1946 from another Raymond Chandler novel, is Robert Montgomery's first film. Again it's a detective story, but also the first systematic attempt at so-called subjective cinema. Ever since 1938 Montgomery had dreamed of a work shot entirely "in the first person singular." Orson Welles all but stole his idea in 1940 for *Heart of Darkness,* a subsequently abandoned project. Finally MGM gave Montgomery his chance, and *The Lady in the Lake* came to be.

The result is on the whole extremely disappointing. The condition necessary to a film's success lies in the spectator's identification with one of the heroes. But how could there be any rapport when all that was known of detective Philip Marlowe, the "I" of the film, was the sound of his voice, his forearms, the smoke from his cigarette, and sometimes his fleeting reflection in a mirror? Added to which, the long-windedness of the dialogue, the acting of characters forever seen face-on, the complexity of the script, which added up to a major failing here, inevitably doomed this experiment to semifailure.

Mainly, though, *The Lady in the Lake* has shown that the procedure, a highly valuable one when judiciously used—as in certain passages of *Murder, My Sweet,* or in the admirable opening sequence of *Dark Passage*—namely, when required by the action, turns out to be gratuitous when one tries to systematize it.

For all that, thanks to this subjective camera there were some excellent moments in *The Lady in the Lake:* the discovery of the body in the bathroom, following an oppressive tour of the dead man's house; or the incredible efforts of Marlowe, after taking a terrible beating, to reach the phone booth. Rasping breathing was heard, one saw hands clawing the gravel of the driveway, and these details gave the scene a feeling of overwhelming verisimilitude.

Lastly, as far as eroticism goes, a winning contribution was to be encountered here. As Phil Mori observes in his study of "The Vertical Screen at the Service of a Sexual Mysticism," "the spectator experiences a highly agreeable sensation when, standing in for the hero, he's eyeballed by some dazzling blondes."[3] There's nothing more fetching that to see the extremely pretty

Audrey Trotter slowly incline her face toward us, closer and closer, until it entirely fills the screen, and to offer her half-open lips to the Marlowe-identified audience. And the sudden darkness: at the contact of those lips the detective had closed his eyes.

Again from 1946, Henry Hathaway's *The Dark Corner* had a few things going for it: a sustained rhythm, smooth acting (Mark Stevens, William Bendix, Lucille Ball, and, above all, the incredible Clifton Webb). Centered, once again, on the theme of the private detective, the film contained one extremely odd scene, typical of the series: Clifton Webb had arranged to meet a bothersome accomplice in the deserted corridor of an office block, in front of an open window. He made as if to take out his wallet to look for money and, with a sharp blow, sent the over-trusting, enormous brute flying into empty space. Then he calmly descended to the floor below, to his dentist's, where he'd also made an appointment.

The hero of *Somewhere in the Night* hasn't just lost his memory. His face was badly wounded in the Pacific, and he had a new one reconstructed. But his past catches up with him: he's an ex–private detective, formerly charged with theft and murder. Joseph L. Mankiewicz, who occasionally lacks rigor, has managed to create an ambiguous, mysterious atmosphere by exploiting the picturesqueness and poetry of the suburban areas of San Francisco. John Hodiak, Richard Conte, and the beautiful Nancy Guild, then just starting out, were faces unknown to the public, and the direction gained in authenticity from this.

The year 1947 brought two major works: Orson Welles's *The Lady from Shanghai* and Delmer Daves's *Dark Passage*.[4]

Journey into Fear and the sparkling beginning of *The Stranger* had shown us a Welles interested by the technique of the thriller and capable, here as elsewhere, of raising himself up to the first rank.

The Lady from Shanghai is a film noir in the full sense of the term. But then the director's personality bursts out at every step, extends beyond the bounds of the series, and streams forth in a whole series of marvelous images.

And yet the subject is no better and no worse than many others. By chance, Michael O'Hara saves a tremendously beautiful young lady from being abducted. The husband, a disabled and more than suspect lawyer called Bannister, suggests he become his wife's bodyguard. He consents to this and embarks with them on a yacht cruise fraught with obscure dangers. One day, Bannister's business partner, who's popped up during the voyage, offers Michael O'Hara five thousand dollars to pretend to murder him. As it is, Michael needs money to run away with Mrs. Bannister, and he accepts. Later, he'll discover he's fallen into a trap: the partner really will be killed. He's arrested and takes Bannister for his defense attorney. But the lawyer easily implicates him during the trial. He escapes from the court, manages to find Mrs. Bannister, then is rejoined by the husband. Shots are exchanged in the haunting decor of a hall of mirrors. Both husband and wife are fatally wounded, but the beautiful woman has the time to admit that she was the real guilty party.

The main characteristic of this confused story is an atmosphere of malaise. In the long episode of the cruise, one senses the murderous intentions hovering around the yacht and its guests. Who'll do the killing? Who'll get killed? And why? The men have something slimy and unwholesome about them. The partner, who sweats and mops himself in the tropical heat, resembles a giant reptile. Added to which, Bannister himself doesn't walk: he *wriggles along* with the aid of two sticks. The crewmen have been chosen for their jailbird looks. One port of call brings other oddball characters aboard: are they killers, spies in the pay of the husband or of the partner? We never find out. The young woman herself is completely mysterious. Her secret schemes don't affect the serenity of her face. What is she up to? And all throughout the voyage the sky is leaden, the oversmooth sea full of sharks, and the heat too muggy. . . . In a sense, Orson Welles has revived the Expressionist tradition of *Caligari*. The decor is always, via contrast or analogy, in keeping with the psychological situation. Let's recall that brief stopover in one of the world's most beautiful landscapes: a magnificent wooded coastline, strewn with white villas that reflect the joys of living. On a sunlit hillock overlooking the bay, the partner, overcome by inexplicable fear, abruptly comes out with some grimly pessimistic and sardonic opinions about existence. Some tourists pass by, and from their jumbled conversation a single word stands out, one that becomes a leitmotif: "money."

Another focus of interest in this exemplary thriller is its idio-syncratic eroticism: *The Lady from Shanghai* reveals a short-haired Rita Hayworth of a marmoreal mattness, radiant and yet out of reach. The scene in which the partner locates her through his binoculars, stretched out almost naked on a reef, pleasuring herself in the sea breeze and completely untouchable, is highly symbolic in that respect. And one won't forget her flight in the threatening darkness filled with the plucking of mandolins, through the slum areas of Mexico City: a woman in sparkling white evening dress runs through sordid streets peopled with motionless shadows, beneath arcades with their pillars covered in torn posters, and is suddenly silhouetted against a background of skyscrapers peppered with lights. Her death will be a lonely one, at daybreak, there on the floor littered with bits of broken mirror. She utters a few words, "I made a lot of mistakes," which will explain neither her life nor her crime.

Other elements have been transposed by Welles here, ele-ments relating to motifs dear to his heart.

In *Citizen Kane,* following the quarrel with Susan, Kane strode along a gallery of mirrors and was reflected ad infinitum in them. An allegorical image, this, which summarized the magnate's insane narcissism. It was to be taken up, moreover, albeit in a banal way, by Mankiewicz at the end of that facile, garrulous pseudomasterpiece *All About Eve.* Now Welles again utilizes mirrors in *The Lady from Shanghai,* but more as a form of dra-matic development: Michael and his lady friend think they're alone in the hall of mirrors, but first a hand resting on a walk-ing stick, then Bannister's sidling along on his sticks, surrounds them on all sides, indefinitely repeated. Then comes the final shootout in the unfathomable depths of this setting, in which the characters don't know whether they're firing at a real person or at a reflection.

Likewise, Kane's cheerless and dignified picnic by the sea finds its echo in the morose party organized at great expense by Bannister in the middle of a crocodile-infested swamp in the overwhelming heat of the Equator.

But *The Lady from Shanghai* is mainly impressive for its extraordinary technical mastery. Forsaking the tradition of *Kane* and *The Magnificent Ambersons,* Welles rarely uses depth of field. He even resorts to extremely long static shots, when these are necessary to the analysis of a character or event. The first half of the film is intentionally slow; it has a documentary rhythm: we let ourselves be lulled by the mounting undertone of menace. But when the drama begins to take shape, the virtuosity of the direction becomes more perceptible: a motley assortment of mobile shots, tilted framings, unexpected reframings, long, circular panning or tracking shots. Welles piles up the bits of bravura and makes light of the worst difficulties. For example, scorning a classic rule of photography, he frames Rita Hayworth's legs or back in reverse shot, following a close-up of her face.

Finally let's cite, in the course of various sequences:

- The crime Michael simulates in the vicinity of a casino on pilotis. At that precise moment, a crowd invades the deserted pontoon bridges from every side, and its all-enveloping procession cuts off the hero's retreat.
- The scene of the trial, entirely in ellipses: during the time it takes to describe a professional ploy on Bannister's part, following a police officer's deposition, the camera glides over the spectators, isolating a face here and there, as in a newsreel; next, there's a strange image of some Chinese listening at home to a radio broadcast of the court proceedings.
- The lovers' rendezvous in the halls of an aquarium stocked with octopuses.
- The Chinese theater silently invaded by the police, the rolling eyes of the hieratic actors among the sound of cymbals and tiny bells.

- Michael's waking up in the amusement park, in the midst of the big dippers, distorting mirrors, labyrinths, and conveyor belts, this episode providing us with a wonderful "avant-garde" moment.
- Finally, on top of all this, the call of the sea, the immense panorama of San Francisco Bay beckoning one to adventure.

It's regrettable that certain scenes relating to the relations between Mrs. Bannister and the Chinese community have been cut.[5]

Made in 1947, and based on an excellent David Goodis novel, former scriptwriter Delmer Daves's *Dark Passage* also has its place in the very first rank.

This director had made some extremely uneven works: a good war film, *Destination Tokyo,* and a curious, much-discussed movie filmed almost entirely on location, *The Red House.* Aside from being an engaging *crime passionnel,* it presented a startling picture of rural life in the United States, while the easy-going morals of teenagers of both sexes recalled that of the Scandinavian countries.

The drama of *Dark Passage* is a new version of the theme of the man on the run. A prisoner, Vincent Parry, escapes from San Quentin Penitentiary. On the road, a beautiful stranger picks him up in her car. In San Francisco, a taxi driver takes him to a surgeon who's been struck off the register, who gives him a new face. He has a rendezvous with his only friend in the city, and . . . comes across a corpse! He finally discovers the person who's really guilty of the crime he'd been imprisoned for, a woman who'd sought to wreak her revenge on him. She jumps out the window, thereby depriving him of his one chance to prove his innocence. Everything's stacked against him, but he is to succeed in crossing the border and will rebuild his life with the beautiful stranger who'd picked him up.

It's hardly necessary to underline the oneiric side of this scenario. This is a nightmare in which everything conspires against Vincent Parry. When some providential allies come to his aid, they loom up as in a dream. Coups de theatre, inexorable fate:

this whole absurd logic is amply authenticated by the systematic use of real locations. The steep streets of San Francisco, with their white house fronts bathed in sunlight, lend a highly disturbing presence to this imaginary plot.

The nightmare ends happily, though. Like a powerful river swollen with slack water, the vista broadens enormously and opens onto the immensity of the Pacific. We're in Mexico. Free and all alone, Vincent Parry awaits his beloved. Smiling, she suddenly appears, and the two of them twine around each other while whirling against the eternal background of the ocean.

Delmer Daves has magisterially guided the narrative to its conclusion. In the ideal museum of film noir, some images will undoubtedly endure: the truly repulsive surgeon; the *necessary* murder of the blackmailer on the deserted San Francisco dockside; the suicide of the demoniacal woman, played by Agnes Moorehead; lastly, the hero himself, who—and the idea's new— *changes face* during the course of his adventures. And Daves has, in the first part of the film, risked a fresh stab at subjective cinema. Until Vincent Parry's been operated on, his face isn't seen. The "I" is here the escaped man. The experiment is motivated by the script, and that's why it proves more convincing than Robert Montgomery's.

Dead Reckoning relates the violent adventures of Captain Murdoch, who's making inquiries into the suspicious death of Sergeant Johnny Drake, an old army buddy of his. John Cromwell's brilliant and expressive direction is chiefly remarkable for the relations between the hero and Cora Chandler, a prostitute to whom Lizabeth Scott lends her finely chiseled features, her singular gaze. The unusually stylish ending is beautiful and totally in keeping with the ambience of the film and the personality of its main actor, Humphrey Bogart. Cora Chandler is stretched out, deathly pale, on her couch. She knows she's going to die and is very afraid. Bogart, who holds her hand, exhorts her to be brave and transforms her final minutes of agony into a story about leaping into the void, about bailing out. At the final moment, he shouts "Geronimo!" And the final, highly documentary image is that of a parachute that unfurls and gets smaller as it recedes into the distance. For the first time in the cinema we've seen death in the first person. The film ends on a fall into nothingness.

Out of the Past raises the extravagance of film noir to its highest pitch. This absurd restlessness, these useless murders, this odd nocturnal atmosphere, and these episodes of a fulgurating brutality could only end in the death of the three protagonists. One thinks of Alfred Jarry's words: "So I'll kill everyone, and then off I'll go." Jacques Tourneur's elliptical direction, the photography, and the location shots in particular are truly remarkable. Robert Mitchum lends his wicked ingenuity to the now-classic character of the private detective.

In 1948 Anatole Litvak directs an uneven, but often successful, work, *Sorry, Wrong Number*. What's more, it's surprising that this precursor of the thriller—Litvak, it will be remembered, had made *The Amazing Dr. Clitterhouse* in 1938—waited so long to reembark on this style.

Sorry, Wrong Number was originally a radio play. A half-paralyzed, bedridden woman isolated in a huge empty mansion made a phone call to try and reach her husband. By chance she cut in on an anonymous dialogue: two killers were arranging a crime that would take place at 11:15. And little by little, phoning here and there to get in touch with the absent husband, she realized that this murder was her own. Too late: the killer was already on his way up through the deserted building. An ideal subject for a radio broadcast: the listener took part in the drama under the same conditions in which its heroine was living it, *as something heard a long way off,* yet urgent and inexorable.

Litvak transposed this subject to the visual plane by following it very closely. He shot his film in interiors, with long scenes in the sick woman's bedroom, by respecting the temporal unity of the radio formula. He denied himself several classic ploys, then: the usual gangsters, the chases, the literal violence. But then the narrative had an implacable toughness, and those bizarre or frightening phone calls are impressive as a use of the theme of the strange. Finally, let's recall the camera movement that ended the film, starting out from the hall, from the front door the assassin was opening, and ending up in the victim's bedroom.

The same year, abandoning his researches into pure technique, Robert Montgomery was to come up with a fascinating opus, *Ride the Pink Horse,* based on a script by Ben Hecht and Charles Lederer.

The film was impressive, first of all, for its enigmatic situations. A man got out of a car in a small Mexican town. Who was he? Gangster, killer, cop, or "dabbler"? The first shots, without dialogue, described in detail his odd behavior with a key and a small suitcase in the bus station. Then the man got caught up in some bizarre goings-on, suffered a severe "going over" in a hotel room, barely escaping with his life, and encountered a few providential allies: a fat, bearded Mexican, the owner of a merry-go-round with wooden horses, and a petite Indian girl, the exquisite Pilar. The raucousness of the fiesta, arousing the dormant echoes of the little town, and the miserable ambience of shadowy cantinas (with their apathetic silhouettes whose eyes sometimes shone with a singular light) were seized in their raw, urgent poetry.

A somewhat barbarous poetry, this, at one with the chill violence of events: as in the punishment inflicted by two hoodlums on the old Mexican, in front of a whitewashed wall, while the wounded hero remained spread out on the merry-go-round that went on silently turning.

The face of the Indian girl introduced an additional note in the register of ambivalence, however. This child-woman of limpid gaze and slender body, who would have charmed André Breton, instinctively awakened to love, and her attentions, her childlike astonishment, the endless devotion she surrounded the American with, made for an unstable emotional mix that lent interest to the scene of their goodbyes. Pilar and her man friend have something important to say to each other, but after a few hesitant starts, the man keeps silent: the "words-that-would-have-made-a-woman" of the Indian girl are not forthcoming. He brusquely leaves her, turns one last time, then quickens his pace, as if in a hurry to have done with it all. Disappointed, Pilar reverts—for how long?—to childhood. Surrounded by a clutch of young friends, already oblivious, she recounts her heroic adventures with "el americano."

In *The Big Clock* John Farrow uses, in a plot à la Fritz Lang, the impersonal machinery and interiors, of a sometimes staggering size, of an ultramodern office building. With his customary energy and meticulousness Charles Laughton plays the part of a newspaper tycoon who's killed his lover. Without being a masterpiece, *The Big Clock* (following a recent viewing) remains one of the better titles in the series.

In Hollywood, even more than elsewhere, new tendencies quickly descend into conventionality once commercial profit feels sure of itself. Film noir is no exception. From 1946 onward the big studios confided to their second-string directors, whether novices or old hands, minor productions in which a highly reliable technique often served a poverty-stricken script, in which the genre lost its edge in an insupportable compromise with "noble sentiments."

In all likelihood, *Gilda, The Lady from Shanghai,* and *The Big Sleep* will go on being outstanding titles in the history of cinema: despite everything, they pave the way (directly or not) to something new. Despite their undoubted qualities, it seems difficult to say as much of the following movies, which visibly mine a seam:

George Marshall's *The Blue Dahlia* (1946), based on a Raymond Chandler script, brought the couple from *This Gun for Hire,* Alan Ladd and Veronica Lake, back together again. A reasonably honest work, it contributed nothing of any great value, aside from putting us in the previously unknown presence of an uncouth gangster with delicate feet.

Frank Tuttle's *Suspense* (1946) has its principal attraction in the diversity and picturesqueness of the sets, sets in which the most unlikely situations develop. In *Fear in the Night* (1947), written and directed by Maxwell Shane, the murder-through-hypnosis makes its appearance, with nightmarish special effects and tricks with wall mirrors. Arthur Ripley's *The Chase* (1946) and, above all, *Fear* (1946), by the writer-director Alfred Zeisler, more or less successfully reworked the oneiric theme of Fritz Lang's *The Woman in the Window*. Let's again cite from 1946: *Nocturne* by Edwin L. Marin, *Decoy* by Jack Bernhard and Bernard Brandt, *Black Angel* by Roy William Neill. From 1947: *Johnny O'Clock* by Robert Rossen. From 1948: *I Love Trouble* by S. Sylvan Simon and *Hollow Triumph* by Steven Sekely.

Apropos of one of these secondary works, Raymond Barkan has rightly noted that "Of course, one really admires the technical perfection many American commercial productions display. . . . Nevertheless, despite their strong appeal, the images fade in the mind once the showing is over. . . . One is conscious of the *industrialization* factor that intervenes in what, for us, seems to be artistic quality."[6]

A psychology of crime

On the fringes of authentic film noir, Tay Garnett's *The Postman Always Rings Twice,* made in 1946 and based on the James M. Cain novel, inaugurates the noirified criminal psychology series of 1946–48. Cain's work had already been adapted on two occasions: in 1939 by Pierre Chenal (*Le Dernier tournant*) and in 1942 by Luchino Visconti (*Ossessione*). It will be necessary to wait until 1946 for the Hays Office to lift a veto maintained since 1937 and to authorize producers at MGM to undertake an American version. This is a sign of the times: the new style had circumvented former constraints, introduced a certain audacity. The theme of the woman who encourages a murder had recently been treated in Edward Dmytryk's *Murder, My Sweet* and Billy Wilder's *Double Indemnity.*

The plot of *The Postman Always Rings Twice* revived the three-way *drame passionnel:* the young Cora had her lover kill her husband, with the crime going unpunished. Some time after this, she died in an accident. The lover, innocent this time, was accused of murder and condemned to the electric chair. This story was potentially remarkable for the character of Cora alone. As it is, Tay Garnett hasn't attempted to reexploit the perfidious sensuality of Barbara Stanwyck in *Double Indemnity*. He has turned his heroine into a radiant and relaxed individual, not at all sinister, whose aspirations seem perfectly legitimate: to eliminate an aging husband, marry a handsome young man, and get her hands on a little money.

This salubriousness, this genuine simplicity in the service of crime goes much further, to be sure, than the tortuous intrigues of Barbara Stanwyck. It is rare to find a lady as dubious as this in everyday life, however, and *Double Indemnity* remains, due to its very improbability, extremely remote from us.

Of a "noirness" just as pure, the character of Cora was, on the contrary, typically everyday. And Lana Turner, almost always dressed in white, embellished it with her figure, with the movements of her hips. Beneath this whiteness one instinctively sought to divine the roundness of a breast or the contour of the buttocks. But then these were the breast, the buttocks of a criminal, and, all things considered, the slogan for the launch of the film could have been: "If you'd known her, you'd have done as he did," or "The crime of passion within everybody's reach."

The dealings in open court between the district attorney and the defense lawyer played by the excellent Hume Cronyn and the punishment meted out to the blackmailer, severely beaten about the face, are quality scenes. And one can't pass over a beautiful dramatic discovery in silence: the falling of a simple lipstick opens and closes the tragic parenthesis of Cora and Frank's love affair.

While of very uneven interest, other movies will be able to claim kinship with film noir on different grounds. For all that, classical, even noirified, criminal psychology visibly loses ground in Hollywood after 1946.

The "costume-drama" series still has a few sequels, such as *Dragonwyk* (1946), a curious period melodrama. Joseph L. Mankiewicz accentuates the ritual gesticulating of stereotyped characters in a morbid atmosphere in which one senses, with every image, the influence of German Expressionism. Vincent

Price plays an anachronistic nobleman, a descendant of the first Dutch pilgrims. He lives not far from the banks of the Hudson, in a mansion that sometimes receives the visit of his great-grandmother, a lover of the clavichord. A new Bluebeard, he kills his wives, who are incapable of giving him a male heir, and he shuts himself away in a tower in order to consume drugs, because the rise of socialism makes him break out in a cold sweat. Sam Wood's *Ivy* (1947) is a classic tale of a female poisoner, of which several images would deserve to remain: the beach at Dover circa 1900, which recalls a Degas; a milliner's where Mrs. Lexton, still married, already picks out her mourning hat; or the plunge in the elevator that will put an end to the court proceedings.

So Evil My Love, made in 1948 in the British studios, is ranked among the three or four outstanding works of this tendency. Olivia Harwood, a missionary's widow, falls madly in love with her lodger, Mark Bellis, an abject, smiling con man, a painter in his spare time; that's to say, when the police are on his trail. Bellis profits from this passion to use his mistress for his own crapulous ends. Olivia's discretion, her good conscience, the bitter fruits of an earlier, probably highly austere life, make a hypocrite out of her à la Choderlos de Laclos: because she proceeds to practice fraud and blackmail, then, crowning her new career, she brings off a poisoning, for which her best friend will be accused in her place. She gives herself up to the police after having stabbed the unfaithful Bellis in a cab. Of calculated slowness, the tale of the downfall of this fine soul, well served by the acting of Ann Todd, with her face of fire and ice, is a model of intelligence, dramatic progression, and subtle psychology. One rediscovers with pleasure the typically English atmosphere and its smell of fog, the high railings giving onto rich residences, the wealthy apartments with heavy curtains that filter the noise and the light, the vast staircases, the conversations in a subdued voice, the feverish looks, the stifled hatreds, the opulent dresses that emphasize the waspishness and flexibility of the women's waists . . . in short, the oppressive charm of *Gaslight.*

Undercurrent (1946) by Vicente Minnelli, *The Sign of the Ram* (1947) by John Sturges, *The Two Mrs. Carrolls* (1947) by Peter

Godfrey, *Sleep, My Love* (1947) by Douglas Sirk (a special mention for this female-victim story à la Hitchcock, as well as for one of its actresses, the astonishing Hazel Brooks), *Act of Violence* (1948) by Fred Zinnemann, *Kiss the Blood Off My Hands* (1948) by Norman Foster, and *Moonrise* (1948) by the excessively underrated Frank Borzage have their good qualities. Lewis Milestone's *The Strange Love of Martha Ivers* (1946) merits particular attention, however. This is perhaps the masterpiece of a career that includes many excellent productions, the latter all too often overlooked in favor of *All Quiet on the Western Front* (1930). Verging on pure criminal psychology, this complex and corrosive study of provincial mores is built around an incontestably noir couple, public attorney O'Neill and his wife. The last scion of a dynasty of respected industrialists, Walter, spineless, alcoholic, and jealous, has married, for love and for family reasons, Martha, a woman who detests him but who remains bound to him because of a dark secret they share (in the past their false testimony has sent an innocent man to jail). She has had a troubled girlhood as a runaway orphan, in conflict with an aunt who will die in dramatic circumstances. Her treacherous sangfroid doesn't prevent her from still being attracted today to Sam, a childhood friend, whose vagabond existence has always represented the ideal of a life without constraints for her. One day she vainly suggests to him to murder her husband, who's fallen down the stairs in a drunken stupor. Walter, meanwhile, tries to have this rival killed by his police cronies. But Sam disappoints all these hopes and arrives to spit his scorn in the face of the couple, which, faced with this hopeless situation, commits suicide.

We will only extract three scenes, here, from this extremely rich work. First, the erotico-sadistic episode of that stroll in the forest in which Martha, convinced by her husband that Sam wants to denounce them, begins putting on a show of being in love with him. She promptly snatches a burning brand from the wood fire, which she hides behind her back, and offers her lips. Sam trustingly bends forward, she attacks, he dodges her smartly, pins her down, and forces her to give in. The look on her face immediately alters, and she tries in vain to conceal her agitated state of mind. A few days later, Sam falls into O'Neill's trap. Savagely beaten by pros, he's left for dead by the roadside. A striking image shows his battered face slowly emerging above the parapet of a bridge. And it's in this state, his clothes blood-stained and torn, that he goes to present himself at the O'Neills'. There, he curses them and leaves, and, from the garden fence, he is present in the twilight at their twin suicide on the other side of a lit-up window. Martha has pensively watched, from behind the curtains, her last hopes slip away with Sam. Walter approaches, a revolver in his hand. She takes the barrel of the weapon and, in a gesture of acquiescence, points it toward her chest. A shot rings out, then a second. From afar Sam perceives two Chinese shadows collapsing one after the other in a sort of derisory reverence.

There remains the case of Hitchcock. From 1946 to 1948 he signed three films that can, on different levels and in varying degrees, be linked to the noir series: *Notorious, The Paradine Case,* and *Rope.*

The Paradine Case (1947) is an excellent documentary about English justice. The preparation of a criminal trial, the encounters under the watchful eye of a policewoman of the defense lawyer and his female client in a glass-fronted dock, the particular role played in England by the prosecuting attorney, the dealings of the lawyer and the judge in town, marked by mundane coldness, the subtle precautions the lawyer takes during a skirmish with a prosecution witness; in a word, the progress of a major court case at the Old Bailey: all this gives the work its testimonial value.

The basic subject, and for once it doesn't matter in Hitchcock's case, appears to be extremely solid. It involves a criminal lawyer who, for the first time in his career, departs from the legendary sangfroid of English men of the law and falls in love with the woman he has to defend. A violent, unforeseen crisis, which undermines the trial, turns his world upside down. It's a crisis he'll maybe overcome.

One rediscovers the director's chief qualities: the art of choosing his actors, of rendering their most trifling gestures necessary, of submitting the filming to the subtlest of intentions, of creating atmosphere with a few touches. In that respect, the beginning of *The Paradine Case* is a complete success. The heroine is about to be arrested. With the arrival of the police several years of her life will be reduced to nothing. Hitchcock has sought to sum up this earlier existence in the icy elegance of the first few images. It is, then, *another film* that comes to an end in the initial sequence, that of the worldly era. As for the images of the trial, they are perhaps the best courtroom scenes the cinema has given us, on a par with Dreyer's *La Passion de Jeanne d'Arc*, Mervyn Le Roy's *They Won't Forget*, or Orson Welles's *The Lady from Shanghai*.

The work has certain somber aspects that involve our subject matter more: to begin with, this crime disguised as suicide, which the final testimony of the accused will only partially explain; then the character of Mrs. Paradine herself, an enigmatic Lady Chatterley who has perhaps been a streetwalker in Italy; finally, the sensual, sadistic, physically repugnant old judge, played by Laughton. He's been spurned, with a gesture of disgust, by the lawyer's young wife. During the trial, Mrs. Paradine will put a stop to his hypocritical smiles with a chilling glance. Following the verdict, he ostensibly quivers with delight. One thinks of another justice-lover's countenance, that district attorney in the old James Whale film *Wives Under Suspicion,* who totted up the death sentences he'd obtained on the little ivory skulls of an abacus.

Rope (1948) has as its point of departure a gratuitous crime committed in the very room a cocktail party will be thrown in, to which the murderers have invited the parents and friends of the victim; the body is still in the drawing room, summarily hidden at the bottom of a chest. This beginning is typically noir. Yet due to its well-studied development, of a classic logic, *Rope* remains a film about criminal psychology, and a remarkable one at that. Let's not leave this work—the summit of Hitchcock's career prior to *Strangers on a Train*—before recalling its exceptional technical interest. The absolutely linear plot unfolded in a tiny apartment and covered a mere hour and a half. The movie, the editing of which remained inconspicuous, seemed itself to be shot during this lapse of time. The camera, of an unimpeachable mobility, sensitivity, and intelligence, *defeated* the theater on its own terrain.

Of these three works, *Notorious* (1946) is the one that comes closest to the noir series. Espionage is involved here, but the insistence of the author in describing, not without humor, the most extreme situations bears the mark of the period.

It has to be said that the script, which is signed by Ben Hecht, is one of the most extravagant Hollywood has exploited since the war. The affair takes place in South America, after the German defeat. The daughter of a Nazi spy, Alicia (Ingrid Bergman), falls in love with a secret agent of the American government, Devlin (Cary Grant), who's been instructed to follow her. Out of love she goes over to the good side and accepts to work for the United States. She's requested to seduce an old friend of her father's, Alex Sebastian, who is himself also a spy. She marries him out of professional duty, but a crucial discovery soon recompenses her: in the cellar, some of the bottles of Veuve Cliquot contain uranium! Sebastian realizes he's been betrayed and, despite his affection for Alicia, he decides to lock her up and slowly poison her. His mother, a jealous and fanatical old woman, helps him do this. Nevertheless, Devlin is watching over her and, in the nick of time, he'll succeed in getting a poisoned, half-dead, but always trusting Alicia out of the Nazi stronghold.

Hitchcock has handled this harrowing tearjerker with the utmost rigor, and it's this mismatch that has made *Notorious*—a hugely successful film, commercially speaking—a much-misunderstood work. One thinks of Charles Vidor's *Gilda;* it, too, was misconstrued for similar reasons. But then it's easy to see what might have seduced the director here. First of all, the story possessed an ideal victim: a woman powerless to struggle against her executioners. And Hitchcock has no equal when it comes to subtly capturing the slightest nuance of doubt and panic on the face of his adorable female leads. Here, Ingrid Bergman deploys her talent in an extremely difficult noir role, built on an unhinged sensuality, because Alicia, as Maurice Scherer observes, "is never physiologically normal, but in a state of inebriation, illness, or erotic ecstasy."[7]

Another valuable aspect of the film was the description of a decadent group of Hitlerite émigrés; the director has always liked, even in old films like *The Ring,* to have his supporting cast play a strong part. In one of the best scenes in *Notorious,* the camera assumes the place of Alicia when Sebastian presents his friends to her, which yields us a fine retinue of suspects, each bowing in turn: a weasel-faced fellow; a fat individual, breathless and simpering, with a myopic's round face and sparse, plastered-down hair, who won't tarry in getting himself killed for "weakness"; and a Prussian patriot, exceedingly edgy and ruthless.

Ultimately, Hitchcock rediscovered in this melodrama the climate of malaise and suspicion so dear to him and which often comes close to the emotional tension of the thriller. In the ever-increasing anguish, the slightest object can assume an extraordinary importance; for example, the key that opens the cellar door and which Alicia has stolen during an official reception. In an uninterrupted high-angle shot, one of the most beautiful and justified in cinema, the camera sweeps down from the ceiling, from where it surveyed the crowd of guests, to the hand of Alicia and to the key this hand holds. Or there again, the cup of coffee that Sebastian has laced with poison: it passes from hand to hand while we follow it, always in close-up. A slide into oneirism once Alicia has drunk this coffee: the images become blurry, and all that remains are two shadowy figures against a brightly lit background; the voices take on new relief, and the staircase toward which the heroine is driven undulates like a reflection in the water.

On top of that, *Notorious* remains an impeccably shot, cut, and edited film. Its chief originality lies in the expressive mobility of the often admirable close-ups. One of the most beautiful examples of erotic cinema—we'd draw attention to that uninterrupted sequence of kisses that Ingrid Bergman and Cary

Grant give each other around a telephone—the film is also a technical feat of which few people in the business are capable. Let's consider Alicia's madcap journey at the wheel of her car: the pale light of dawn on an imprecise landscape and the shifting shadows of palm trees bordering the road aren't perceived through the wisps of her hair floating in front of her eyes and forehead alone, but also in the semi-unconsciousness of her drunkenness. Other, rightly celebrated, images depict the nauseating disarray at the end of a party, the leaden faces of the exhausted drinkers: a single couple still teeters, all but immobile, gasping for breath. Finally, various, always very handsome, exteriors punctuate the story: an aerial shot of the bay at the moment the airplane flies over Sugarloaf, a sun-drenched beach, the colorful crowd at a race track.

We cannot resist the pleasure of evoking the final scene here, one that attains an extraordinary mastery in terms of suspense. In the vast entrance hall of the villa, three groups develop in opposition to each other. First, Alicia and Devlin, who are trying to get away. Then Sebastian and his mother, who have unmasked them but cannot denounce them without themselves being lost, since the spies don't tolerate any failure. Lastly, their bemused accomplices. Now the camera takes the place of the Alicia-Devlin couple and descends the staircase with measured tread, toward Sebastian, who waits at the foot of the stairs; now it accompanies them side-on; now it stays on the impassible group of henchmen. The hero and heroine will owe their salvation to the ambiguity of relations within the opposing group. They cross the threshold, but Sebastian follows and begs them to take him with them. Faced with their refusal he reascends in the dark toward the light-filled rectangle of the doorway, as if to the sacrificial altar. We hear a distant voice: "Alex, will you come in, please? I wish to talk to you"—and the door closes.

The denouement was somewhat cynical. Devlin knew he was sending Sebastian to certain death, yet he readily rid himself of Alicia's husband. Here was, in short, a crime as perfect as it was patriotic.

Notorious has been the equivalent for Hitchcock, perhaps, of

The Lady from Shanghai for Orson Welles. There's undoubtedly a parallel to be drawn between the two men: both dominate the last ten years of American output and have been, with a few months' difference, attracted by the noir style. But then Welles has played the game straight, and *The Lady from Shanghai* remains in the line of *The Maltese Falcon* and *The Big Sleep*. Hitchcock has shown himself to be more reticent and only retained those elements compatible with his favorite themes. In the two cases, however, one perceives the latent humor, the discreet irony of an exercise in style.

Police documentaries and gangster films

The influence of film noir on the police documentary may, it seems, be dated to the years 1947–48. Up till then, the two series had developed in an almost autonomous manner. Later, they will come together to the point of merging into one another.

From the historical point of view, a film like Alfred Werker's *He Walked by Night* (1948) has a certain importance, therefore. The script is based on a true story. An ex-auxiliary policeman has become a thief and a killer, but in a singularly "scientific" and solitary way, without links of any kind with the underworld. The narrative is tough, without letup. In front of our eyes the wanted criminal extracts a bullet from his own arm. Such audacity would have been inconceivable in a prewar American production. The noir style has had its impact here. It has also left its mark on the last few scenes: a manhunt in the sewers of Los Angeles.

In Robert Stevenson's *To the Ends of the Earth* (1948) an investigation, undertaken in China, Egypt, Havana, and San Francisco by an inspector from the U.S. drug squad, ends in the arrest of a young Chinese woman whose inoffensive appearance masks a dangerous gang boss.

The same influences are found in the gangster film, which seems both crueler and more authentic than ten years ago. Max

Nosseck had shown the way with *Dillinger* (1945) by insisting on details like the vengeance of Public Enemy Number 1, who disfigured, with a broken beer glass, a barman who'd once humiliated him. Likewise, a terrible "hammering" inflicted on Burt Lancaster will save Byron Haskin's *I Walk Alone* (1947) from complete mediocrity. Due to its theme of the hunted couple, Nicholas Ray's *They Live by Night* (1949) occasionally recalls Fritz Lang's *You Only Live Once*. Yet it remains conventional, despite the amorous and sensual spontaneity of Farley Granger and Cathy O'Donnell. From Henry Hathaway's *Kiss of Death* (1947), one will remember that nasty little creep with the wild eyes and high-pitched laugh, neurotic to the core, which Richard Widmark has turned into one of his finest roles. *Raw Deal* (1948), by Anthony Mann, has an edifying ending, but is worth it for several scenes: a final showdown in a blazing apartment, for example. *Born to Kill* (1947) brought renown to the name of Robert Wise. And in John Huston's *Key Largo* (1948), a prelude to *The Asphalt Jungle,* there are gangsters who through some highly acute psychological touches defy the then-current model.

Between 1946 and 1948, however, this "neo-gangster" tendency, at the boundaries of film noir, has given us three outstanding works: *The Killers, Criss Cross,* and *Brute Force. The Killers* (1946) bears the signature of Robert Siodmak, and from the first sequences onward one expects something extraordinary, worthy, through its intensity, to figure alongside Howard Hawks's *Scarface*. At nightfall, in a peaceful American small town, two men with cruel and scornful expressions have just arrived by the main highway. After a brief scene of clipped violence in one of those diners that in the United States spring up alongside the road, they make off for the house of their victim.

The man they're going to kill listens, panting, to footsteps resounding on the stairs. The door is suddenly opened, a blast of air obliterates the darkness and the silence, then the shadows are restored.

With the appearance of the investigator the rhythm gets weaker, and the atmosphere becomes more commonplace. We steal in the direction of the well-made, but classical, crime film.

Nevertheless, throughout the narrative a number of success-fully assimilated influences are made manifest. The use of low-key lighting to create a tense atmosphere reveals a Siodmak visibly impressed by the procedures of his compatriot, Fritz Lang. Other images belong more to the Orson Welles manner: during the robbery of the factory payroll, the camera follows the crimi-nals who mount the stairs and break into the offices from out-side, and it describes a long, vertical tracking shot up the façade of the building. The free-for-all with the police has the authen-ticity of a news report. Lastly, the device of the flashback, recre-ated in some sense in *Citizen Kane,* is all-important here and reestablishes, in brief episodes, the brutality of the beginning. Thus there will remain fixed in our memory one of the tough-est ever studio-shot boxing bouts and the scene in which the Swede, crazed with pain due to his mistress's betrayal, smashes the furniture in his hotel room to bits.

Criss Cross (1948 [1949]) marks the summit of Robert Siodmak's American career. To be sure, it never attains the unal-loyed ferocity of certain scenes in *The Killers,* but the work is much smoother, more profound, more *truly* distressing.

It's both a noirified gangster film and a study of the abase-ment of a weak and passionate man. Slim Dundee would like to have the former husband of his protégée Anna, Steve Thomp-son, join his band of crooks. Steve does so, thanks to the wiles of the beautiful woman, whose charms still have a hold over him. He perceives, however, that he's been tricked, and he con-trives to upset the gang's plans. Slim, maddened by jealousy and rage, surprises him in the arms of Anna, who he was trying to convince to resume their former life together. He kills them both, before being killed in turn by the police.

While there are still "bits of bravura"—the attack on an ar-mored truck in the midst of a cloud of tear gas; the anguishing hospital scene, which Hitchcock would surely not disown, in which Steve, his arm in traction, waits to be abducted by the accomplices he's betrayed—these episodes blend into a system in which the most minor sequences retain the intensity of the whole. This complete mastery and strength in reserve, which feel no need to broadcast themselves, are the lot of very few directors in Hollywood. Thus the banal death of a gangster in a hail of police bullets has been dispensed with at the end of the film. The amplified wailing of the police sirens suggests the final outcome in a much more dramatic way.

In the last analysis, the fundamental complexity of Siodmak's human beings demonstrates—if such were really necessary—that even within the framework of film noir we're in the presence of one of the finest psychologists of the screen. The return of Steve Thompson (Burt Lancaster has encountered a role worthy of him here) to his hometown would be sufficient to convince us of this. His apparent indolence belying the millstone of a lost love affair he bears around his neck, he invariably fetches up at the counter of a shadow-filled bar, where he knows he'll reencounter "her." As for Anna, her ambiguity will be maintained right till the end. We'll never know if she was a "bitch" or a shallow-minded young woman, a victim (as they say) of the company she keeps, yet sincerely attached to Steve.

Siodmak will rediscover neither the brilliance of *The Killers* nor the "finish" of *Criss Cross* in the over-rushed, too uneven, *Cry of the City:* for all that, one will remember the figure of a forever famished masseuse, a real "phallic woman" who, with a flick of the wrists, has a "tough guy" at her mercy.

Brute Force was produced in 1947 by Mark Hellinger and directed by Jules Dassin. This is a documentary on American penitentiaries and the description of an escape attempt. Some skillful flashbacks, which evoke the life on the outside of various prisoners in a cell, also turn it into a compilation film.

The essential interest of the work, however, is that it gives carte blanche, if one can put it that way, to the most unbridled sadism. There's the crushing of a stool pigeon under a stamping machine. There's the beating up of a prisoner, immobilized in a chair by a system of straps. There's the scene of the escape, the fearsome energy that turns it into a pitched battle, with a truck that, like a tank, staves in the main gate of the penitentiary. There's the taking of the watchtower: one of the insurgents, fatally wounded, has had the strength to hoist himself up as far as the lookout post and to grab hold of the chief warden; he lifts him above his head and tosses him into empty space. Above all, there's the figure of the warden, a sort of puny fascist, buttoned up tight in a dark uniform, who listens to Wagner while bludgeoning his victims to death. The scene eloquently reveals the attraction exercised on certain American social classes by the Hitler regime.

Canon City (1948), a low-budget work by Crane Wilbur, is an escape story handled in the neorealist style: a dozen convicts overwhelm their guards and make a break for it. Stopped short by a snowstorm, they seek refuge in various isolated houses. A roundup is organized, and all the men are recaptured or killed: one is brained by a hammer-wielding woman, another felled atop a viaduct. The deserving will get their medals, and the chief warden will become a national hero.

References

1 Clearly, this is a *délire d'interprétation* on the part of the authors: Gilda is simply wearing long evening gloves. —*Trans.*

2 *L'Ecran français* 101.

3 *St-Cinéma des Prés* 3 .

4 In contemporary filmographies *The Lady from Shanghai* is usually dated 1948. —*Trans.*

5 It would be something of an anachronism to link Orson Welles's two Shakespearean works, *Macbeth* (1948) and *Othello* (1952), to the noir series. Nevertheless, even without gangsters or detectives, the "blood tragedies" of the Elizabethan period prefigure the thriller in more ways than one. The ambivalence of *Macbeth* is striking—"Fair is foul and foul is fair"—and the witches' incantation that opens the play could provide a motto for the series as a whole. While his *Macbeth* remained profoundly faithful to Shakespeare, Welles conceived *Othello* as a free variation on a classical theme. This much-queried work, often wrongly so, is undoubtedly his greatest success to date in terms of visual poetry. But then again, Iago and Othello are prime candidates for a criminal psychology of the most modern kind, and this *Panorama* ought to mention the death of Desdemona, in which the "sumptuous and stagnant exaggeration of murder" (as Mallarmé said of *Hamlet*) that suffuses the whole work is concentrated.

6 *L'Ecran français* 154 (8 June 1948).

7 *La Revue du cinéma* 15 (July 1948).

6

Decadence and transformation (1949–1950)

From 1949 on, the career of the noir genre, properly so called, comes to an end. There were hints of this effacement in the preceding period, and it seems mainly to have to do, on the one hand, with a certain crisis of the subject, which the theme of "the strange" had duly brought about and, on the other hand, with a strong taste for realism shared by both directors and audiences, in which the influence in the USA of European and especially Italian productions has to be perceived, at least in part. From now on, the idea is to "make it real" down to the very last detail, and even minor B-movies will be shot on location. This move, in fact, was much more compatible with the traditional series of criminal psychology and gangster films. It was even more so with the police documentary, which, beginning that year, is to experience a major boom. As things stand, the noir style doesn't disappear, it *tends to be absorbed* into adjacent series; and, at the very moment neorealism modifies certain of its traits, it ups the dosage of atrocity, psychopathology, or sensuality that it already contained.

Two titles, however, defy this regrouping of styles and, given their strangeness, appear to prolong the orthodoxy of the genre: Lewis Allen's *Chicago Deadline* and Ted Tetzlaff's *The Window* (both 1949).

Chicago Deadline, by the adroit Lewis Allen, who uses the flashback with unerring skill, is mainly of interest because of its scenario: a beautiful young woman dies of tuberculosis in a seedy hotel in the red-light district. An enterprising journalist, played by Alan Ladd, falls in love with this "exquisite corpse" and decides to rehabilitate her memory. Right from the start of his inquiries among the relatives and friends of the dead woman, however, he runs up against a rigid mask of unspeakable terror, and bodies are soon littering his path. Badly wounded himself, he will manage to fathom the secret after a remorseless gunfight in a gigantic car park. If the scriptwriters had insisted on the bizarreness of the investigations and the morbid nature of this attachment to a dead woman, spontaneously endowed with every kind of virtue; if the exhausted but triumphant hero of the final scene had succumbed to his wounds after hearing an entire Mass said for the final rest of this now purified martyr's soul; if Alan Ladd had not played the superman whose mere gaze controls every situation; if, finally, a director of talent had handled the mise-en-scène, we'd undoubtedly have been in the presence of a major work, romantic-noir in tone, not unlike Delmer Daves's *Dark Passage.*

Ted Teztlaff, the cameraman on *Notorious,* now a director like his confrere Rudolph Maté, gained first prize for direction at the 1949 Knokke-le-Zoute Festival for his film *The Window.* Skillfully but without genius, he exploited the talents of Bobby Driscoll in the role of a mythomaniacal little boy who happens to witness a murder. Alerted to the fact by the boy's own mother, the murderous couple try to do away with this embarrassing witness. We won't insist on the intense sadism of an interminable pursuit of the boy across the rooftops, down the streets, through a half-demolished apartment block in which staircases collapse under the weight of the visitors, nor on the *Third Man*–style exploitation of the young actor's likeness to Orson Welles in some of the terrifying chase images. Even the interesting use of New York locations didn't justify an international award. In *Johnny Allegro,* also made in 1949, Ted Tetzlaff timidly attempted to rework, during the course of a botched espionage affair, the memorable theme of Ernest B. Schoedsack's *The Most Dangerous Game* (1932).

Examples of the "criminal psychology" genre are abundant. To be sure, they don't overtly break with such classic themes as, say, the female killer in whom sensuality is allied to treachery. The output of the time oscillates between recourse to all the usual tricks and a gratuitous virtuosity that is ultimately tiresome. Neorealism, however, sets certain standards of authenticity, and its complete assimilation of the noir series is expressed now by a redoubled cruelty, now by a thickening of the atmosphere, which willingly accommodates "trance" or pathological states (drug addiction, mental illness, hypnosis, etc., etc.).

This is patently obvious in *Under Capricorn* (1949), one of Alfred Hitchcock's masterworks and surely the only one in which there is not the slightest trace of humor: it is, tragically, the most beautiful. Enhanced by a discreet Technicolor, the exotic setting of New South Wales around 1820, with its population of adventurers and ex-convicts, serves as a backdrop. Hitchcock pays particular attention to the downfall and intimate breakup of a couple, to their unceasing struggle between the present and the cruelest of pasts. Some highly welcome slices of horror—notably the appearance of a Jivaro-style shrunken head— are striking, especially as the direction attains, what's more, an extreme sobriety. In the interiors the director takes advantage of his technical experiments in *Rope:* all the moments of dramatic tension have been filmed in a single take. The long, fixed shot of the confession of Ingrid Bergman evoking her memories of Ireland is moving for the charm of the actress's voice and face alone: Hitchcock demonstrates that the use of the flashback is often an easy way out in the rhetoric of cinema. The theme is not without echoes of *Notorious* or *Rebecca,* and Ingrid Bergman embodies a sort of martyr to the cause of secrecy, slowly poisoned by a demoniacal housekeeper.

Stage Fright, which Hitchcock makes in 1950, is less interesting. On the strength of a mendacious flashback, all our sympathy goes, right up to the final sequence, to the murderer, whom the fall of a theater safety curtain will crush in the very last images.

In 1950, Otto Preminger signs two films of unequal merit. *Whirlpool* is a somber tale of mesmerism about a young female kleptomaniac and a charlatan who tries, by hypnotizing her, to make her take the rap for a murder. The direction is faultless, and Gene Tierney perfect in this new character role, which will not cause us to forget, however, her creations in *Laura, The Shanghai Gesture, Leave Her to Heaven,* and *Tobacco Road.*

Where the Sidewalk Ends brings together the couple from *Laura* once again. Dana Andrews returns to his role as a detective, but this time he's the son of a gangster shot down by his own men, and he's redirected all his hate toward his father's one-time "mob." In an excess of zeal, he accidentally kills a gang member he's chasing and covers up his crime in such a way that the dead man's father-in-law is charged. A terrible dilemma takes hold of him when he falls in love with the victim's widow. Everything, of course, will turn out right in the end. All the same, this will have permitted us to witness the odd moment of chilling violence, entirely in keeping with the director's style: the extremely brutal relations of the police among themselves, a fascinating manhunt pitting Dixon against a sneering gangster. Without matching *Laura, Where the Sidewalk Ends* deserves a special mention and clearly ranks above most current production.

Gerald Mayer's *Dial 1119* (1950), a film very close, incidentally, to *The Window,* ushers into the series a subgroup of noir neorealism based on psychopathology. A criminal madman escapes from prison, takes refuge in a bar, and telephones, with the intention of murdering him, the psychiatrist who'd put him away. Unmasked by a TV broadcast, he shoots the owner of the bar. The shot, however, has alerted several passersby, and the police machinery goes into action. The story ends with a final gun battle "meting out justice" to the guilty man.

Owing to its exceptional economy of means, *Dial 1119* announces Henry Hathaway's *Fourteen Hours* (1951), which also has a lunatic as its main character, but this time one who's a danger only to himself. This is the cinematic exploitation of the sensational news story with a hint of sadism, and it will enable the gawkers who missed the real event to relive such moments better than in the pages of *Samedi-Soir, France-Dimanche,* and other American "radar beacons."

Manhandled (1949) by Lewis R. Foster (in which a psychoanalyst puts his science in the service of theft and murder), *Trapped* (1949) by Richard Fleischer, *Red Light* (1949) by Roy Del Ruth, *Woman in Hiding* (1949 [1950]) by Michael Gordon, *The Capture* and *Mystery Street* (both 1950) by John Sturges, *The Second Woman* (1950) by James V. Kern, and *Woman on the Run* (1950) by Norman Foster all have excellent moments. The same could be said of two evocative titles: *Too Late for Tears* (1949) by Byron Haskin and King Vidor's *Beyond the Forest* (1949), with its bitchy heroine devised by some frenetic Georges Ohnet,[1] yet whose final sequence is not lacking in violence. Both are underpinned by an impeccable technique, and the suspense is maintained right to the end. Each of their scripts is so lacking in originality, however, and the repetition of clichéd situations is so tiresome, that they only deserve passing mention. We will end this list with *The File on Thelma Jordan* (1949), which bears the signature of a somewhat breathless Robert Siodmak. The subject is noir: a woman makes use of an attorney to work various criminal rackets and then, when she has no more use for him, leaves him for a sleazeball. This female shark is played by Barbara Stanwyck, who's made a specialty of these "vice-ridden murderess" roles. And if virtue triumphs right at the end, it's by a final gambit that won't fool many viewers. Yet the work is slow, leaden, barely convincing; but for the director's name, it could be taken for a B-movie.

We've already evoked the police documentary. After Henry Hathaway's *The House on 92nd Street,* which related the methods of the American secret services during the last war, the series never got very far. From 1949 on, it's the taste for realism in relation to murder that is to give this formula its crucial importance.

Indeed, though any film may use real locations, the police documentary offers the added advantage of being based on wholly authentic facts, and this without the risk of a libel suit. It's into this over-facile recourse to the reportage-type thriller that, for the moment at least, neorealism has degenerated in

America. But then, of course, the persistent presence of the noir style is going to guide the choice of scripts: a super-spicy dossier will always be exhumed from the criminal archives, one capable through its excesses, through the pathological aspect of different kinds of behavior, of making Sunday matinee spectators (who are nevertheless well versed in the matter) shudder in their seats.

One of the best titles from this period is surely William Keighley's *The Street with No Name* (1949 [1948]). Its basic premise is simple: a young inspector infiltrates a bunch of gangsters and manages to hand them over to the police. The film momentarily transcends its documentary feel and effortlessly attains pure drama. Each scene seems lifelike, whether it involves a run-of-the-mill hotel, a ferryboat wharf, or some training gym, a lowlife hangout with its regular crowd of boxers and onlookers, its paraphernalia, its hustling, and its stupid bets. Richard Widmark confirms his gifts in a complex role as a drug-taking tough guy afflicted by a morbid fear of drafts. What's more, the mass killing at the end has been remarkably well orchestrated.

Joseph H. Lewis's *The Undercover Man* and László Benedek's *Port of New York* (both 1949) also find their inspiration in this police-style neorealism. Without equaling the great exemplars of Hathaway or Kazan, they have the narrative sureness, the rhythm, and the care given to the choice of locations and actors that these two have. The government agents are perfect, as usual—courageous, lucid, and incorruptible. These are puerile, cartoon-style police officers, with the heinousness being reserved exclusively for the gangster milieu. Be that as it may, these works arrive too late to renew a worn-out formula.

A certain importance might have been attributed to Rudolph Maté's *Union Station* (1950), if Alfred L. Werker's *He Walked by Night* hadn't appeared before it. The chasing of the killer-cum-kidnapper along the disused tunnels through which high-voltage cables pass takes a conventional turn here. The film is interesting, though, for showing how the security services of a big train station work. Aside from the ill-treatment inflicted on a blind girl by her kidnapper, there are two scenes of momentarily authentic noir cinema: a gangster flattened during his escape by a stampeding herd of steers maddened by gunfire; the pressing invitations to spill the beans exercised by the cops on an untalkative accessory to a crime. After giving him a working over using state-of-the-art methods, they drag him onto a platform overlooking the railroad track. "Make it look accidental," the police inspector orders. When a train passes beneath, they grab hold of the "tough boy" and make as if to push him off. The guy immediately screams that he'll "talk," and he's led away distraught, ready to sell out father and mother alike.

We finally arrive at one of the of the genre's most indisputable successes. *The Enforcer* (1950 [1951]) has revealed to the public the name of a director who will henceforth have to be contended with: Bretaigne Windust.[2] His work has the documentary feel of Jules Dassin's *Naked City* (1948) and the starkness of setting, the cruelty, and the sober tension of a world without hope of a Fritz Lang. It involves, the credits tell us, a vast criminal affair the American police found out about in 1948: the existence of a band of contract killers organized on a commercial basis by a businessman in crime. The disclosure is important: reality thus confirms some of the more sadistic enterprises of earlier film noir.

We evoked, at the beginning of this panorama, the razor killing of an awkward witness and its astonishing mise-en-scène. Let's add to it the episode of the reciprocal killings among the band hunted by the police, the almost gratuitous violence of which causes a certain shudder, all the same. One will also remember the final scene, shot entirely in the city streets. Loudspeakers warn a girl lost in the crowd that two men are looking for her in order to kill her. She's asked to phone the police as quickly as possible and to state exactly where she is. The district attorney receives the message, which comes from a post office, and rejoins the young lady squatting down low in a phone booth. He cautiously opens the glass door in time to see the killer coming toward him. He slowly takes out his revolver, then suddenly spins round and shoots. The gunman staggers, lurches forward, fires his weapon into the ground in one last reflex action, and collapses between the swing doors of the exit, which eject his body onto the sidewalk.

The gangster film undergoes a change at the contact of the noir series with the police documentary. If it cannot work with authentic case files, it will accentuate its reportage style by means of a rapid, action-packed narrative shot in real locations. It will outdo its previous violence: in intensity, through a more unexpected sadism; in universality, by making all the soldiers of "the army of crime" equally ruthless. From the noir genre it borrows, with an arsenal of pathological cases, the odor of corruption that now penetrates every last corner of its social world.

Raoul Walsh's *White Heat* (1949) is of an exceptional toughness. It's the chronicle of the final months of a gang boss, a sort of megalomaniac killer that James Cagney has undoubtedly transformed into his best-ever part. The description of two jobs he masterminds—the attack on a train and a holdup in an oil refinery—has all the interest and intensity of a news report. The gangster's mother plays a key role. When she appears, one thinks she's going to drive him into the arms of repentance and morality. But no, she's just as cruel as her son, and the scriptwriter has clearly referred, here, to another famous mother in American gangster history: "Ma" Barker. A policeman insinuates himself into the gang, working as an informer within it. Cagney quickly accords him his friendship and his trust. But the informer will be ruthless. As a brassy blonde with a wicked charm, Virginia Mayo plays one of those women existing on the fringes of the gang world, undoubtedly frigid but always ready to betray someone and give herself to whoever comes out on top. Walsh intentionally accumulates certain details: a man has been badly burned during the attack on the train; Cagney bears him off to a hideout in the mountains, and the police will later find him there half-frozen, scalded, and dead from the cold. While at least as tough as gangster films from before the war, *White Heat* is, however, much less summary. In it, one rediscovers the obvious influence of realism and of psychoanalysis. Cagney is an epileptic and a borderline psychotic, and the cinema has rarely gone this far in the description of a true Oedipus. Madly attached to his mother, he will suffer, when he learns of her death, an attack of impulsive violence that gives the episode the feel of a medical case history.

Two films, not of the best, yet curious in certain respects, are still worthy of attention: *The Damned Don't Cry* (1950) by Vincent Sherman and *Kiss Tomorrow Goodbye* (1950) by Gordon Douglas. In the first, the affinities between the underworld and high society are exhibited with complaisance. Female emissaries of the leading gangs are introduced into the most exclusive circles, where they devote themselves without risk, beneath the mask of utter respectability, to corrupt practices, as well as various lucrative deals on the side. In the second, it's the entire social order that appears to be rotten from top to bottom. Police officers and prison guards sell themselves for a few hundred bucks and put up, if necessary, with the wrongdoing or escape of the crooks, as long as they get their cut. As for the local senator, he controls all the casinos in the area and is in more or less direct charge of a small troop of armed men.

Let's also point to a whole set of well-shot, but not particularly interesting, movies like Nicholas Ray's *In a Lonely Place* (1950); *The Crooked Way* (1949) by our compatriot Robert Florey, which once again explores the theme of the amnesiac; and Anthony Mann's *Side Street* (1950), which is clearly superior to the other two, and whose conclusion could be "Crime sometimes does pay." Hugo Fregonese's *One Way Street* (1950), illuminated by the fatal charms of Marta Toren, remains a highly conventional melodrama, bearing more of a resemblance to the French noir genre. Fate has a primordial role in it: the hero played by James Mason gets out of the grimmest of situations, only to be run down by a car at the very end. *Highway 301* (1950), written and directed by Andrew L. Stone, and Richard Thorpe's *The Black Hand* (1950 [1949])—a Mafia of sorts exploits a colony of Italian immigrants at the beginning of the century— are inspired, it seems, by genuine news stories.

The simultaneous showing in Paris during winter 1951 of Elia

Kazan's *Panic in the Streets* (1950), Jules Dassin's *Night and the City* (1950), and John Huston's *The Asphalt Jungle* (1950) was the cinematic event of the season. The mutual resemblance of these works didn't end with just their dates of release. All three thrust aside the glistening folds in which the modern big city garbs itself by night, in order to plunge into the feverish and desolate world of gambling joints, lowlife types, and nightclubs. The symbolic search for illegal immigrants carrying the plague (*Panic in the Streets*), the scientific ceremonial accompanying the cracking of a safe by a group of gangsters (*The Asphalt Jungle*). and, under the blazing lights, the fight to the death of two huge wrestlers streaming with sweat (*Night and the City*) lead to one single end: the chase, the hunted man. Only the setting changes: the deserted docks and the chaotic landscape, strangely petrified, of the quays of a port in the Deep South; the anonymous streets and unmysterious façades of an American town; the bomb sites and alleyways of London, seething with bizarre shadows and beggars straight out of *Der Dreigroschenoper,* in which a miserable thug will vainly attempt to escape the omnipresent clutches of the English underworld.

It's interesting to witness the results obtained by Elia Kazan in shooting his film "à la Rossellini"; that's to say, in actual locations. Within the province of pure oneirism and strangeness, he's managed to outstrip his confrere Dassin, an equally convinced advocate of Italian methods. During the first five minutes of *Panic in the Streets,* one anticipates a vaguely police-style documentary on the workings of a hospital service. But we're not long in taking the path to the more dubious parts of town. The masque of the plague is lurking in the moistness of the shadows, and the disorientation functions effortlessly, thanks to cameraman Joe MacDonald's dark, lustrous images. Humble tradesmen are transformed, once night falls, into ruthless villains. A man is murdered, backed up, knife in hand, against a picket fence, with the noise of blaring jazz completely deadening the echo of the gunshots; one meets unemployed types, game for anything for a fistful of money; a gangster, whose face seems carved in wood with a knife, is unknowingly contaminated at the bedside of a dying henchman, whom he underhandedly harries, without ceasing to lavish the signs of a deep affection on him.

In *Night and the City* Jules Dassin has described a case history: that of Fabian, a washed-up mythomaniac, irascible and deceitful, who awakens the mother in every woman. The psychic liberation of this coward will come about at the end of a desperate flight in which he'll voice his feeling of universal betrayal. He'll overcome a morbid fear and throw himself into the arms of his executioner. This role enables Richard Widmark to create one of the most remarkable compositions of his career.

In *The Asphalt Jungle* John Huston has mainly applied himself to destroying certain preconceived ideas. His finely drawn gangsters aren't abnormal people, thirsting for murder and pillage, but simple, everyday folk. Their caste barely differs, in its organization, from law-abiding society. There are businessmen, crooked or straight. Intellectuals intervene as experts, dancing attendance on minor criminals, often married and good family men to boot. In their crummy rooms, crucifixes hang above miserable iron beds. For want of something better, most of them exercise this profession in order to survive—with the exception of Doc Riedenschneider, the head of the gang, and the crooked lawyer Emmerich, who work "for the hell of it." The pessimistic ending has nothing conventional about it. Most of Huston's works have their little scene, meticulously timed, of murky sensuality. Here it's the appearance of Angela, Emmerich's mistress, a gluttonous, lascivious doll whose body seems made for the contact of springy sofas and silk cushions. There's also the piquant bobby-soxer who, in exchange for a few dimes for the jukebox, launches into a wild dance that causes her young breasts to quiver in front of Doc's obscenely immobile face. Once out of the sterile ferment of an obstinately closed world, and for the first time in Huston, a great blast of country air blows through the final sequences. Killer Dix Handley, the deracinated son of horse breeders, comes to die in the lush grass of his native Kentucky.

Aside from an exemplary cast, the talent of each of the directors lends these three films a joint perfection: the unity of an indirect style, polished and unfaltering, disdainful of effect, in Kazan; a warmer and more "human" mise-en-scène in Dassin; an icy conclusion, in Huston, due to an extremely rigorous control: the plot develops with clockwork precision.

Gun Crazy (1950) by Joseph H. Lewis merits a place apart. First, because it's an almost unclassifiable work. A gangster film? But here the gang is reduced to the minimum, to the partnership of two killers. A film about criminal psychology? But it contrasts absolutely with the tone of that series. Then again, the ambivalence of the narrative makes for two very different interpretations. In point of fact, it involves a maniacal lover of firearms and his desperate efforts to affirm his virility in some way other than by murder. His companion, who plays a decisive role in their career as "outlaws," is a fine, bitchy specimen. She has a marked predilection for trousers or a cowgirl outfit, and she polarizes the aggressiveness of the couple. The final episode in the swamp turns into a vengeful killing of the woman by her companion: he prefers the life of a police officer, a childhood friend she's prepared to shoot, to hers.

But then rather than consider *Gun Crazy* as a story with an edifying ending, with pathological causes in support—as it seems we're invited to do—we ourselves prefer to provide it with a justification, by regarding it as one of the extremely rare contemporary illustrations of an *amour fou* (in every sense of the word, of course) that, as André Breton put it, "assumes *all power*" here. *Gun Crazy* would thus appear as a sort of *L'Age d'or* of American film noir.

Never has so much insolent and solitary beauty been seen as in these rivals of Monsieur Verdoux. Passion, violence, eroticism are unleashed and somehow purified here by their very excess, transforming the protagonists into the unwonted heroes of modern times, victims of misfortune and human viciousness. The fusion of their two existences is indeed "that block which, due to its very structure, thwarts any factor of division," exalted by the Surrealist theoretician, and each of their acts springs from it, both outside and against a seedy-looking multitude, trampled underfoot with sovereign contempt.

Will it be said that the poetry leads us somewhat astray? But then everything is visibly arranged here so that the spectator, oblivious of their behavior as killers, crosses, with John Dall and Peggy Cummins, to the other side of the barricade. The recollection of their death will spontaneously rank, in the viewer's mind, with the memory of the death of other famous lovers in the cinema and in literature. Dall, setting aside his few last scruples, decides to become an outlaw. This means being instantly greeted by a triumphant wife stretched out on the bed, wearing only nylons and a white bathrobe. Gripped by a true frenzy of love, nostrils quivering and lips apart, she awaits her companion's embrace in silence; their attitude—they appear to want to voraciously gobble each other up—bespeaks an uncommon craving. And in the presence of such blazing passion, one understands how, in the most natural way in the world, the tried and tested categories of traditional morality may lose their meaning.

One will nevertheless recall, with regard to this film, technically of the highest order, but in which, incidentally, children serve as hostages, in which the anguish of killing is but an added pleasure, the negative attitude of almost all the critics: the frustrated censors' complete lack of understanding or their concerted stifling of the film is something to be pondered at length.[3]

References

1 The authors are evoking the French titles of these films—*La Tigresse* and *La Garce*, respectively; that is, *The Tigress* and *The Bitch*. Georges Ohnet (1848–1918) was a French writer of titillating novels, much read in the 1880s. —*Trans.*

2 It's now generally accepted that Raoul Walsh directed much of this film. —*Trans.*

3 The commercial career of this film has been so brief that of the two authors only Etienne Chaumeton has had the chance to see it.

The Maltese Falcon (1941), dir. John Huston. *L to r:* Elisha Cook Jr., Sydney Greenstreet, Humphrey Bogart, Mary Astor.

Double Indemnity (1944), dir. Billy Wilder. Fred MacMurray, Barbara Stanwyck.

Laura (1944), dir. Otto Preminger. Dana Andrews, Gene Tierney.

The Woman in the Window (1944), dir. Fritz Lang. Edward G. Robinson.

The Big Sleep (1946), dir. Howard Hawks. Humphrey Bogart (*l*), Lauren Bacall (*c*), Bob Steele (*r*).

Gilda (1946), dir. Charles Vidor. Rita Hayworth.

The Killers (1946), dir. Robert Siodmak. Ava Gardner, Burt Lancaster.

Crossfire (1947), dir. Edward Dmytryk. Steve Brodie (*l*), Robert Ryan (*r*).

Dark Passage (1947), dir. Delmer Daves. Lauren Bacall, Humphrey Bogart.

Dead Reckoning (1947), dir. John Cromwell. Morris Carnovsky (*l*), Humphrey Bogart (*c*), William Prince (*r*).

Out of the Past (1947), dir. Jacques Tourneur. Robert Mitchum, Jane Greer.

The Asphalt Jungle (1950), dir. John Huston. *L to r:* Sam Jaffe, Sterling Hayden, James Whitmore, Anthony Caruso.

Gun Crazy (1950), dir. Joseph H. Lewis. John Dall, Peggy Cummins.

Night and the City
(1950), dir. Jules Dassin.
Richard Widmark.

The Big Heat (1953), dir. Fritz Lang. Glenn Ford (*l*), Lee Marvin (*c*).

Du rififi chez les hommes (1954), dir. Jules Dassin. Carl Möhner (*l*), Jean Servais (*r*).

7

The demise of a series (1951–1953)

We've dated the resurgence of the noir series to the first few months of 1949: from that period on, filmmakers were to assimilate various conventions from Italian neorealism and orient themselves toward documentary. Development is to continue, sometimes in a different direction. In any event, by 1951 noir is no longer American production's dominant shade. Neorealism has become second nature, and an examination of cinema receipts betrays a certain saturation. Hollywood is on the lookout for new formulas in which "escapism" is the order of the day.

Out of a desire for exoticism and, above all, for cutting costs, many films are shot in the famous locations and big cities of Europe. If necessary, a studio is rented in situ. Such was the case with William Wyler's *Roman Holiday,* John Huston's two most recent films, *Moulin Rouge* and *Beat the Devil,* and with Mervyn Le Roy's *Quo Vadis.*

The enormous progress of Technicolor turns the heads of the majors toward spectaculars once again, with a preference for biblical subjects (Henry King's *David and Bathsheba*), big-game hunting and the picturesque mores of African peoples (*King Solomon's Mines* by Compton Bennett and Andrew Marton), and tales of piracy like Robert Siodmak's *The Crimson Pirate* and Edward Dmytryk's *Mutiny.* Finally, the series of musicals and variety films reaches its apogee (*An American in Paris, Singin' in the Rain*). Two stars shine with a phosphorescent brilliance here: the dancer, choreographer, and director Gene Kelly and, above all, the great director Vincente Minnelli.

Science fiction (*The Thing* by Christian Nyby, *The Day the Earth Stood Still* by Robert Wise) has broken out of its narrow confines and absorbed the clientele for detective films by communicating the awesome thrill of the cosmos to it. The same phenomenon is produced in literature, what's more. Lastly, 3-D has marked the reemergence of the horror film, with André de Toth's *House of Wax.*

The role of the Korean War has undoubtedly been much more decisive, however: the armed conflict has repercussions on the choice of dramatic themes and the content of popular entertainment. Reaffirming one of his cherished ideas, Pierre Kast noted, furthermore, that certain film noirs contained exceedingly harsh descriptions of the established order, and he cited the example of *The Maltese Falcon,* "a ferocious entomology" of the police.[1]

Most series evolved, then, in the direction of other, more conformist channels: patriotic productions (*The Steel Helmet* by Samuel Fuller and *I Want You* by Mark Robson) returned to favor, and producers invested a part of their capital assets, formerly given over to the making of spy thrillers, in the anti-Red series, the prototype of which—*Walk a Crooked Mile*—dates from 1948. All that was needed in order to do this was replace the word "Nazi" with the word "Russian." One also saw the scriptwriters of Henry Hathaway's extremely mediocre *Diplomatic Courier* (1952) "transform" Peter Cheyney's novel *Sinister Errand,* the action of which occurred in London during the last war, into a case of Soviet espionage. Let's also cite *Tokyo File 212* (1951) by Dorrell and Stuart McGowan, intended for the Asian market; Vincent Sherman's *Affair in Trinidad* (1952), in which Rita Hayworth vainly attempted to resuscitate Gilda's earlier magic; and *Peking Express* (1951), a wretched, updated remake of Josef von Sternberg's *Shanghai Express.*

The detective film subsisted, to be sure, but set about elaborating the myth of the "thinking cop." Local police stations transformed into purgatories were packed with individuals of caring countenance, a Bible forever to hand. In between two workings over, the cops adopted the attitude of Rodin's *Thinker,* chins propped on the end of their nightsticks. William Wyler's *Detective Story* (1951) will long remain the genre's masterpiece, with the day-to-day atmosphere of a small precinct and its finely etched gallery of psychopathic detainees. Nicholas Ray's *On Dangerous Ground* (1952 [1951]), the self-critique of an over-energetic officer, is in the same vein; and *The City That Never Sleeps* (1952 [1953]), by John H. Auer, relates the misadventures of an inspector who has marriage problems and, in a careless moment, takes up with the very people he's supposed to be fighting against.

Meanwhile, not everything was bad in the bland heritage of the noir series; it will have a happy effect on the evolution of the social film. Let's list a few titles here in chronological order, titles to which we will return: Billy Wilder's *The Big Carnival* (1951), László Benedek's *Death of a Salesman* (1951), Daniel Mann's *Come Back, Little Sheba* (1952), and László Benedek's *The Wild One* (1953 [1954]).

Directors of any renown begin, moreover, to turn away from this series. Only Hitchcock seems once and for all to have chosen the thriller as a form of expression. Most of these films are made with scant resources and entrusted to novices or unknowns.

Josef von Sternberg's *Macao* (1952) must be stressed, however. The emotion felt during the showing of a thriller is, as often as not, cerebral in origin. Things are not like this in Sternberg's films, in which anguish is always accompanied by a certain sexual excitement. Baudelaire's line could stand as an epigraph for his oeuvre as a whole: "The pain that fascinates and the pleasure that kills." Sadomasochists will always be drawn to these mirage-memories of some new Gomorrah.

This very special thrill is felt at odd moments in *Macao,* which marks Sternberg's return to the studios of California. The setting of the story is Macao, a name redolent of magic for the author of *The Shanghai Gesture.* But the rather detective-style script offers almost no latitude on the erotic level, and the film's budget was probably of the slimmest. Notwithstanding this, the old maestro has occasionally rediscovered all his old skill and passion: the dripping corpse, dressed in white linen, that's trundled into the oily water— having searched it, someone re-trieves the dagger planted in its back; the oppressive chase across the moored fishing boats, through screens of hanging nets; Jane Russell in a high-slit kimono, electric fan in hand, rushing at Robert Mitchum, who defends himself with a pillow. The rotat-ing blades of the fan rip the pillowcase and advance inexorably through a cloud of feathers. . . . Sternberg has been ordered by his producer to make the most of Jane Russell's assets. But he's thought too much about his onetime ideal actress. The mo-ment Jane Russell starts to sing "You Kill Me," the specter of *The Blue Angel* is superimposed upon her person. To make up for it, at the beginning of the film she's been very adroitly used dur-ing two scenes in which her "director" has called upon her well-known talents as a vamp. Gloria Graham, the female support in the film, already remarkable in *Crossfire* and *In a Lonely Place,* is the gangster's rejected moll; without turning a hair, she leads her lover to his downfall. The ambiguity of her features and her character, an odd mixture of cold calculation and sensuality, is pleasing. If the producers had given her her big chance around 1946, Gloria Graham would undoubtedly have become one of the key figures of the noir genre.

Let's cite, in addition, two spy thrillers of unequal merit: Russell Rouse's *The Thief* (1952), a non-talkie sound film like they used to make in 1929, vainly attempts to have us share the fears of an atom spy hunted by the police, thanks to the highly ingenious use of sound, a chase in the Empire State Building, and the legs of Rita Gam. The initial bias of the story lumbers us with a stereotyped psychologist who ends up spoiling the film, which promised much on the technical level. Robert Parrish's *Shoot First* (1952 [1953]) is a nutty spy story shot in England, with a manhunt in Waterloo Station that ends up on the roof of Madame Tussaud's.

Much closer to the classic detective film, Phil Karlson's *Scan-dal Sheet* (1951 [1952]) is inspired by John Farrow's *The Big Clock.*

We've already evoked the new police-documentary formula. Due to its brilliant classicism, John Cromwell's *The Racket* (1951) escapes this definition. Political corruption is involved here. Via a third person, the mob takes over an American town. A particularly honest police chief will succeed in destroying the gang and its boss, without, however, getting to the real mastermind, mysteriously called "the old man," who appears to move, untouchable, in the country's top government circles. *The Mob* (1951) describes a detective's fight against a dockland gang. Despite a mawkish love affair, William Dieterle's *The Turning Point* (1951 [1952]) uses urban locations extremely well and contains one excellent sequence: a killer, hired to shoot a journalist at a boxing match, moves around on the catwalks of the hall looking for the best firing position. As he's about to pull the trigger the crowd leaps to its feet to applaud the boxer, who's just knocked out his opponent. He'll only manage to shoot his victim later, at the exit, in the thronging crowd.

The Big Heat (1952 [1953]) is a detective film. But through its tense atmosphere, some unusual details, the instability of the relationships between the characters, and the violence of a few scenes, it reuses the devices of classic film noir. Working with the most banal of scripts, Fritz Lang has managed to develop his favorite theme: human solitude in an ironclad world.

Masters of a provincial town, a gang of hoodlums has the wife of an unbending police detective, Inspector Bannion, killed. Disowned by cowardly and corrupt chiefs, Bannion is nothing but an automaton thirsting for revenge, literally propelled by his destructive instinct. This fascination sets the narrative tone.

Featherbrained or levelheaded, victims or manipulators, ruthless or willing to help, women play a paramount role in this. On their reactions, on their volte-faces, depend the fluctuations of this drama. Their tender flesh is sorely tried during the sadistic episodes: they're murdered in cold blood, burned with cigarettes, disfigured by scalding coffee. Glenn Ford is sensational as the *bel inspecteur sans merci,* and Gloria Graham's half-destroyed face marvelously concretizes the duality of her "soul."

As in Alfred Hitchcock's *The Lady Vanishes,* the action of *The Narrow Margin* (1952) takes place on a train. A policeman escorts a young widow who must hand over to the Los Angeles court her late husband's secret accounts. A bunch of racketeers wish to eliminate the witness, but the killers don't know what their victim looks like. By mistake, they kill a policewoman who's impersonating the widow and was made up to look like a vamp. They'd never have thought that the woman they were seeking had the features of an upstanding American bourgeoise, with a drab and angular face, as maternal as they come. On top of that, she'll marry the young cop, and they'll have lots of little cops. But then the interest of Richard Fleischer's film is that it unfolds in a sort of two-dimensional universe. The external world is seen as if in a mirror, through the train window: for example, the gang's car that follows the train at the end of the trip and which is glimpsed, silent and haunting, out of the wide carriage windows; or the gunman's face, which the glass screen of the compartment suddenly reflects at the very moment the policeman thinks he's safe. Fleischer has managed to get the most out of the enclosed setting of an express train: an obese police officer blocks the corridor of the carriage with his belly in the most exciting chase sequences, and a two-man fistfight in a compartment is of an almost unrivaled violence.

A mention for *Calling Bulldog Drummond* (1951), which attains a kind of dreamlike fantasy because of the stupefying technical nature of the methods employed during a holdup: the team of burglars is organized as a commando unit by a superior officer who is nostalgic for the war and its dangers; the raid is directed by walkie-talkie and comes equipped with radar.

Gangster films continue to have the same vehemence as before, but Hollywood produces fewer and fewer of them. There's one memorable scene in Joseph Kane's *Hoodlum Empire* (1952), inspired by Senator Kefauver's inquiry: a blind priest who's about to denounce the activities of a gang to the police is thrown down an elevator shaft. Gordon Douglas's *Come Fill the Cup* (1951) contains a few episodes in the same vein: at gunpoint a gangster forces a recently detoxed journalist to drink alcohol again. And age causes James Cagney to lose none of his dynamism and violence. Otherwise mediocre, Phil Karlson's *Kansas City Confidential* (1952) benefits from one original idea: the armed robbery of a bank undertaken by three masked gang-sters, none of whom knows the others' identity or that of the boss who's in charge of them.

Films about criminal psychology are still abundant, alone making up three-quarters of the movies studied. This is a highly valuable formula because it offered much broader scope to the social domain, while giving greater importance to sentimental intrigue, to studies of personality, and to individual problems.

The year 1951 was marked in this field by one important production, *Strangers on a Train,* which is surely Hitchcock's masterpiece. In it, he manages to bring together all the components, hitherto dispersed, of his style: criminal psychology, humor, suspense, a study of pathological cases, and an interest in minor characters. He even extended this vision by multiplying the milieus and settings. Looked at one way, this film is a satire, doubtless implicit, yet forthright, of different social strata in Washington.

The essential ingredients of the noir genre are present here in an original cocktail that possesses its share of humor. Only eroticism is missing, although the hypothesis might be envis-aged of Bruno's obscure affection for Haines. The oneirism of the script—adapted from a Patricia Highsmith novel by Raymond Chandler and Czenzi Ormonde—bears a certain re-semblance to that of *The Woman in the Window.* A man of good-will is drawn into a criminal situation he can't get out of. But the plot is handled in the most believable and subtle way, even in the details, which is rare in Hitchcock. A tennis champion, Guy Haines, is approached in a train by Bruno, a young man of independent means. They have a rambling conversation. Bruno shows that he knows about Haines's conjugal misfortunes and his passion for a senator's daughter. The ever-smiling Bruno proposes a curious deal: he'll do away with the wife, and in return Haines will rid him of a father he detests. This exchange ought to lead to two perfect crimes, since the murderers lack any personal motive. Haines believes he's dealing with a mad-man and makes off. A few days later, Bruno precipitates matters: he murders Mrs. Haines and invites the husband, already suspected of the murder, to do his father in. Haines refuses, and Bruno compromises him by leaving the champion's lighter on the scene of the crime. All is resolved after an extraordinary chase that will end on a runaway carousel, amid the terrified screams of parents and children, and the dicey potshots of the overwhelmed law officers.

During the unfolding of the plot, Hitchcock employs, in the setting proper to them, a series of largely new or renewed social types: Haines's vulgar, bespectacled wife who goes out with her friends on a Saturday night, but who'd rather supplement her salary with wealthier young men; Haines's girlfriend and her father, in the deluxe apartments of Washington congressmen; Bruno's milieu, with its eccentric pleasure-seekers, notably his own mother, a refined fifty-year-old with an anxious look in her eyes. The pictures she paints in her Victorian home evoke a carnivalesque Soutine. This response sums her up: "My son would never have had the idea of committing anything so ridiculous as a crime." Haines is painted in broad strokes. Hitchcock gives him the allure of a student; he's a charming young man, quick-witted and complex.

The incidental characters are in no way inferior to the authenticity of the whole: the professor who, the worse for drink, discourses in a deserted carriage on the solving of multiple integrals, the fairground stall holders, or the salon of old ladies with their sheep's or camel's heads, whose gazes betray a ruminant stupidity.

The film's main psychological interest clearly resides in the character of Bruno, unforgettably portrayed by Robert Walker, who was himself to die a few months later in a nursing home. Here, the pathological behavior of the hero is studied both externally and in depth (his Oedipus complex). His huge spoilt child's face, with its ambiguous, rather fixed smile, his profile, his way of dressing, the abnormal rigidity of his bearing, give him an incredible presence. It's enough to see him hanging around Haines, frequenting the same places, telephoning him at all hours, or to observe him, immobile, lost in thought, on the steps of the Capitol in Washington, to experience a feeling of doom. He reveals his madness in flashes during the train conversation: he shies away from, comes back to, reveals his obsession, speaks of something else, and then backtracks. Aside from when his father is mentioned, he displays perfect lucidity. Cunning, prudence in the very midst of imprudence, vigor, decisiveness: these are the trump cards he masterfully plays in order to bring this murder off. In the inimitable language of our psychiatrists, "a total anesthesia of moral feeling" could be diagnosed.

Technically, *Strangers on a Train* is not an experimental film like *Rope*. The direction of this black-and-white movie is sober and of an exemplary sureness. Not devoid of elegance, this clarity of definition is literally found in every shot. Let's take the opening sequence: the camera swoops down in front of the door of a taxi that's just stopped near a station, frames the shoes of a traveler, which it follows through the crowd, meeting the feet of a second traveler along the way. A shuttling back and forth begins, until the moment Bruno's shoe bumps against Haines's in the carriage, and a conversation is struck up. Banal in itself, this procedure is recreated by a master hand. There's the same sureness in the creation of the train sequences; in the discussion in the record store where Mrs. Haines works (the glass booths recall the box in *The Paradine Case*); in the snobbish get-togethers in Washington; in the tennis championship shot in the most brilliant manner, without any of the traditional ploys. It's the sequence of the murder in the amusement park that constitutes Hitchcock's greatest success, however, with its fast cutting between strange images. The little boats full of loving couples gliding through the dimly lit tunnels and Bruno's attempts to approach across the fairground defer the ineluctable tragedy from one second to the next: that paralyzing underwater image of strangulation, reflected and deformed in the victim's spectacles, fallen on the grass. You can't go any further than this in terms of suspense.

Without measuring up to *Laura, Angel Face* (1952) confirms Otto

Preminger's mastery and subtlety where psychological analysis is concerned. The by now banal theme sometimes recalls *Leave Her to Heaven* and, at other times, in the trial scenes, *The Postman Always Rings Twice*. But the precision of the editing, the mise-en-scène, and the directing of the actors attain a wholly classical clarity of definition.

Preminger has managed to give his characters that margin of indecision, even indifference, which confers on certain decisive episodes in our lives a banal and superficial appearance. Nevertheless, behind such appearances an implacable drama is brought to a head. A stubborn and perverse little angel, with eyes obstinately fixed on her own secret, Jean Simmons seems to have escaped from one of Leonor Fini's paintings. Robert Mitchum has perfectly conveyed the clairvoyant masochism of the strong and blasé male. Endlessly attracted by "the power over life or death a face has at its command," he puts a lot of unconscious willing into dying with his lover.

Excellent from start to finish, Roy Rowland's *Witness to Murder* has but the one fault of being a banal suspense story. Like *Angel Face,* it was made five years too late. Whence the impression of déjà vu.

The question of disastrous couples always inspires scriptwriters: one or the other of the couple (almost always the woman) has married out of self-interest. An affair reveals physical love to such people, however, and they attempt to break their chains by recourse to murder.

The subject of *The Prowler* (1951), ably handled by Joseph Losey, is not lacking in this sort of cynicism: a policeman, a former basketball player, kills the husband of his mistress, whom he's got pregnant, in order to marry her and make off with the spoils, a $62,000 life insurance policy.

Sudden Fear (1952), by David Miller, is an excellent suspense film, the Hitchcock-style theme of which recalls a spicier *Suspicion* or Anatole Litvak's *Sorry, Wrong Number*. One will remember, in the final sequence, the extravagant dancer's figure of the very tall Jack Palance, trying to find his wife in the steep San

Francisco streets during a chase that resembles some demoniacal dance.

The script of *Pickup* (1951), written, directed by, and featuring the Czech author Hugo Haas, echoes that of *L'Homme qui cherche la vérité* and reconstitutes the dramatic "triangle" of *Double Indemnity* and *The Postman Always Rings Twice*. A fifty-year-old stationmaster, married to a younger woman, regains his hearing as suddenly as he'd lost it, but keeps his immediate circle in ignorance of his cure. He finds out that his wife has a lover and that the two of them plan to murder him. The ending will be happy. In the mise-en-scène, which adroitly maintains the tempo, we reencounter the sensuality typical of the heyday of Czech cinema, in the shape of Gustav Machaty. Hugo Haas invents a subtle creation of the highest order, and Beverly Michaels is a leggy blonde who has nothing to envy the greatest charmers of the American screen for.

In the glorious Technicolor of *Niagara* (1952) Henry Hathaway ravels and unravels a classic crime story: a high-strung husband, an unsatisfied, provocative wife who'll try and have him killed by her lover. In the grandiose, resonating setting of Niagara Falls, the irresistible surge of this liquid mass symbolizes the blind force of passion. A strangulation scene filmed in cast shadows recalls certain De Chiricos. And then the hysteria of Marilyn Monroe singing "Kiss Me" and her voluptuous tossing and turning in a hospital bed happily reenliven the erotic repertoire. "I once had occasion to write," André Bazin has said, "that since the war cinematic eroticism had shifted from the thigh to the breast. Marilyn Monroe makes it descend somewhere between the two."

Lastly, Irving Rapper's *Another Man's Poison* (1951 [1952]) has been visually put together to make the most of the aging personality of Bette Davis.

Within an excessively limited range, the description of individual clinical cases retains a certain rigor, despite an obvious lack of originality. Henry Hathaway's *Fourteen Hours* (1951) uses a genuine news story, one which also formed the final sequence of Anthony Kimmins's *Mine Own Executioner:* a young suicide case, perched on the ledge of a high building, threatens to jump. The interventions of his parents, his girlfriend, and two desiccated psychiatrists are not enough to make him abandon his perilous situation. Only a wholesome and understanding police officer will be on the point of getting a result. The very sober direction, handled in the style of a newsreel, admits of two endings, as in the excellent *Mr. Lucky* (1943) by H.C. Potter: one tragic, which we feel to be the only right one, and a second, happy ending, which is a concession to public sentimentality. Joseph Losey's *M* (1951) is a worthy Freudian remake of Fritz Lang's famous film, shot entirely, contrary to its model, on location.

Edward Dmytryk's *The Sniper* (1952) is an excellent clinical description that, in this respect, ranks with *Le Puritain* by Jef Musso or Buñuel's *El:* a sadistic loner shoots young women with a rifle equipped with telescopic sights. Other people's pleasure is physically insupportable to him. The film has an extremely disagreeable thinking-cop side to it, however. Dmytryk uses neorealism and Expressionism with virtuosity. Two redolent images: a man is working halfway up a factory chimney; he espies the murderer on a balcony and alerts the crowd; the young man regretfully shoots him, not now because of his neurosis but out of self-defense. Second, the last, very beautiful shot in which the maniac, sitting on his bed, his rifle across his knees, lets himself be captured without resistance. Streaming with tears, his face communicates a tremendous sense of relief.

In *Don't Bother to Knock* (1952) Roy Ward Baker injects humor and cruelty into a story set in a Manhattan hotel about the aberrations of a babysitter. This beautiful girl and her emphatic charms beneath a revealing negligee—Marilyn Monroe, no less—is suffering from a traumatic psychoneurosis brought on by the death of her fiancé. In order to spend a few tranquil moments with a man who reminds her of him, she ties and gags the little girl she's looking after, after first having tried to throw her out the window. The mother arrives unexpectedly, the man disappears, and the madwoman tries to slash her wrists, but will be saved.

Something of a footnote to the series, John Sturges's *Jeopardy* (1952 [1953]) creates a new suspense genre: a couple of Americans and their son camp out on a deserted Mexican beach that was once a fishing port. A rotten jetty collapses under the weight of the husband, who can't release his foot, trapped under a beam. With the tide inexorably rising, his distraught wife signals a fishing boat, which takes her appeals for a wave of greeting. She gets into the car and races off in search of help. She meets a prisoner on the run, who's trying to escape a police manhunt. She doesn't hesitate to help him and even to offer herself to him on condition that he rescues the husband. The rescue will be effected in extremis, and the escaped prisoner will make off into the night. With utmost simplicity, John Sturges uses the minor workings of chance that constitute the warp and weft of our lives. He has us sense the immense indifference of things in the face of human tragedy.

Despite this handful of recent titles, one can say that the noir series is well and truly dead: today it only inspires lassitude. Our blonde viragos already have the smell of stale perfume exuded by Peter Cheyney's posthumous novels. The formal wonders of Lang's or Preminger's recent works are no longer enough to hide the threadbare quality of their content. *Murder, Inc.,* the masterful report by Turkus and Feder, has brought things up to date. Crime in the USA can still provide filmmakers with worthwhile themes, but in another spirit: that of the nonfiction documentary, the sociological monograph. Elia Kazan has just botched a wonderful subject, the hold gangsters have on the unions, by giving in to religious imperatives (*On the Waterfront,* 1954). These commercial concessions are no longer tolerable. A Joris Ivens or a Georges Franju is needed here.

Vincente Minnelli, the most refined man in Hollywood, has chosen this supreme moment, in which film noir becomes fogged in our memory, to give us a sort of poetic transposition of it in the form of a ballet (*The Band Wagon,* 1954 [1953]).

Gene Kelly had already been inspired by *Scarface,* a *Scarface* revised in the manner of Horace McCoy, to compose the final scenes of *Singin' in the Rain* (1953). But then there was such a sense of joie de vivre in this divertissement that the plot became a mere pretext or design. Tragedy vanished in the riot of colors.

Minnelli is a much more tortured aesthete, who may remind us of Sternberg (the "Limehouse Blues" sketch in *Ziegfeld Follies* has the same caustic, desperate exoticism). And the ballet in *The Band Wagon*—a banal production, moreover—is more than a parody, even a subtle one: a final concession to our past, it has the savor of those fated love affairs and wan nights of which all passive adventurers dream. A bit like Yves Salgues's poem, "Clarinet Lament." From the cinema angle it's also one of the most extraordinary shorts in talkies, and, if the print were to disappear, one would wish to preserve this reel in some imaginary cinematheque.

The shooting script draws its inspiration from the novels of Mickey Spillane: Rod Riley, a private eye, a tough guy, traverses the sleeping city. Somewhere, a trumpet solo pierces the night. A gorgeous, slender blonde falls into Rod's arms, terrorized. A man advances, gesticulates. He'd like to talk. Boom! He was an embarrassing witness. The killers rush the detective, who blacks out (a clear allusion to *Murder, My Sweet*). An investigation. Guided by his instincts, Rod breaks into a high-fashion salon: purple satin (*Ziegfeld Follies*), pinups, dowagers decked out in jewels, as immobile as wax dummies (*La Nuit fantastique* and the "Caveau des Illusions"). A pan across a private entrance: Cyd Charisse appears, a dazzling brunette in an evening dress slashed to the hip. She drags Rod to the haute couture workshop, where dislocated dummies are in nightmare poses (the Surrealist theme of the mannequin). Fisticuffs. Rod blacks out. He wakes up, opens a door: "Maybe this was a long shot," he says, "but I've seen some funny ones pay off." And in a set inspired by the animated cartoons of Stephen Bosustov (a metal fire escape taken out of context, descending into empty space, like a sketch on a sheet of paper), Rod pursues his investigations. Office corridors with steel-gray walls. Light coming from an elevated subway. Machine-gun fire, the killers' dance (obviously a parody of the bit of bravura that ends any manhunt). Jazz rhythms: a bar. Drug-addict types surge into a smoky, windowless joint: Sartre's hell with no exit. A pan across the counter, handled in velvety tones of gray and blue. A black-gloved female turns round, opens her green cape, and reveals a glittering red dress. It's Cyd Charisse. The band falls silent. A grotesque musician attacks a trumpet solo. The killers get up, knives in hand, and slowly make for the detective, who's worked out the riddle in a moment of inspiration: "Suddenly, all the pieces fitted together—I knew how the crime had been done!" Fisticuffs. Boom! The grotesque musician peels off her male disguise, and the blonde emerges, the blonde murderess of Billy Wilder, Tay Garnett, Edward Dmytryk. Rod plants four slugs in her belly. She staggers, embraces him, dies. ("Goodbye, baby," Fred MacMurray murmured when shooting Barbara Stanwyck point blank.) The detective reemerges into the sleeping city and its deserted, dangerous streets. A bitter curl on his lips, he digs for a cigarette. A black-gloved hand crosses the screen and proffers a light: it's Cyd Charisse again. "She was bad, she was dangerous." Yet Rod takes her in his arms and their lips mash together.

Truth to tell, a heavily made-up Cyd Charisse also plays the part of the blonde: this ambiguity is indeed the sign of love affairs doomed to a violent end. Sure, Fred Astaire doesn't have the weighty presence of a tough guy. Sure, Minnelli has been inspired by a facile and banalized Surrealism. This ballet is a success, for all that. Never had the noir series been grasped "in its very essence" with such lucid complicity.

References

1 See *Positif* 7.

8

Influences

Film noir is situated within the more general current of American realism. Hasn't there always been something artificial about speaking unilaterally of this style's influence on non-crime series? Often a noir detail in a non-noir film is simply due to a realist orientation. An example: Anthony Mann's *Border Incident* includes scenes that are among the cinema's cruelest: a man, his back broken, held down on the ground, is finished off beneath a tractor; others are sucked down into quicksand. Now, *Border Incident* restricts itself to describing a point of fact: the exploitation of labor passing illegally from Mexico to the United States. Can one speak of noir violence in a work that treats of an objective economic phenomenon and that is inspired, even atrociously so, by authentic news stories?

This is a methodological problem of the same order as the question of film noir's influence on the psychoanalytic film. Here again the genres mutually interfere. The basic ambition of noir characters inevitably recalls that of neurotics. This remains so true that we've made *Gilda* and *Leave Her to Heaven* into implicitly psychoanalytic films.

Moreover, all these tendencies are so interconnected that the same names keep cropping up in them. It's significant that Robert Siodmak, Curtis Bernhardt, John Brahm, Alfred Hitchcock, and Otto Preminger have made film noirs as well as psychoanalytic films. It's also highly remarkable that most of the great names in social documentary already figure in the noir series: Billy Wilder, Edward Dmytryk, John Huston, Jules Dassin, Robert Wise, Anthony Mann.

The question of dates is crucial, though. Wilder filmed *Double Indemnity* (1944) before *Sunset Boulevard* (1949), and Dmytryk *Murder, My Sweet* (1945 [1944]) before *Crossfire* (1947). Huston made *The Maltese Falcon* (1941) long before *We Were Strangers*

(1948 [1949]). Dassin tried his hand at police documentary before directing *Thieves' Highway* (1949). Anthony Mann directed a movie about Treasury agents, *T-Men* (1947), before *Border Incident* (1949). Of Robert Wise, lastly, we knew *Born to Kill* (1947) before his extraordinary document on boxing, *The Set-Up* (1949). Furthermore, film noir's glory days end around 1948, and from then on it undergoes a change in spreading to other, parallel series. In any event, if noir details were the exception in social documentaries, one could attribute them to the desire for realism alone. But then it's an ongoing tradition for so-called American "realist" films to include noir elements. One even gets the impression that the Hollywood producers only accept a realist screenplay to the extent that it's capable of being noirified. Noir sells, and it permeates the documentary.

It isn't forcing things, then, to speak of the "influences" of film noir on the non-crime series. But then the phenomenon continues as we write, and it would be absurd to try and be thorough on such shifting ground. Whence some all but inevitable gaps.

From 1945 to 1947 social documentaries of a noir kind are rare. On its release in France Billy Wilder's *The Lost Weekend* (1945) had been classified, somewhat superficially, as belonging to the noir genre, doubtless because of the hospital scenes and the description of delirium tremens. Strangeness and crime, however, were absent from it, and the psychology of the drunk offered one of the most classic examples there are of the all-powerfulness of a rudimentary desire. *The Southerner* (1946 [1945]) and, it must be added, *The Woman on the Beach* (1947), with its bitter and anguishing atmosphere, bore Renoir's mark much more than that of the new American style. *Nightmare Alley* (1947), directed by Edmund Goulding, an old hand at melodrama, was more ambiguous. In this movie there was a documentary about fairground booths and circuses, a love story of little or no interest, but also two striking figures: a psychoanalyst who recorded the confessions of his patients on disk; and a professional drunk, consumed by alcohol, whom the circus owner exhibited as a freak and whom he fed on raw meat.

Edward Dmytryk's *Crossfire* (1947) merits closer attention, however. It's been too rapidly pigeonholed among films dealing with American racial problems. It is, in effect, a description of anti-Semitism, along with a successfully conducted criminal investigation, since it involves the murder of a recently demobilized Jewish GI.

There was, however, another aspect to this work: the difficulty soldiers have in readapting to civilian life, their disarray when faced with the new responsibilities that are their lot, and the uncertainty of their status. In this respect, *Crossfire,* even though it was shot in twenty-four days on a meager budget, is vastly superior to that stodgy and complacent William Wyler film, *The Best Years of Our Lives,* the very title of which is more than suspect when you think that the years in question are the war years.

This is because *Crossfire* owes the greater part of its qualities to the noir style: a rapid-fire, brutal narrative; a reduced number of sets, confined ones that end up communicating a physical sensation of malaise: a bar, a cinema balcony, the police station, some furnished rooms; few long shots, yet an almost constant use of the medium shot and the close-up, which further increase this sense of isolation; plus edgy, terse dialogue.

One remains in a state of stupefaction before the indolence and emotional misery of these men: their persistent drinking bouts, along with casual pickups; their soul-destroying days spent at the movies; their gratuitous quarrels; their pointless brawls. The love theme comes up against the same lack of horizon: Dmytryk has symbolically situated the dance, full of spleen, that one of the soldiers has with Ginny, the understanding hostess, in an interior courtyard surrounded by high walls. A little later, the girl's boyfriend will have bitter things to say about the impossibility of love. Roy Hunt's photography, which, it must be said, is very fine, adds its harsh glare to this sensation of deep-seated impotence.

As always with Dmytryk, this haunting theme is accompanied by cruel touches. *Crossfire* opens with a roughhouse that soon turns into the slaying of one of the two protagonists. Of the tussle only the play of shadows on the wall is seen, while the hammering sound of punches landing home is heard. A lamp crashes to the ground; darkness ensues. One of the two men is dying, and the camera executes a tracking shot of the legs of the murderer, who takes to his heels. There's the same technical sureness, the same curtness, in the final scene. The killer's been unmasked, and he runs off down a badly lit street. The police officer calls twice for the customary surrender; then he draws a bead, bags him like a jackrabbit, and calmly puts his gun back in the holster. Dmytryk has attended the school of film noir, and this is felt in every sequence. Here, the influence is indisputable: without *Murder, My Sweet, Crossfire* wouldn't have had this style.

The insurgents in John Huston's *We Were Strangers* (1948) are part and parcel of a career that, from *The Maltese Falcon* to *The Asphalt Jungle,* is situated under the sign of noir or noirified film. One will not forget the cruel and bestial policeman, played by Pedro Armendariz, who "invested libidinally" in food, or the excavating of a tunnel in the earth of a cemetery filled with human remains. Once again the film illustrated, in the context of a revolution in Havana, one of Huston's main themes: partial failure.

The qualities of Anthony Mann's *Border Incident* (1949) have been alluded to. We'd also have to stress the Dantesque sequence of the ambush in the marshy canyon and the death of the Mexican farm workers who'd crossed the border without a work permit.

Finally, in the brief series of exotic social documentaries, *Rope of Sand* by William Dieterle (1949) gave a striking description of diamond mining in South Africa, with Paul Henreid playing the mine's chief security officer, an out-and-out sadist, in a style very reminiscent of the Wagnerian warder in *Brute Force.* Unfortunately, the melodrama deprived this indictment of much of its force.

In another sphere, *All the King's Men,* the highly remarkable Robert Rossen film (1949), and *Flamingo Road* by Michael Curtiz

(1949) have shown that political life in the USA can be an extraordinary machine for corruption, blackmail, and, at times, death, with Broderick Crawford and Sydney Greenstreet portraying politicians who have nothing to envy the gallery of racketeers.

Jules Dassin's *Thieves' Highway* (1949) may pass for a documentary about the fruit and vegetable trade in a big American city, and it makes us think of that old Lloyd Bacon film, *Invisible Stripes* (1938 [1939]). But there are also a few noir details: a settling of scores by night, some killers, a hand smashed with an ax handle, an ambivalent heroine who amorously rakes her nails down the naked torso of the man she's meant to betray. And these touches seem a little too insistent to be inspired by a realist ambition alone. It's films of this kind that we were thinking of when we proposed the hypothesis that Hollywood production arbitrarily noirifies social statements.

Boxing is one of American cinema's most venerable themes. Yet up until recently it had all too often merely inspired mediocre productions of the overly sentimental kind. Siodmak devoted a few images to it in *The Killers*. In 1948 [1947] Robert Rossen made a hit-and-miss movie, *Body and Soul,* which had an extremely dour opening. In 1949 Mark Robson turned *Champion* into a study of the character of a prizefighter whose career is governed by a desperate wish to succeed.

In *The Set-Up* Robert Wise directed, also in 1949, a work of impeccable craftsmanship that we rank among the greatest titles of recent world production. In addition to its intrinsic perfection, this film had the merit of blazing a new trail. Here was the most implacable statement about professional boxing in the small towns of the USA. Wise abandoned the convention of the great champion and the world-title eliminator; for a couple of hours he riveted our attention on the progress of a burned-out unknown fighting for ten-dollar purses. Nothing was hidden of the fixing of fights by managers and bookies, the sordid setting of the arena, the cheap hotel rooms, the pitiful existence of ring professionals once they're over the hill. The unity of time, which was respected in this film, created an extraordinary effect of tension and malaise. Finally, the match itself, then the score settling in that alley where the hero has his hand broken with a brick, had all the asperity of certain newsreel films.

The Set-Up would have been unthinkable before the noir genre came along. This is because the film has inherited its narrative speed, its audacity of detail, its veracity in the minor roles, and its cruelty from noir. This cruelty and audacity are never gratuitous, however. They are placed in the service of a work that's much more than an indictment: it's a sociological document. *The Set-Up* reveals what might be expected of American technique if Hollywood directors made decent scripts more often. In that respect, Robert Wise's work is the finest example of the successful integration of noir style.

Since 1950, the social documentary series has experienced a new lease of life by consistently using some of the techniques of the thriller.

Illegal immigration has been a consistently privileged theme: Joseph H. Lewis devoted an uneven work to it, *Lady Without a Passport,* in which some bizarre lowlife scenes in Cuba and the pursuit of a boat through the Florida swamps are insufficient to redeem a conventional story. Michael Curtiz had a surer touch when directing a version of Hemingway's novel *To Have and Have Not, The Breaking Point* (1950). The American title is more fitting than the French, *Trafic en haute mer* [Traffic on the High Seas], to this tragic tale of the honest man tempted by money and the fatal charms of a blonde hetaera magisterially played by Patricia Neal: it involves the lamentable adventures of a boat owner who agrees to smuggle some Chinese into the United States. As a result, he's forced to become the accomplice of a team of gangsters. This life-and-death struggle on the high seas bears comparison to the one in John Huston's *Key Largo.*

Cy Enfield's *The Sound of Fury* reembarks on the tradition of the strong indictment. The subject recalls the Fritz Lang of 1936–38: an unemployed man is drawn into a criminal affair (*You Only Live Once*) and will be lynched (*Fury*), following a hysterical campaign mounted by the yellow press. The prison assault remains one of the most brutal sequences in postwar American cinema.

Centered once again on the baleful role of a certain muck-raking press, Billy Wilder's *The Big Carnival* makes more of a concession to conformity, because of the rather too providential death of the journalist. But then the film is remarkable for its intelligence, its narrative toughness, its rigorous analysis of the reactions of the crowd. Any direct influence of the noir series seems to be minor, but its underlying contribution is enormous. Twenty years before, the censors would never have passed this ferocious chronicle, inspired by an authentic news story. A man goes digging in a cave formerly inhabited by Indians. He's caught in a rock fall. Charles Tatum (Kirk Douglas), a hard-drinking and histrionic hack reporter, makes a deal with the support team and the sheriff (the elections are near) to have the rescue work take at least a week. Radio, television, and the dailies seize on the event. A tent city springs up in front of the tragic cliff in a fairground atmosphere. A train stops in this austere New Mexico landscape: the crowds charge toward the site of the accident. . . . The entombed man's wife suggests a feebler version of the heroines of *Double Indemnity* or *The Postman Always Rings Twice.* She will kill the reporter, whose demise is one of the most striking images in the film: Tatum advances toward the camera and pitches forward in front of the lens, the perfect expression of death already on his face. *The Big Carnival,* an extremely fresh and highly valuable sociological document, is one of the rare instances of the successful integrating of noir style. Its soundtrack is perfectly true to life.

No Way Out by Joseph L. Mankiewicz (1950), *The Lawless* (1950) by Joseph Losey, and *The Well* (1951) by Leo Popkin and Russell Rouse describe racial conflict in the United States. The best of the three, *The Lawless,* has Mexicans in California pitted against a group of rednecks inflamed by the tabloids. *No Way Out* situates the racism in a highly special milieu, that of gangsters. Panic is the dominant aspect of the film: the terror of a white man about to be operated on by a colored surgeon, the agonizing stupor of a fourth-part black man in the face of "reprisals." Despite some pleasing images, *The Well* remains a low-budget B-movie with an ambiguous conclusion. But then again, in all these works there are the same unfeeling, sadistic reactions, the same punitive forays, the same lynchings.

A Streetcar Named Desire (1951) is the intelligent transposition by the former stage director Elia Kazan of the cruel, debased, extremely artificial world of playwright Tennessee Williams. The minute description of the sordid apartment in a working-class district of New Orleans employs the methods of the Free Theater once again. On a neighboring theme, the everyday life of the American lower-middle class, *Death of a Salesman* (1951) by László Benedek and *Come Back, Little Sheba* (1952) by Daniel Mann are valuable testimonies. László Benedek cut his teeth on the police documentary and has retained from this a taste for rigor, for the telling detail, for high-contrast photography. As for *Come Back, Little Sheba,* this film will endure as a document on alcoholism, along the lines of Wilder's *The Lost Weekend* and Goulding's *Nightmare Alley.* Come to that, these two play adaptations bear a resemblance to the naturalism of a Simenon.

Lastly, one of the finest social works of recent years, László Benedek's *The Wild One* (1953 [1954]), reveals the diffuse influence of the noir series.

For almost a decade now the American public has been preoccupied by the rise of mental maladjustment. The cinema has not been slow in taking advantage of this interest. There again, psychiatrists have recently perfected some spectacular techniques: curative drug treatment, shock therapy, etc. In this arsenal, psychoanalysis was the least obtuse method of cure or improvement, the easiest to vulgarize, and the one that best lent itself to certain dramatic effects. Given the initial enigma, the minute sifting of bits of evidence and of people's confessions, the sudden story shifts and the final dramatic turn, psychoanalytic investigation—at least the way it's currently taken to be—is not without its similarities to a police inquiry. This is the angle, it seems, from which the genesis in Hollywood and elsewhere of a psychoanalytic series must be explained.

It's remarkable that psychoanalysis makes its appearance on

screen under the cover of murder. Is it the audacity of the subject that has prompted producers to seek an alibi? Is simple commercial expediency involved? The prudence of the Hollywood moneymen is legendary, and psychoanalysis combined with crime investigation offered the twin advantage of renewing the interest of the detective film and of not disorienting the spectators by suddenly presenting them with overly "intellectual" works.

There's murder afoot in Charles Vidor's *Blind Alley* (1939) and in Alfred Hitchcock's *Spellbound* (1945). A perfect crime, which would go unpunished but for a number of tests of an analytic persuasion, furnished the plot of Robert Siodmak's *The Dark Mirror* (1946). Curtis Bernhardt's *Possessed* (1947) is a classic story of criminal psychology, with some images of drug therapy. The same director's *High Wall* (1948 [1947]) is much closer to the thriller than the psychiatric document. *The Locket* (1947 [1946]) by John Brahm is a technical shot in the dark. Never has the device of the flashback been taken so far. Narratives are jumbled up, parentheses opened, exploits slot one inside the other like those Chinese toys sold in bazaars, and the figure of the heroine gradually comes into focus: beneath her somewhat obscure charm there lurks a dangerous and perverse mythomaniac who's been the death of all her husbands.

For a number of years, then, the psychoanalytic series remained on the periphery of film noir: the same climate of malaise (*Spellbound*), the same technique of suspense (*High Wall*), the same seeking after the cruel detail. We have to wait until 1949 to witness a film of pure psychiatry: with *The Snake Pit* by Anatole Litvak,[1] American cinema tackles the problem of mental treatment without looking for a cover or a pretext. The psychoanalytic series goes beyond the noir series while assimilating what was most valuable within it. And in that respect *The Snake Pit,* with some unrelenting images (we're thinking of that high-angle shot of an asylum courtyard which gives the impression of a hole in which the madwomen seethe like worms), plays an analogous role to the one that, in a different genre, *The Set-Up* had.

It's banal to say that there are no more good Westerns. It would be more correct to speak of a transformation of the genre. The "neo-Western" is less spectacular but more human. Eroticism has staked its claim (*The Outlaw*); heroes are occasionally cowards (*Along Came Jones*); the attack on the stagecoach may not even occur, and the main thrust of the film may be to show why the attack fails, by analyzing the internal tensions that cause the band of outlaws to disintegrate (Hathaway's *Rawhide*).

Film noir was bound to contribute some neurotic and sadistic types to this new epic. Ray Enright's *Coroner Creek* (1948) is an important work in that respect: henceforth, the gratuitous violence and occasional bit of bloodletting form part of the conventions of the Far West. And Raoul Walsh will describe the ambush with exceptional cruelty.

Another influence: the new role played by women. Up to this point, the Western utilized them in the roles of compassionate fiancées (the daughters of a sheriff or judge, in general) or in troupes of fiendish saloon girls. This was in line with the summary mythology of the adventure film: on the one hand, noble sentiments and marriage; on the other, the unfettering of the "lower instincts," sexuality, crime. Exceptions were rare: *Stagecoach,* for instance, but the film was a one-off, almost; or, in certain respects, William Wyler's *The Westerner.* With the films of Raoul Walsh, the ambivalent heroine makes her appearance in the Western, marrying a man in order to have a better chance of killing him (*Pursued*) or resolutely placing herself in the service of "evil" (*Colorado Territory*).

Film noir wouldn't form a series worthy of the name if it hadn't given rise, in Hollywood itself, to various parodies. *Arsenic and Old Lace* (1944) by Frank Capra plus *And Then There Were None* (1945) by René Clair had paved the way, but there it was a question of faithful adaptations of the theater and literature. The merit of Richard Wallace's *It's in the Bag* (1945), Elliott Nugent's *My Favorite Brunette* (1947), Lloyd Bacon's *The Fuller Brush Girl* (1950), Sidney Lanfield's *The Lemon Drop Kid* (1951), and the beginning of George Marshall's *Murder, He Says* (1945) is, on the contrary, to have grounded the parody on purely cinematic terrain. With unequal success, these films used, by amplifying them, the actual stereotypes of Hollywood noir style: the rogues' gallery of killers, the suspense, the strangeness. *Behave Yourself* (1951), by the writer-director George Beck, remains the best of these pastiches.

John Huston has parodied one aspect of American film (adventurers, killers, hoods) in *Beat the Devil* (1953). Preston Sturges, lastly, has adroitly handled the comic noir detail. The sequence in *Unfaithfully Yours* (1948) in which a jealous orchestra conductor imagines, at the same tempo as the piece he's conducting, that he's slashing his wife to death with a razor would make an excellent noir episode if isolated from its context.

There are even cartoons that bear the mark of this cruel humor. Fred Quimby "succeeds in making wounds and swellings irresistible, along with bruises and blisters, a set of teeth stove in by a hammer, a stump a voracious maw tears to ribbons, flesh that burns, body hair that's singed."[2] Tex Avery takes pleasure in traumatic themes: the geometrical anguish of changing size (*King-size Canary*), obsession (*Slap Happy Lion*). With *The Cuckoo Clock* he will create a pastiche of the noir series. Paramount, too, goes on producing *Popeye* with less success but as much sadism as in the Fleischer Brothers era.

Another question is worth bringing up: has the noir series influenced international film production? For the USSR and its allies the answer is obviously no. Once the Allied war effort was over, contact between the Communist and non-Communist world gradually went by the board. There again, the making of a film doesn't have the same aim in both instances. On the one side, it mainly involves creating exchange values, making money, and therefore pleasing audiences in one way or another. Elsewhere, it means, first of all, exalting collective work or, more generally, reinforcing the uniformity of collective awareness. And crime films in particular, whether noir or not, are incompatible with this attitude. Where both subject and atmosphere are concerned, there's seldom a common standard between a Hollywood production and one from Moscow, Prague, Warsaw, or Peking.

Film noirs have long been spoken of in France, with something very different being meant by this, something that, roughly speaking, the following tendencies would embrace:

- First, the tradition from the years 1935–39 (*Pépé le Moko, Le Jour se lève, Quai des brumes*); that's to say, the Fatefulness of Destiny, the Impossibility of Redemption, the Brevity of Great Passions. In the worst of cases, melodrama is involved. In the best, a social study that, for no particular reason, ends tragically. Yves Allégret with *Dédée d'Anvers* and René Clément with *Au-delà des grilles* have been the immediate heirs of this current in the postwar period.

- Second, a sort of realism attracted by some of the more sordid aspects of existence: Anouilh, Clouzot, Gilles Grangier in his only good film, *Au P'tit zouave,* Yves Allégret with *Une si jolie petite plage* and *Manèges.* As Claude Roy writes: "I'm a man, thinks the adolescent who leaves the bordello. I'm a realist, thinks the filmmaker who reenters it."[3] But none of these films is deliberately set in the gangster milieu. Not one is strange or oneiric. A Zola-style naturalism is often involved, occasionally filtered through Freud.

For a long time, the influence of the American series was almost nil, then. A few months ago, however, French producers discovered that the formula made money. And French film noir has suddenly experienced such a boom that it's necessary to devote a special chapter to it.

In Italy, more readily than in France, realism takes the form of a social testimony and occasionally reworks the style of Soviet films. Few of its details echo the noir series, even in the more disenchanted works. Nevertheless, Giuseppe de Santis has handled certain sequences in *Rizo amaro* (1949) in the style of American films: the settling of scores in the butcher's shop, amid the sides of beef, the scene in the silo, or the thrashing Vittorio Gassman gives his mistress. In *Anna* (1951), Silvana Mangano performs a dance number and an exotic song that are meant to recall those in *Gilda*. In this uneven film there is, furthermore, a fight to the death in the cellars of a watermill that's inspired by the Hollywood tradition, some of whose dramatic devices the director, Alberto Lattuada, has managed to assimilate. *Senza pietà* (1948) is another example of this. More to our liking, Ferdinando Cerchio's *Il Bivio* (1951), with its police inspector–cum–gang boss, would be more reliant on the gangster film.

On the Scandinavian front, the cinema is, finally, traditionally split between mysticism, the theme of prostitution, old-style melodrama, implicit psychoanalysis, and visual research: as of now, it's hard to see how the inspiration that concerns us could have installed itself there.

In England, on the other hand, film noir quickly found itself at home. Let's note, in passing, that a single European writer, Peter Cheyney, has made a genuinely original contribution to the noir detective novel, and he was British. Let's also remember that Graham Greene has been the source of one of the first American movies in the series, *This Gun for Hire*. Finally, James Hadley Chase is English.

England and the USA share two common themes in their cinematic repertoire: the hunted man and the chase in an unexpected urban setting. The hunted-man motif recurs in Carol Reed's *The Third Man* (1949), Cavalcanti's *They Made Me a Fugitive* (1948 [1947]), and Robert Hamer's *It Always Rains on Sunday* (1948). This is so typically English a theme that Jules Dassin used it when he wanted to set one of his films in London (*Night and the City*). As for the bit of bravura of the chase, even a documentary like *It Always Rains on Sunday,* which comes close to *Domenica d'agosto* or *Antoine et Antoinette* in its depiction of normal, everyday people, doesn't shun it. Added to which, the common language and constant interchange of actors between Hollywood and London could only favor the development of film noir.

After all, puritan, obsessed England has had its own very particular annals of crime for a century or more. Perhaps more than any other, this is the country of sophisticated murder, of abiding cruelty, and also of sadistic outbursts: the Pritchard affair, the case of Dr. Palmer, Jack the Ripper, John Christie, or the Coronation Sadist.

Since 1946, all these factors have successfully played their part in the development of an authentic British noir series. In it, one rediscovers most of the Hollywood themes: police-style realism, ferocity, ambivalence, and, sometimes, strangeness. This seam has given some of the best and some of the worst. Let's cite at random, among the more worthy titles: *Brighton Rock* (1947) by John Boulting; *The Upturned Glass* (1947), a remarkable film by Lawrence Huntingdon; *Obsession* (1949) by Edward Dmytryk; *The Third Man* (1949) by Carol Reed; and various sequences from the collective film, *Dead of Night* (1945), the oneiric theme of which recalls *The Woman in the Window* and *Clouded Yellow*. And among the less good, *No Orchids for Miss Blandish* by St. John Legh Clowes or *I'll Get You for This* by Joseph M. Newman.

References

1 Usually dated 1948. —*Trans.*

2 Abner Lepetit [Robert Benayoun], "Bilan du dessin animé," *L'Age du cinéma* 1. Quimby was in fact an MGM producer. A humorless man, he did engage Hanna and Barbera to make the *Tom and Jerry* series and gave Tex Avery his head. —*Trans.*

3 *Cahiers du cinéma* 7.

9

French film noirs

In France the recent 1954–55 season has been placed under the aegis of the "noir." Fascinated by the miraculous encounter between Eddie Constantine and Lemmy Caution, the producers use, to the point of exhaustion, a formula they'd have been wrong not to exploit: it makes money. Almost without a break, inveterate wasters of celluloid as woeful as Willy Rozier shoot low-budget movies that have an aggressively vulgar title as the ace up their sleeve. The fashion is for noir. Foreign films are rebaptized. An Italian melodrama by Guido Brignone, *Processo contro ignoto* [Trial of an Unknown], becomes *C'est la faute au grisbi* [Blame It on the Loot]. *Black Tuesday* is called *Mardi, ça saignera* [Tuesday Will Be Bloody] in France. An unspeakable light comedy takes *Les Pépées font la loi* [The Broads Lay Down the Law] for a title.

Sometime in the future sociologists will be called on to study this phenomenon. Why, ten years later, has French cinema adopted formulas that in the USA are running out of steam? Is this about coming to the rescue of American cinema, perhaps? There would be, then, a constant and irrepressible need for violent spectators. Come to that, military publicity has turned the parachutist into the somewhat sordid hero of our times. Judo extends its hold as far as the provinces. Killers have returned from overseas covered in medals. And one is struck by the youthfulness of the audiences (many sixteen-to-twenty-year-old youngsters of both sexes) whenever a film noir is shown at the local cinema.

Another factor: international détente. The American noir series really took off in 1945; that's to say, with the close of hostilities. It spoke to the passive adventurers of peacetime. The image it presented of the United States—a venal and vicious society—would scarcely have been suitable to the ideology of a country at war. One may assume that the French series owes its own development to the likelihood of peace that, given the euphoria of the negotiations, is about to happen with the settling of the Indochina affair.

Most of the films are mere parodies. One goes to see *Ça va barder* the way one used to go to a Fernandel. The noir series *à la française* doesn't seek authenticity. Let's add that the bourgeoisie has retained a certain nostalgia for prewar American comedy. The gentle eccentricities of *My Man Godfrey* or *The Awful Truth* correspond to the "easy" days of the Third Republic.

In 1949, an unknown, André Hunebelle, attempted to reconcile the taste of the day—the totally amoral, vaguely anarchist man of action and his simple, violent pleasures—with the fond memories of a social class in a state of crisis. His *Mission à Tanger* marked the beginning of the French series. The film's hero was an investigative journalist partial to whiskey and women. He recalled those easygoing detectives of which William Powell was at one time the prototype. Raymond Rouleau, flanked by his resourceful and blundering photographer, Bernard Lajarrige, was very entertaining in this role.

Méfiez-vous des blondes, made the following year, marked a step forward. Its technique was more polished, the female characters more ambiguous. Repartee began to give way to aberrant action. Henri Crémieux cut a delicious figure as a petit-bourgeois hired assassin, who took off his slippers with regret, cast a wistful glance at the steaming soup tureen, and left to do the business, machine gun tucked inside a violin case.

Massacre en dentelles (1951) is the final film in this series, with Hunebelle shooting the exteriors in Venice, a setting he managed to convert into something strange. It's true that a group of black gangsters, deserters from the American army, added spice to the City of the Doges.

Bernard Borderie's first film dates from the same period. *Les Loups chassent la nuit* is a conventional and extremely well resolved spy story. Paul Paviot parodies the American noir series in a *Chicago Digest* that's good for four or five gags, but which didn't equal *A toi de faire, Archibald* by Marcel Cravenne. Lastly,

Lemmy Caution makes a humorless appearance in 1952 in the third segment of Henri Verneuil's *Brelan d'as,* entitled *Je suis un tendre.*

It's Bernard Borderie who really opens fire with *La Môme vert-de-gris.* He utilizes all the rules of the genre, albeit without conviction: chases, fistfights, nightclubs, unusual settings, knowing winks at the public. Eddie Constantine, who's far from having the FBI agent's physique described by Cheyney, was hired to play the role of this superman, and his ugly mug on an ad for toothpaste brought him instant success. Better constructed, *Cet homme est dangéreux* gave Jean Sacha the opportunity to bring off two or three ingeniously framed shots. The genre is now well into its stride, and Constantine has lost his self-conscious air.

In *Votre dévoué Blake* by Jean Laviron—a despicable philistine who works in variety theater and nude revues—Eddie Constantine plays a new tough guy who resembles Lemmy Caution like a brother. The fights are always of a singular improbability. There's one good idea in it, though: a gang boss who resembles Jacques Fath is the lover of a dopey but very rich dame. He suggests she throw a big charity ball in a tiny amphitheater. Some Dominican friars are to pass the plate around. The gangsters get dressed up as monks and hide their machine guns under their sackcloth robes. The amphitheater is surrounded by an iron grille through which an electric current passes at just the right moment, and charity-loving Tout-Paris falls victim to a mega-stickup. This sequence is extremely well done, yet one dreams of what the marvelous Louis Feuillade would have made of it at the time of the *ciné-romans.*

Ça va barder deserves a mention, perhaps. The screenplay is consistently insignificant, but the broads are better chosen. The American John Berry, who has signed the mise-en-scène, has more nerve and skill than our pathetic lot of third-raters, who race through their work with one eye fixed on the cash drawer. The supporting roles have unusual prominence. Roger Saget puts in a savory performance as a fat drug dealer, a lover of the little delicacies a pretty individual in scanty clothing prepares for him. As always, the film ends with a bit of bravura in an unusual setting. Here, it's a fight in a lighthouse.

Eddie Constantine's success encouraged other "crooners" to try their hands at the noir series. Georges Ulmer, a pop singer and judo expert, has appeared in Jean Sacha's *Une balle suffit*. A fine start, shot on film tinted red as in the silent days, a brawl in the wings of a variety theater, and an oddly strange "baddy" (a cranky collector who's always stroking, with calculated slowness, a very beautiful cat): this is all that's worth retaining of a decidedly mediocre film. In *Pas de coup dur pour Johnny* the latter is played by Armand Mestral, a basso cantante in operetta, and the film is of no interest.

This lamentable series draws to a close, for the time being, with a Willy Rozier film, *A toi de jouer, Callaghan.* An Englishman, Tony Wright, a well-built blond actor with insipid features, imitates Eddie Constantine. The worst kind of commercialism no longer even bothers to hide. This is as badly made as Monsieur Emile Couzinet's *Le Congrès des belles-mères.*

All these films have been a caricature of the noir series. Neither the eroticism of *Gilda,* nor the frenetic oneirism of *The Lady from Shanghai,* nor the rigor of *The Enforcer* had the slightest chance of interesting producers who work with film the way some women work the streets.

Over the past year, though, a number of figures have created a French school of noir or noirified film that has other ambitions. Up till now three formulas have been used:

- Criminal psychology based on suspense (*Obsession, Bonnes à tuer, Les Diaboliques*)
- The police documentary (*Razzia sur la chnouf*)
- Films about the underworld (*Touchez pas au grisbi, Du rififi chez les hommes*)

Suspense, such as it is practiced today, runs little risk of violating the habits of the general public. A degraded prolongation of a certain shock cinema—that dared to make *Nosferatu* many moons ago—suspense has become the dramatic spice of safe family entertainment. Jean Delannoy adapted a William

Irish novel, *Obsession,* which deserved a better fate. Delannoy represents a tradition of commercial efficiency and academicism. He follows the latest fashion, has a schoolteacher's mentality, will receive the award for the best worker in France. *Obsession* was an overfastidious drama in which every image was foreseen three seconds in advance. This is the kind of cinema we hate.

In *Les Diaboliques* Henri Clouzot created a pleasantly sordid, minor work that met with enormous success. Such pseudosuspense didn't go very far, but it has to be said in Clouzot's defense that the film he dreamed of making, a script about Indochina, never got beyond the first hurdle of the censors.

Henri Decoin's *Bonnes à tuer* is the adaptation of an American novel by Pat MacGerr. Was this choice really necessary? Pat MacGerr, who's a Catholic, has centered her tale on the moral tortures of a cynic: no man is completely lost, and even in the most depraved mind there's a little light burning beneath the memories of childhood. Here the morally blind figure is a journalist, Larry Rock, who's risen from nothing and is ready for anything. He arranges the murder of his first wife because she symbolizes Good. This edifying tale is underpinned by a well-worked suspense and, from the pure detection angle, his "fall" is really sensational. It has to be said that Catholicism has an incredible capacity for adaptation: God is present in a detective novel in which His name is never uttered. Such is the road traveled since *Fabiola.* . . .

A subject like this was difficult to adapt in France. In a country that, fortunately, turns away from Christianity, the moral coup de theatre would have had trouble reaching the screen. Henri Decoin has modified the text by emphasizing the versatile personality of Larry Rock. The spectator thinks more in terms of a madman's crime, of the gratuitous act of an intellectual. This journalist intoxicated with luxury has a Chinese butler, like some Edwardian lady's man. He's a Lafcadio and no longer the average American of Pat MacGerr's novel.

The direction is very skillful. Decoin has long been a specialist in atmosphere (*Les Inconnus dans la maison, L'Homme de*

Londres, La Vérité sur Bébé Donge). He has handled his subject in the "society scandal" style: a luxury terrace overlooking the Champs-Elysées, well-bred glamour pusses in evening dress, crystal chandeliers. A number of flashbacks evoke the journalist's rise. Certain acts of blackmail make one think of currency trafficking. When viewing this film it's hard not to think of what the press was like just after the Liberation, what it's become in the context of Laniel-Pinay.[1]

Finally, some visual innovations will please the movie buffs. Decoin was obliged to reconstitute, in flashback, the impressions of an amorous young woman who's a bit drunk. Setting: a nightclub. He isolates the orchestra and the couple against a black background. The photography is beautiful, in the Expressionist style. A bit later, the danseuse feels unwell and heads for the bathroom. The cameraman uses the same black background: to the right, the oversized sign, "Ladies"; to the left, the young woman on a chair; in voice-over: "She's pregnant, your little lady. Didn't you know?"

These few seconds of true cinema are to the credit of a director who will manage, perhaps, to escape the "tradition of quality."

It's to Decoin, once again, that we owe a police documentary that dares not speak its name: *Razzia sur la chnouf*. This discreet eulogy to the forces of law and order is the culmination of a campaign of rehabilitation that began in 1947 with Maurice de Canonge's *Un flic* and H.-G. Clouzot's *Quai des Orfèvres*. Three years later, Hervé Bromberger directed an English-style reportage on the Criminal Investigation Department, *Identité judiciaire*. A bit of bravura, a chase after the sadistic lawyer in a warehouse, ended the documentary on an American note. Recently, *Série noire* eulogized both the informer and the virtues of the police. It's to this need for justification that the theme of *Razzia sur la chnouf* responds. Henri le Nantais, a big shot who's shown what stern stuff he's made of in America, lands at Orly airport. His mission is to take a narcotics gang in hand. He's initiated into the different operations: the receiving of the raw product, its refining, its marketing at the wholesale and retail level. He probes the weak points, weighs up the volume of sales. He's a sort of specialist consultant who has the power over life and death: something to warm the cockles of the heart of all those functionaries who nourish dreams of power. Le Nantais, who's a boy in blue disguised as a bad lot, now knows all the workings of the gang. One last haul, a catch too good to be true, and the crooks are in the hands of the CID.

Razzia sur la chnouf deserves to be compared to one of László Benedek's first films, *Port of New York* (1949). The theme is the same. A policeman is introduced into a narcotics organization. Decoin, though, has souped up his plot by revealing the identity of Le Nantais right at the end. The use of this ploy is stupid. A cop's a cop, and Andromache is Andromache. There's never been a masterpiece based on a commercial hoax. It would have been better, from every point of view, if the credits had been followed by a notice: "The French police long suspected the existence of a gang specializing in drug pushing. A CID inspector whose service record guaranteed his relative honesty was given the mission, etc. . . ." The film would gain in authenticity and be judged on its own merits.

That said, Decoin hasn't done too badly. Less constricted than Benedek by puritan censorship, he has given us a view of Paris by night that the history of mores will perhaps bear in mind. Two aging queens interviewed in a bar are "1955" the way Robert de Montesquiou was fin-de-siècle. In them, fashion literally sublimates homosexuality. They already have something of the period engraving. Another image deserves to stick in the mind: the opium den in a luxury setting—walls in mat tones, discreet moldings, Chinese antiquities. For the general public this is a kind of résumé of the Champs-Elysées atmosphere of La Boëtie.

This desire for verisimilitude has given the film the look of a series of news flashes: the crooks' dice game in the smoky cellar of the bistro, the refinery in the sticks, the sale of the white powder in a Métro station and in the toilets of a cabaret. . . . There's one good, effective scene: in an illicit dance hall where marijuana is smoked, a drugged girl is seduced by a black man to the rhythm of tribal music. A less good scene, that of the big boss, recalls the English novels of Edgar Wallace. Everyone has dreamed of being a drug baron and resembling the sophisticated gang leader played by Dalio. It was necessary, then, to give a wide berth to Dalio. As for the killers, who fill the screen to overflowing, it's merely a question of knowing whether they correspond to something real in France. In *France-Observateur* (258), H.F. Rey gives a negative, albeit partial, response: it is based on two unverifiable testimonies.

There remains Gabin: Decoin has been reproached with copying a character from *Touchez pas au grisbi*. Here and there, in effect, Gabin plays the aging heavy in an impeccable shirt. He has the same gestures as always. He eats cooked ham and potted pâté, brushes his teeth and tootles around like a pensioner.

This criticism is beside the point. For ten years, Humphrey Bogart has played the same character in the American noir series (*The Maltese Falcon, The Big Sleep,* etc.), and nobody's dreamed of hauling him over the coals for it. Let's say, rather, that Gabin is irksome because he's Gabin, to wit, a famous actor, and that an anonymous face would have been better. Since the war, Gabin has played men of substance: the romantic gangster of *Pépé le Moko* or the violent yet good proletarian of *Le Jour se lève* has become a property owner. He's created the myth of the bourgeoisification of the big cheese (*Le Miroir, Touchez pas au grisbi, Razzia sur la chnouf*) and of the revenge of the parvenu (*La Marie du port, Martin Roumagnac, La Vérité sur Bébé Donge*). Before the war, Gabin worked wonders in populist versions of *amour fou*. Today, he has sex. And he always has sex, and not by accident, with women younger than himself (from *La Marie du port* to *French Cancan*). This Prévertian rebel has become an expert in sleeping around. The black-market nouveaux riches can rest easy: life begins at forty. Because it's indeed to them that Gabin addresses his character. He embodies the small French capitalist who owes his wealth to the war years. A comparison could be made with the pre-1914 self-made man: Gabin is a modern version of Henri Bernstein's *Samson*.

Whatever its weaknesses and its pro-cop side, *Razzia sur la chnouf* will have a certain historical importance. In the USA the noir series evolved after 1948 in the direction of reportage. The strangeness of the first few movies (*The Maltese Falcon, The Lady in the Lake, Ride the Pink Horse*) soon evaporated. The public got tired of confused stories that no longer provided new thrills. In France, cradle of Surrealism, it was hoped that quality film noir would exploit such strangeness to the hilt. None of this occurred. Like their American colleagues, the producers of *Razzia* have opted for reportage and the established order.

The appearance of a typically French gangster film is due to two Gallimard novelists, Auguste Le Breton and Albert Simonin.

Touchez pas au grisbi was a faithful adaptation of a Simonin novel that had psychology and myth as its goal: the psychology of a middle-aged gangster, the myth of indestructible friendships. Jacques Becker, however, had condemned his art to insignificance. The photography, studied in the extreme, recalled Robert Bresson: a lot of staircases and doorways, as in *Les Dames du Bois de Boulogne*. And the same slow gestures: Maria Casarès, a woe-begotten lover who hadn't much to say, found her ideal partner in an elegant and banal Gabin. The minor detail "à la Becker" (the bachelors' bedtime, for instance) assured the film of success. An admirably constructed entertainment, this: Guermantes among the lowlife.

We prefer *Du rififi chez les hommes* to such exercises in style. This is because Jules Dassin has never taken cinema for an art of amusement: "To go five years without making a film is terrible," as he said in an interview published in *Cahiers du cinéma* 46.

In the USA, Dassin has had to fight to defend his oeuvre. *Brute Force* and *Naked City* have been cut to ribbons; *Night and the City* has been reedited to make it more commercial. He has been and still is on the blacklist. In France, the cops of the CISL, the International Confederation of Free Trade Unions, have managed to prevent him from shooting *L'Ennemi public no. 1,* and a famous actor has been found to back this conspiracy plus a hack to direct the film. *Rififi* is Dassin's temporary revenge on the imbecility of the self-righteous. He has other projects, like adapting Verga (*Mastro Don Gesualdo*), Ibsen (*An Enemy of the People*), Thomas Mann (*The Magic Mountain*). He's working on a life of Victor Hugo. Will he be condemned to silence?

The human analysis and psychosocial content of Auguste Le Breton's novel aren't what's best about *Rififi*. An obvious Manicheanism oversimplifies this underworld. Two gangs, one good and one bad, are pitted against each other. The ones who are good are absurdly—namely, religiously—good, making the sign of the cross, medals, playthings for the kids. This was already a failing in *Grisbi*. This rehabilitation of the hoodlum in terms of a certain right-wing anarchism seems as suspect to us as justifying the forces of law and order. Gangsters become the natural supporters of capitalism in a revolutionary situation, the most recent example being the gambling franchise in Saigon-Cholon.[2]

Some doggedly average types undertake a burglary, then, one that requires the utmost professional skill. In the group there's an exile with a face marked by misfortune; a jovial, Italian bon vivant; another, more reserved, Italian obsessed by bits of skirt; lastly, the strapping young fellow, a good husband and father. For twenty years the American novelist W.R. Burnett (from whom John Huston borrowed *The Asphalt Jungle* story) has exploited the notion that gangsters adore family life and picnics in the country. In *M* Fritz Lang had already shown that there's little difference between an underworld that metes out justice and official justice itself. But then Lang was perfectly aware of the link between the underworld and fascism and never made concessions to such sympathy, so fashionable today, for the gangster class.

The work is original for reasons external to the subject. The poker game had lasted till morning, and the bistro's iron shutter was raised on a rain-soaked street: this is one of the first images of a film in which Paris is constantly present, not the Paris of smart comedies, but a mist-shrouded and hostile big city. "What interests me is the truth," says Dassin in the interview cited above, "and I think I find it in the framework of documentary. A certain poetry must complement the documentary aspect, however. . . . What you see in my films, this mixture of documentary and poetry, is my modest investigation of an expression of truth, even when one is limited to thrillers or detective stories."

Such a feeling for detail is only given to the great filmmakers. Through it, dialogue, gestures, and settings become meaningful. For example: the murder of the junkie at Saint-Rémy de Chevreuse; Mario's funeral along the Seine, with the cortege of empty cars covered in flowers; the Chinese shadow silhouettes at the "L'Age d'or" cabaret; the dummies in the basement. . . . Dassin uses fast cutting and an inordinately mobile camera. There is no better formula.

But the high point of the film is that interminable burglary in which the suspense consists of professional gestures. Ever since Pudovkin died and Lang succumbed to commercialism, we find it hard to imagine who else could have brought this scene off. Much has been said about this already classic sequence, apart from that it renews the *drama of objects*.

In terms of their everyday handling, some objects are bound up with impending danger: a truck gets bogged down in the mud, a tire bursts, an ineptly felled tree flattens a worker, a trench collapses. One of the most fecund traditions of American cinema is to subordinate a human story to the endurance of an engine or a scrap of material. In *Air Force,* will the patched-up airplane manage to take off? Will the Joads' truck, in *The Grapes of Wrath,* make it to the Promised Land? Clouzot had already subjected the fate of a group of men to a rotten plank or a bumpy road (*Le Salaire de la peur*). In this *Rififi* sequence the suspense is of the same order, since too strong a mallet blow would, in short, have set off the "super-alarm."

As so often in Dassin's work, the film ends with a desperate race through the city streets. Tony le Stéphanoise is all but dead at the wheel of his car as he crosses the south suburbs and the Left Bank. The murderer in *Naked City* was gunned down on Brooklyn Bridge. The remarkable neurotic in *Night and the City* met a derisory end while fleeing along the Thames.

Rififi, then, is the only "authentic" film in the French noir series. It's the culmination of a style. Due to the quality of the narrative, it bears comparison with an American masterpiece,

The Asphalt Jungle. The picturesque human aspect is less emphasized. César le Milanais is only a pale copy of the astonishing Doc Riedenschneider, that erudite-looking old German who liked innocent young girls. In Huston's film the strapping young fellow was possessed by a strong yearning: to see the open fields of his native Kentucky once again. Here he's a simple family man. Dassin, though, has surpassed Huston in the burglary sequence.

Alas, *Rififi* is merely a happy exception. At the time of writing, unadulterated rubbish goes on being churned out. The producers announce *Pas de whisky pour Callaghan* and *Les Salauds vont en enfer.*

It's a matter of some urgency to put a stop to this squandering of celluloid and to make some *serious* film noir. We suggest some titles: *Le Ratissage du Cap Bon, Le Quadrillage de l'Aurès, Napalm sur les Viets,* and *L'Affaire Guingoin.* We can also envisage different biographical accounts: *El Glaoui* for instance.[3] This would be genuinely noir and genuinely French. To be sure, there's little chance of seeing these projects happen in standard format. But what are the amateur filmmakers with their 16mm cameras waiting for? Is the Jean Vigo tradition dead and buried?

References

1 In 1954, the right-wing coalition government of Joseph Laniel and Antoine Pinay was scuttled by the politicking of its arch enemy, De Gaulle. —*Trans.*

2 A reference to the protection money exacted by local Binh Xuyen gangsters, in collusion with the French military, on the casinos, opium dens, and brothels of this teeming sector of the city. The colonialist strategy was to use the racketeers' self-interest to keep the Viet Minh Communists at bay. —*Trans.*

3 These invented titles allude sarcastically to the colonialist machinations of the French government in Indochina, Algeria, and Morocco, and to the internal politics of the French Communist Party. —*Trans.*

10

A balance sheet

Noir isn't so noir . . .
—Paul Valéry

In order to arrive at a conclusion, and setting all metaphysics aside (notwithstanding current fashion), let's define the range and the limits of this "panorama."

To a greater or lesser degree all criticism, and cinema criticism in particular, combines *aesthetic appreciation* and the *sociology of art,* two attitudes that are very different in their viewpoints, their methods, and the validity of their judgments.

To describe and classify particular themes and genres, to determine their origin, the reasons for their evolution, and their influence is to pronounce judgments about reality, within the framework of *sociological analysis*. One therefore aims at a scientific kind of objectivity, and research in this field can never be too rigorous. But in order to exactly establish the contours of the noir series, to define its sources, describe its history, and pinpoint its repercussions a mass of facts would be necessary that are difficult to obtain—a more detailed chronology of all the movies in question; data about their financing and their commercial success; various inquiries among their creators and critics; surveys made after test screenings, among correctly sampled audiences; an exploration of the widest possible social context—as well as sometimes complex methods of interpretation.[1] Due to a lack of time and means, but also a lack of lucidity, "impressionism" remains the norm in such matters. If we haven't avoided this ourselves, it has been at all events consciously so. The interest of this panorama is not in supplying definitive responses to a subject that is still virgin territory (at least in France); it's in offering to the curiosity of film lovers, and perhaps to the more in-depth studies of the future, a set of hypotheses that one has endeavored to make the least unilateral and most likely possible, given the main facts available.

Aesthetic appreciation consists, on the other hand, of value judgments proffered on certain aspects of a work, on a set of works, or on whole groups of works. The need for objectivity doesn't have a lot of meaning here, especially today. In terms of its justification, the opinion of a film critic is only as singular as the opinion of any other spectator. When we found some character or other created by Barbara Stanwyck "erotic" or some manhunt or other "impressive," our feeling remained linked to an arbitrary system of references. In many respects, however, this principle of relativity is attenuated: in the technical domain (mise-en-scène, photography, sound, set design, acting styles), the notion of competence may, in a given time and place, have a certain meaning. Thus the specialized press as a whole has offered judgments very close to, or identical with, our own, not only on the technique of works we take to be important within the noir series but also on the general technical value of this series. As to the actual "subject" of the film and to its various possible facets (psychological and social content, political orientation, dramatic and poetic nature, etc.), it is answerable to a *critique of veracity* when science has its word to say about the situations it presents. The noir genre seems favored in this respect, since it can be confronted with psychoanalysis, with well-known criminological data on gangsterism in the USA, even with the sociology of "elementary groups" (account being taken of the sometimes hypothetical nature of these systems themselves). Lastly, in the often extremely wide area of appreciation, which is not dependent on technical or scientific expertise, not every assertion has, of course, the same interest: some are more original or more suggestive than others. Here—but only here—criticism becomes, or should become, a work of art. If from this angle the noir style has not always elicited a reaction of any quality from its judges, it has managed to elicit intense and diverse ones from them.

Another distinction is called for between the *elementary components* of the series and its unique atmosphere. Let us explain.

In its more typical creations, film noir was striving to give birth to a "new frisson" that was indivisible and inimitable. It juxtaposed certain themes within the framework of a particular technique: strange intrigues, eroticism, violence, psychological ambivalence within criminal groups. It's the convergence of these dramatic factors, some of which were not new, that created a style.

It was legitimate, therefore, to isolate these constitutive elements, to analyze them separately, to draw up an autonomous balance sheet of them before offering an overall judgment of film noir as a historical moment in sensibility.

As to an overall assessment, it would be difficult to situate this in other than in terms of time. Besides, do worthwhile criteria exist for delimiting what will remain of an artistic phenomenon and what will disappear? Let's resolutely take our own risks, despite an obvious lack of distance. What's more, we haven't had the chance, in such a brief period, to reexamine all these film noirs. Some of them have been definitively withdrawn; others are still circulating as 16mm versions in the provinces. Here, one touches on the problem of the material conditions of filmological research: you'd have to be able to "consult" the works under study as you wished, which presupposes their deposit in a cinematheque. But that's another story.

One last remark: as in all cycles, there are productions of very uneven merit in the noir series. In the preceding chapters we have stressed the important films. Account will have to be taken here of the genre's *average quality,* which can sometimes modify the perspective.

Technique is almost always excellent: polished but never "finicky" photography, an incisive mise-en-scène, and a vigorous tempo are never found wanting. Two successive formulas have to be distinguished, however.

In the early days, which correspond to low-budget productions, interior sequences dominate, these being handled in the classic style of prewar detective movies. Whence the feeling of claustrophobia, of "no way out," encountered in both *The Maltese Falcon* and *The Glass Key.*

After 1946, the modus operandi changes: street scenes, often shot at night, real locations, chases in an unusual setting; in a word, expensive virtuosity. Directors have substantial means at their disposal, and they perfect methods whose realism, whatever its inflection may be, will be put to good use.

Having agreed on this, all one can do is juxtapose a number of widely differing characteristics. Let us note the German influence and its taste for high-contrast photography. Systematic researches into depth of field are rare. They suit certain "psychological" films better, films in which it is necessary to illustrate the complexity of the relationships between many characters, placed in the one image at varying distances from the lens. Likewise, rightly or wrongly, color has only been used on the periphery of the series, in noirified works, but each time in an extremely fruitful way (*Leave Her to Heaven, Rope, Under Capricorn*). Films like *The Lady in the Lake, Murder, My Sweet,* and *Dark Passage* have introduced the device of the subjective camera. Finally, as a type of introduction or a means of linking sequences together, the voice-over had a certain success during the years 1945–47 (*Laura, Double Indemnity, The Lady from Shanghai*), but today it seems reserved for the police documentary.

As for the *subject,* the balance sheet is, on the contrary, negative. The choice of themes is undoubtedly banal: crimes or gangsters. Yet the noir series has sought to renew these themes by imparting a quality of strangeness to the action. It has only managed this in part. During the first few years, the spectator's disarray was real: the classic parameters of the detective film had disappeared. There was an ambiguity to the suspense: obscure motives, shifting interests, absurd corpses. In that respect, film noir was very much of its time. It was inscribed within a more general tendency: the exploitation of incoherence, the heritage of Surrealism, the influence of Kafka.

As it was, the method contained the seeds of its own rapid downfall. The first private detective's inquiry in a nightmarish nocturnal setting was impressive. By the time the tenth such adventure came around, the theme had become stereotyped, and *the strange, being itself denied, became a new point of reference.* It was to degenerate because it remained on the surface. It affected neither the setting, nor the social context, nor the actors' gestures, nor the profound structure of perception.

Although it may often have been imitated, Dalí's painting retains its shock value. The visions of Kafka—we're thinking of *The Metamorphosis* here—are always stirring because of their across-the-board power of deracination, which makes them identical to the creations of the dream. Here, on the other hand, the incoherence is limited to the plot (chaotic vicissitudes, incidental characters, obscure undertakings) and, on second viewing, the incoherence often gave a mere impression of being disjointed or improvised.

On 12 January 1953, the Toulouse Cine Club attempted an experiment when showing *Murder, My Sweet* a few weeks before the distribution rights lapsed. This involved finding out whether this film would create in the viewer the state of tension and malaise that the critics had been unanimous in describing seven years before. The experiment was negative. Marlowe's third blackout, which at the time had elicited a genuine feeling of anguish, provoked a general outburst of laughter. During the discussion, it was claimed that this was a parody of terror.[2]

The works that, on this point, are still valuable are those that displayed much greater daring: the sets of *The Shanghai Gesture,* the fairground scenes in *The Lady from Shanghai,* the concentrating of the anguish on an oneiric fact in *The Woman in the Window,* or the dream sequence in *Spellbound.*

Actually, the noir series has lost out on two counts: on that of the strange, through a lack of boldness, and on that of documentary realism, through the conventional structure of scripts.

One can easily understand this disenchanted statement by one of the creators of the thriller, Edward Dmytryk, who, in order to avoid such uncertainty, advocated a much franker option in favor of social or economic realism: "To you French, it may seem odd to hear an American director use words like 'economic,' 'political,' or 'social.' But you should know that even in Hollywood there is a small group of men who understand that few stories or few films can be worthwhile if the situations and characters they put forward aren't solidly rooted in what these three words represent."[3]

From 1947 on, the producers themselves sensed that the semi-incoherent plot had had its day, and they resolutely turned toward the documentary. But then neorealism was almost wholly limited to matters of murder and to the world of the police. The seam was already played out. Although we know about the underworld's role in the United States, about which a recent book, Burton B. Turkus and Sid Feder's *Murder, Inc.* has provided impressive data, we find it hard to believe that crime has the same importance in the country's affairs as it has in the scripts filmed in Hollywood (more than 50 percent). There's a lack of proportion here that's all the more irritating for being weighed down by repetition and convention.

The series has died due to a crisis in the subject. *Uninteresting strangeness or police realism: the series has been unable to escape this dilemma.*

American audiences seem particularly sensitive to the *eroticism* of the thriller. As it is, this is more often a question of a veiled eroticism—or an eroticism of the veil, if you prefer—at one with noir ambiguity. Here, though, the understatements have to do with the puritanism of the Hays Code, the rigor of which poses a genuine headache for the men of Hollywood. In film noir one is obliged to create an atmosphere of latent sexuality, nebulous and polymorphous, that, as in projective tests, each individual can people with his own desires and "structure" as he sees fit. On this subject a French film lover—since the formula also has its connoisseurs outside of America—has written that, "There's a science of dissimulating the flesh and of arranging the folds of a dress that's more evocative than the most provocative dishabille." This is "the supreme refinement of an eroticism that dares not speak its name . . . because it is totally disembodied and reduced to the knowingly calculated lines of clothes which draw all their lewdness from their rigor and discretion."[4]

In its way of playing with official censorship, this eroticism recalls the elaboration of the dream, according to Freud: instead of showing forbidden realities, one introduces seemingly neutral elements that will evoke them through association or symbolism. Thus dance is an immemorial transposition of the sex act itself. But then the thriller has occasionally succeeded in employing such trite allegory with finesse. There are the "poses" struck by Gilda or the frenzied whirling of the bobby-soxer in *The Asphalt Jungle*. Certain fetishistic themes could be explained in a similar way: the boots and gloves of Rita Hayworth in *Gilda*, the delirious ornaments Ona Munson (Mother Gin Sling) wears in her hair in *The Shanghai Gesture*, Barbara Stanwyck's ankle bracelet in *Double Indemnity*. The sadomasochistic episodes, in accordance with the very subject of film noir, lent themselves particularly well to this technique of allusion. In the pleasure/ violence pairing, the exhibiting of the second term will sometimes add up to a substitute for the first, the presence of which will be implied by a few details. The slap in *Gilda* has remained famous; Cagney brutalizes his mistress with gusto (*White Heat*); and Dan Duryea doesn't conceal his pleasure when mistreating Joan Bennett in *Scarlet Street*. The masochist inclination has undoubtedly formed the basis of the theme of the blonde criminal (Lana Turner, Peggy Cummins, Barbara Stanwyck) and the vampire woman (Lauren Bacall). At times one guesses at sexual situations that are abnormal or on the verge of anomaly: for example in *Gilda*, in which several touches hint at the murky relations between men. On this point, however, the novels went much further than the films: the latent homosexuality that Dashiell Hammett introduced into *The Glass Key* disappeared from the screen. Some of the faces of the child-woman or of the woman-child—the Indian girl in *Ride the Pink Horse*, the young sister in *The Big Sleep*, the lawyer's niece in *The Asphalt Jungle*— have been evoked with tenderness (Pilar) or ferocity (Carmen).

This is a very special optic, then, yet its oblique rays have their charm. Hollywood has made a virtue out of necessity here. European cinema displays more daring in the actual description of sexual attitudes, and a part of the audience will show a preference for this more direct eroticism, of which French and Swedish filmmakers have made a specialty. Film noir has never, for instance, evoked the issue of lesbian love affairs, nor the rapes instigated by old men, nor the passionate fear of a virgin spying on a couple making loving, nor the torments of a frigid woman.[5] In passing, let's also protest against a fraudulent kind of advertising that, in France at least, tends to have the thriller pass for what it isn't: a libertine film.

One touches here on a more general question: that of the relationship between the noir genre and morality. Doesn't this truck with the seamy side of life, with a jungle in which, in back of all the crime, blackmail, and corruption, all kinds of desire lie in wait, lend a sort of anarchist accent to the whole series?

Let's lend an ear, however, to the opinion of an H.F. Rey, writing about *Double Indemnity*, which "becomes, thanks to the character played by Edward G. Robinson, a sort of lesson in morality, ending with the obligatory, semipublic confession in finest Salvation Army style. Here the famous dogma of the sin that's too heavy to bear has found illustration. At no moment in this movie does morality forgo its rights. Of course, the devil is shown in the astonishingly erotic shape of Barbara Stanwyck, but this is merely to obey Christian tradition, which doesn't hesitate to show evil when it has to. In this film, it's a question of demonstrating that crime does not, and never will, pay. This is an intelligent propaganda piece which, far from denying certain social defects, willingly describes them, the better to stigmatize them."[6]

Applied to the series as a whole, these lines would call for many reservations. It's true that Christian moralists depict evil whenever they deem it useful: yet rarely without "morose delectation" (to borrow their language) and always in order to present a repellent image of it. In fact, film noir tends to grant an attractive side to evil, while having the long shadow of the gallows fall over the representatives of law and order. It's true that the story ends badly for the guilty (even in *Gun Crazy*):

prison, madness, or death put an end to their heinous crimes. But then in many instances this denouement seems, indeed, to be the likeliest outcome from the realistic standpoint itself. Besides, is a film's deep-seated effect on the viewer completely effaced by the final five minutes of the screening?

Having said this, H.F. Rey's opinion is interesting in that it reminds us that film noir cannot be considered "immoralist" in the Nietzschean sense or revolutionary in ethical terms. We've made an exception for *Gun Crazy*, given the Surrealist atmosphere it lends itself to. It is one of the genre's traits to be neither moral nor immoral, but *ambivalent vis-à-vis morality* (the ambivalence being more or less pronounced, depending on the case). Its social universe is a world in which morality is breaking down: it retains the power to disturb our sensibility and to distort our vision of the real, but it no longer has the power to inhibit or to convince; and, in this twilight world, no new moral outlook is really in sight. In it, "vice" is seductive; it is nevertheless experienced as "vicious," and the lawbreaker seems obsessed by a sense of anguish and a feeling of guilt. Set against this, the policeman, even when he doesn't stink to high heaven, never smells very good: but one doesn't see how to dispense with his services.

The *violence* of film noir has first of all to do with its desire for realism. The cinema is here the outspoken witness of a society in which savagery is a daily affair. Its audacity extends even further, however. In modern life an important sector, violent and bloody, exists *even in peacetime* (felonies, social or political conflicts; police methods; violent sports; illnesses; diverse accidents; medical and surgical interventions; different kinds of brutality in everyday human intercourse; incidents involving animals or in the relations between people and animals, etc.). Right from the start, whenever a scriptwriter met with such situations, conventions as hypocritical as they are inane ordered him to attenuate or glide over them. It indeed seems to be the case that the noir genre has played an important part in the weakening of such prejudices. Along with films about war (*She*

147

Defends Her Country and the newsreel montages *Stalingrad* and *Guadalcanal* contain some impressive shots), noir has paved the way for, or gone hand in hand with, a whole series of documents that, for years now, indicate a new state of mind: surgical operations (in France, *Sous le ciel de Paris, Un grand patron*), disabled people shown matter-of-factly (*Los Olvidados, The Men, The Best Years of Our Lives*, or that overwhelming documentary by "Major" John Huston about the reeducation of mentally disturbed war veterans, *Let There Be Light*), fights between animals (*In the Sands of Central Asia*, from the USSR), abattoir scenes (*Le Sang des bêtes*).

It will be all the more regretted that this bias toward authenticity is, in the series that concerns us, often limited by a certain refusal of the image shot from life. Of course, the same prohibitions are still in play almost everywhere, but the Hays Code maintains, in Hollywood even more than elsewhere, a sort of academicism in the midst of the violence, according to which it would be as out of place to present *real* images of suffering as to illustrate a recruiting poster with photos of soldiers with serious head wounds. The dying retain a twinkle in their eyes; mothers of newborn infants are chic and attractive; there are few mangled faces following a fistfight. The killing, here, is impeccable: none or almost none of those awkward acts or gruesome details frequent in real crimes. Dead vamps remain vamps: no contorted corpses, no ludicrous postures, no stockings around their ankles. We're a long way from a noir "kino-eye."

But then violence is also a privileged theme for pathos, and in the noir genre a taste for gratuitous cruelty exists that hasn't been seen since the Surrealist films of the 1930s. It's this that some critics, educators, and moralists have denounced in these productions.

Is the theme blameworthy in itself? Of course not. Rejecting it on principle is unjustifiable. Violence is a fact, and there's something suspect about any systematic camouflaging of certain facts. Added to which, it isn't true that in individual or collective life violence has only ever had destructive consequences. Some of the most powerful works in the history of world cinema contain sequences of great brutality. *Battleship Potemkin, I Am a Fugitive from a Chain Gang, Caccia tragica, Dead End,* and *The Grapes of Wrath* are far from being milk-and-water films. The theater has made an essential dramatic lever of it at all times. Evangelism is dangerous in art as well as in morality. On the screen, as in real life, for individuals as for groups, the relative value of aggressiveness is a matter of proportion, lucidity, and context.

This puts us that much more at ease when judging noir violence, which gives rise to a series of reservations on that score. Through its simplistic excess, crime is already the very model of sterile violence. Organized, standardized, underworld crime becomes a form of social squandering, however. And if murder has sometimes been seen as the least appreciated of the fine arts, it is perhaps the thriller that is the most distanced from it. It brings to bear an ambience of cowardliness (the theme of the unequal struggle), of anxiety (the theme of self-punishment), and of mediocrity. The mental level of the hero—detective or killer— is run of the mill, if not lower than average: only Bannister in *The Lady from Shanghai,* the gangster in *He Walked By Night,* Mendoza in *The Enforcer,* and Riedenschneider in *The Asphalt Jungle* evoke the uncommon intelligence typical of characters from the classic whodunit. Raymond Chandler has the ex-policeman in *Farewell My Lovely* say: "And as for the top men . . . they didn't get there by murdering people. They got there by guts and brains—and they don't have the group courage the cops have either. But above all they're businessmen. What they do is for money. Just like other businessmen." Gang bosses are involved here: Al Capone or Frank Costello would undoubtedly correspond to these criteria. The punks, gunsels, and lickspittles put one in mind, rather, of Rimbaud's words: "Criminals are disgusting, like the castrated." This viscous ferocity as well as the moral confusion we were referring to just now are strongly opposed to the poetic and ideological context that gave meaning to the virulence of the great Surrealist or social classics.

Is it necessary to add that such brutality serves the propaganda of war? It will doubtless be objected that there is, here, a stifling atmosphere that is unpropitious for heroism, for "radiant and joyous" warmongering, and the demoralizing nature, for the viewer, of the corrupt world the series delights in will still be called to mind. It is nevertheless a fact that the presentation in massive doses, for years on end, of crime films probably has, in a period of international tension, a dangerous effect on the collective aggressiveness of the public, even if the production of these movies has had financial considerations as its only motive.

In the last analysis, the *psychosocial substance* of the series is perhaps its most original and most solid contribution. There is an astonishing contrast between the inconsistency of most of the scripts and the *presence* of the characters they bring into play. Placed in more valid situations, one is persuaded that the significance of these figures would stand out even more. There are two reasons for this.

First, the bias toward ambiguity of character: an ambivalence of attitudes, a complexity of motives. Part of this, of course, is convention. While the characters may have many facets, these are almost always the same ones: self-interest, sensuality, an instinct for power, etc. And yet they derive a lasting density and opacity from this. All this enriches cinematic language, in general terms. If fully fledged heroes become increasingly untenable on the screen, as they already are in literature, then film noir will have really served for something.

Second, this series has lent a new importance to the criminal milieu. Notwithstanding certain exaggerations, it will one day provide the sociologist and the historian with precious material. The mob and the hoodlum gangs have their own existence here. Supporting roles cease being simple walk-on parts, as in *Scarface* or *G-Men*. They are described and established with extreme care. One shows the multiple interactions that draw them together and the changing tensions that drive them apart. Film noir has definitively imposed the fecund formula of the *drama centered on the vicissitudes of a small group*. American filmmakers have acquired genuine mastery in this area, and they've subsequently made it the basis of their principal movies on the Second World War (the fighting, as lived by a small army unit). Other countries has exploited this formula, which is at the origins of many an interesting film, notably in France (*Le Salaire de la peur, L'Auberge rouge*), in the USSR (*The Great Turning Point*), in Italy (*Il Cammino della speranza*), in Czechoslovakia (*Bílá tma*), and, occasionally, in England. One may ask oneself if, originally, there wasn't a transposing of the "microsociology" (study of elemental social groups) that was an American specialty from 1920 to 1945 (Thomas, Park, Thrasher, and their collaborators; then Mayo, Moreno, and Lewin): it's worth remembering that the gangs were one of the objects of their earliest investigations.

In a word, all these films add up to invaluable documents. If it were easier to work on 35mm copies while they were in distribution, one could imagine an ideal montage in which the politician from *All the King's Men*, the maniac from *Strangers on a Train*, the gang boss from *The Enforcer*, and the cynical dilettante from *Laura* would go to form the characters in a world worthy of Jean Vigo.

If it were necessary to draw the conclusions from this analytical balance sheet, we would propose the following list:

On the credit side—

Without reservations:

- Technique
- A refined psychology; the attention given to small criminal groups and their changing structure; the sociological document

With reservations (which would also be true for many of the works of world cinema):

- Eroticism
- Violence

On the debit side—

- The failure of strange themes and, more generally, the choice of subjects
- Moral confusion

Considering, now, the four main nontechnical components of this style (strangeness, eroticism, violence, the refining of psychosocial realism), it is conceivable that the legacy of the genre could, at least in theory, be exploited in various directions:

- As to the primary "impetus" of the series, one can imagine an even "darker" thriller liberated from the restrictions that often take the edge off it.
- Or, instead, a comic orientation through the integration of a strangeness inflected toward slapstick and of a brutality that the humor would render inoffensive.
- Or, there again, a leap into poetic fiction, sanctioning a more essential strangeness and, incidentally, a utilization of the three other themes.
- Lastly, a shift to realism, through abandonment of the bias toward incoherence, the violent themes and psychosocial content of the genre being subsequently subordinated to a rigorous, original script.

The odds in favor of these few formulas are very uneven, however. The investigation of an absolute kind of noir would come up against the veto of censorship and, above all, wouldn't be able to overcome the fundamental contradiction of the genre: the conflict between an overly artificial strangeness and an unrelenting realism. Noirified slapstick already exists and is nourished by an extremely meager vein, extending between the disquieting cartoon and the pastiche per se. As for the systematic poeticization of noir imagery, this would end up in neo-Surrealism. While the noir genre guarded a valuable echo of the avant-garde film, it remained far short of this most of the time. Perhaps there will be a renaissance of cinematic Surrealism: it's unlikely that it has much to learn from the archives of the thriller.

It's probably in the realm of realism that the more productive aspects of the series will be incorporated. The notion of realism isn't always clear: the main thing is to avoid banality, concessions, and the already known while keeping as close as possible to the "genuine minor incident," which is often more unexpected, more interesting, than the finest screenplay turned out by a professional. The psychologist's clinical document has its place here, along with the serious social inquiry, the genuine ethnographic report, and a lot of other things besides. Many excellent films have shown what filmmakers formed in the school of the noir series could do in this respect: Litvak on a psychiatric case in *The Snake Pit,* Wise on professional boxing in *The Set-Up,* Dmytryk on war veterans readapting to civilian life in *Crossfire,* Mann on the existence of certain labor issues in *Border Incident.* Even before film noir there were promising signs on this front in two of Ford's works inspired by recent rural change, *The Grapes of Wrath* and, in particular, *Tobacco Road.*

It's a remarkable thing: no matter which track we follow, there is always at least one element of the original style that disappears. Obviously, each person tends to value what best corresponds to his temperament; but the "new frisson" linked to the series implied a constellation of themes. Our affirmation of the noir genre's historical importance is not, therefore, without a certain skepticism as to the lasting nature of its power of suggestion.

More so than for the other arts, the emotion a film series arouses in the public is bound up with the ambience of the moment, and the evidence of retrospective viewings is often extremely cruel. Comedy and tragedy, poetry and truth are only too precarious here: after an interval of twenty years, at a distance of a thousand kilometers, one rarely sees a film in the same way. Right now one might be forgiven for thinking that the Soviet public, for instance, would greet the thriller not as a work of art but as an extraordinary condemnation of capitalist mores. And what will the spectator say of it in his cine club (if such things exist) in 1970? Many experiences have shown that dramas resisted these kinds of evidence better, went out of fashion less quickly, when they had a documentary aspect. Film noir has one such, and the future will find in it at least a vigorous description of certain sections of American society at a particular moment in time. But temporal distance will accentuate its stereotypes.

Keeping to French cinema, what became of the "new frissons"

certain celebrated series dedicated themselves to? Does much remain, for example, *pace* Fernand Léger and Marcel L'Herbier, of *L'Inhumaine,* which summed up the whole avant-garde society drama (1924 style), with its merry-go-round of subliminal passions and its neo-Cubist sets? In another genre entirely, *Quai des brumes* has aged, and *Le Grand jeu, La Bandera,* and *Gueule d'amour* occasionally provoke a smile, a bit like the "realistic" songs of the period ("Mon légionnaire," let's say).

Once its contribution to world cinema has been acknowledged, will the thriller rejoin those snows of yesteryear? And, if so, would it be necessary to bemoan this? The debate remains open, and only the future will tell us whether the noir series was something other than a "season in hell."

References

1 Added to which, some seemingly important film noirs haven't been screened in France: *Force of Evil, The Web, The Brasher Doubloon, Dark City, Cause for Alarm,* and *Cornered,* for instance.

2 *Murder, My Sweet* program note from the Inter-Club Cinématographique du Sud-Ouest.

3 *L'Ecran français* 161.

4 Pierre Duvillars, *L'Erotisme au cinema* (Ed. Du XXe Siècle, 1951), pp. 71, 67.

5 We're alluding here to *Olivia, Deux sous de violettes, Fröken Julie,* and *Minne, l'ingénue libertine,* respectively.

6 *L'Ecran français* 157.

Postface

Nineteen-fifty-five. An era draws to a close. Film noir has fulfilled its role, which was to create a particular sense of malaise and to transmit a social critique of the United States. Robert Aldrich gives this adventure a fascinating and somber conclusion, *Kiss Me Deadly*. This is the desperate flip side of the film that had opened the noir series fourteen years earlier, *The Maltese Falcon*.

The theme is the same: the search for a treasure, a statue or iron strongbox. The hero is the same: a private detective, both tough and vulnerable, who adores pounding a face, pummeling a belly, and who is the victim marked out by fate of she who will remain his objective counterpart: the grasping, desirable, and frigid female.

But between 1941 and 1955, between the eve of the war and the advent of consumer society, the tone has changed. A savage lyricism hurls us into a world in manifest decomposition, governed by dissolute living and brutality; to these intrigues of wild men and weaklings, Aldrich offers the most radical of solutions: nuclear apocalypse.

Kiss Me Deadly is in every respect, then, a point of no return. Film noir is to be reborn around 1965, but it will be very different from the kind of oneiric violation that was the thriller of the 1940s. Many things will have changed, audiences first of all.

The latter gave a huge welcome to the spy stories the success of James Bond had brought into fashion. Linking up again with the movie serial, these big-budget productions provided exoticism, the atmosphere of the big capital city, escapism on a planetary scale. Their futurist, fairy-story climate, replete with strange discoveries, proposed an elaborate ceremony of death and imposed the car chase (cf. *Dr. No*), which was to become one of the stereotypes of the new detective film. Violence and sadism were rehabilitated in a series that was, all things considered, the *Thousand and One Nights* of our time.

Next came the moment of retrospectives and remakes. The posthumous glory of Humphrey Bogart and the legend he inspired coincided, in the 1960s, with a certain return to traditional film noir: new versions by Don Siegel of *The Killers* and *Ride the Pink Horse*, rebaptized *The Hanged Man;* B-movies such as Edward Dmytryk's *Mirage,* Roy Rowland's *The Girl Hunters,* in which the novelist Mickey Spillane played the role of his hero, Mike Hammer, and especially the remarkable *Harper* by Jack Smight.

What has changed is the way of perceiving the characters. A sort of derision—a distance, in any event—is introduced between actor and act. The old series gave the impression of a no-holds-barred fight against death and chaos. The new series announces itself through far more nuanced states of mind, Freudian analyses, furtive relationships in which time and introspection are to play a preponderant role. The putrescence overwhelms human beings whose main concern it is to survive, not to fight back. Machiavellianism takes precedence over a brute strength that will only burst forth in the last resort, with lightning speed.

Let's compare Robert Siodmak's *The Killers* (1946) with its remake by Don Siegel (1964). The police investigation, the brutal and classic document marked by the influence of *Citizen Kane,* gives way to the viewpoint of the killers themselves: one of these about to retire, the other neurotic to the point of madness. We are gripped by an icy delirium, an unswerving cruelty the bright light no longer bothers. At the same time, however, the lusterless, ugly colors represent a standardized world in which people already have the look of the condemned.

All this will result in a new, specifically American series, mainly about the police, shot in real locations, yet giving the impression of being great entertainment and marking the cinema's return in force in a market monopolized by television.

For the motivations are many. Productions like *Point Blank* by John Boorman, *Bullitt* by Peter Yates, *Coogan's Bluff* and *Dirty Harry* by Don Siegel, *The French Connection* by William Friedkin,

The Stone Killer and *Death Wish* by Michael Winner, *Magnum Force* by Ted Post, and *Badlands* by Terrence Malick, which dot the dazzling renaissance of film noir on other bases, are first of all a return to the professional job of work, following the parenthesis of independent—that's to say, amateur—cinema.

To this economic factor there is added the raising of certain prohibitions. After a century of silence, the word "Mafia" can be uttered (*The Godfather* by Francis Ford Coppola, *The Don Is Dead* by Richard Fleischer, etc.). Black gangsters and cops equal and surpass their white counterparts (*For Love of Ivy* by Daniel Mann, *In the Heat of the Night* by Norman Jewison), and one actor alone, Sidney Poitier, is the symbol of integration. But more than anything else, sexual taboos go by the board. The cinema has played a part in this. The noir series has made the most of it. In the Lauren Bacall and Rita Hayworth era, many acts of depravity were suggested by ambiguous words, facial expressions that told their own story, and a vague atmosphere of latent sexuality. Now, a spade is called a spade, the female body is stripped naked, erotic minorities are explored.

Kept under wraps until then, or evoked with such a sense of shame that it was only discernible to the expert eye, homosexuality affirms itself as an essential feature of American violence. In Blake Edwards's *Gunn,* Daisy Jane, linchpin of the plot and proprietor of a floating brothel whose residents are pairs of twins, is a transvestite. Marion Marshall, who plays her, has the weary and voluptuous authority and bearing of a "matchmaker," and when Gunn snatches off her wig the surprise is total. In John Guillermin's *P.J.,* the private detective gets beaten up by twenty or so homosexuals, their fingers laden with heavily bejeweled rings. In Gordon Douglas's *Lady in Cement,* a transvestite belongs to the police special branch, and in *The Detective,* likewise by Gordon Douglas, the investigation shifts toward the gay world: the accursed race is hunted down in the docks, in shady hotels, and beneath the tarpaulins of trucks.

This freedom of tone appears to have been established first of all in certain adults-only cinemas where "hot" versions of the detective film were shown. We remember having seen on

Broadway in 1968 a traditional film noir in the Mickey Spillane style, *Aroused,* which contained some extremely risqué scenes, scenes restricted to a few major cities. Be that as it may, the change seems irreversible, even if this desire to show everything, which strongly resembles an act of public confession in a puritan society, were to arrive at saturation point.

Color has intervened. It makes the mistake of "prettifying" things, and the splendid blacks and whites, with their high-contrast lighting, which Jewish directors fleeing Nazism had brought from Germany, are missed. But then color confers on the urban setting of steel and glass, which has been visually transformed over the years, a preponderant place, as if the actor were no more than the emanation of this. And this victory of color values, which is most mysterious by night, suggests a new kind of morbid toughness.

Is it necessary to say anything more than that the noir series of the 1940s was German in inspiration, while this one is evidence of an Anglo-American osmosis? Have Englishmen John Boorman, John Guillermin, and Peter Yates brought to the cinema of the New World the intellectual poisons of Old Europe: the ambiguity of human relationships, a willingness to describe these, some subtle camerawork, more "English" colors, and an aesthete's virtuosity? This is doubtless true, but the worm was already in the bud.

The main novelty lies in the effacement of the private detective in favor of the official police force.

The private eye had been the standard character of 1940s film noir. Arriving from the novels of Dashiell Hammett and Raymond Chandler, he moved around in a twilight world, on the borderline of legality. Accepting of dubious clients, mixed up in suspect affairs, he symbolized the rottenness that comes inevitably from contact with crime. Yet at the same time he played the scapegoat's role, he stomached all the wrongdoing so that the police might remain above suspicion. In that sense, he was American cinema's alibi, and it interposed his pervasive myth between spectator and society.

It's now the turn of the "good cop" to put up with the mud

baths, the ignominious pressures, the beatings. The key film, it seems, may well have been *The Detective* (1968): the honest Inspector Leland, tricked by a powerful organization of property speculators, sends an innocent man to the electric chair, is promoted to captain, and discovers the truth. Tired and disgusted, he will resign. But then in *Bullitt* Steve McQueen will be merely tired: "Do you let anything reach you, I mean really reach you? Or are you so used to it by now that nothing really touches you?" his girlfriend Jacqueline Bissett asks him. "You're living in a sewer . . . day after day." "That's where half of it is," he replies. "You can't just walk away from it."

Sidney Lumet's *Serpico* (1973), which has a lot of defects, which is listless and badly acted, marks the furthest point of this denunciation: here, it's the entire New York Police Department that is corrupt.

But the response of the "healthy" part of the social body was to come from the police itself, with *Dirty Harry*. And Harry (Clint Eastwood) will find the remorseless cops of *Magnum Force* even harder and more justice-loving than he is.

The noir series of the 1970s is, then, very important: in this way the drama of America is enacted before our eyes, an America crushed by delinquency, suffering from a generation gap, and asking itself if it shouldn't, as in the era of the Far West and its vigilante groups, mete out justice itself.

One step further and the policeman will be replaced by the citizen: Charles Bronson has recently played a "justice-lover in the city" (as the French title of *Death Wish* puts it), an average Joe driven to extremes by the violence of a society that's falling apart.

Other films will present a stagnant vision of the ailing United States, a vision both taut and tepid, close to nightmare (*The Long Goodbye* by Robert Altman) or coldly technological (*The Conversation* by Francis Ford Coppola), yet forever disabused. Beyond traditional political discourse, a petrified world, a sort of immobile present, harbinger of apocalypse, begins to dawn.

Deriving from the world of the novel, from the gratifying frisson of fear, and from a certain qualitative notion of pleasure, the noir series has, over the years, linked up with the anguish of a society that no longer knows where it's headed. It has taken the place of social cinema, devoured this, and it is exemplary that the series may have found its provisional conclusion in the most terrifying film in the history of cinema: *Soylent Green*.

—*RB & EC* (1979)

Chronological index
of the main series

1942 *Shadow of a Doubt,* Alfred Hitchcock
      King's Row, Sam Wood
1944 *Double Indemnity,* Billy Wilder
      The Woman in the Window, Fritz Lang
      Laura, Otto Preminger
1945 *Hangover Square,* John Brahm
      Conflict, Curtis Bernhardt
      Leave Her to Heaven, John M. Stahl
      Love Letters, William Dieterle
1946 *The Spiral Staircase,* Robert Siodmak
      The Strange Love of Martha Ivers, Lewis Milestone
      The Postman Always Rings Twice, Tay Garnett
      The Locket, John Brahm
1947 *The Paradine Case,* Alfred Hitchcock
      Born to Kill, Robert Wise
      The Two Mrs. Carrolls, Peter Godfrey
1948 *Sleep, My Love,* Douglas Sirk
      Rope, Alfred Hitchcock
1949 *Under Capricorn,* Alfred Hitchcock
      Whirlpool, Otto Preminger
      House of Strangers, Joseph L. Mankiewicz
1950 *Night and the City,* Jules Dassin
      Gun Crazy, Joseph H. Lewis
1951 *Strangers on a Train,* Alfred Hitchcock
1952 *The Sniper,* Edward Dmytryk
      Angel Face, Otto Preminger

Crime films in period costume
1941 *Dr. Jekyll and Mr. Hyde,* Victor Fleming
1944 *Experiment Perilous,* Jacques Tourneur
      Gaslight, George Cukor
      The Suspect, Robert Siodmak
1946 *Dragonwyck,* Joseph L. Mankiewicz
1947 *Ivy,* Sam Wood
1948 *So Evil, My Love,* Lewis Allen

Gangsters

1946　*The Killers*, Robert Siodmak
1949　*White Heat*, Raoul Walsh
　　　Criss Cross, Robert Siodmak
1950　*The Asphalt Jungle*, John Huston
1951　*The Enforcer*, Bretaigne Windust, Raoul Walsh (uncredited)
1953　*The Big Heat*, Fritz Lang

Police documentaries

1947　*Kiss of Death*, Henry Hathaway
　　　Crossfire, Edward Dmytryk
1948　*He Walked by Night*, Alfred Werker
　　　The Street with No Name, William Keighley
　　　The Naked City, Jules Dassin
1949　*Port of New York*, László Benedek
1950　*Where the Sidewalk Ends*, Otto Preminger
　　　Panic in the Streets, Elia Kazan
1951　*The Enforcer*, Bretaigne Windust, Raoul Walsh (uncredited)
1953　*The Big Heat*, Fritz Lang

Social tendencies

1945　*The Lost Weekend*, Billy Wilder
1947　*Nightmare Alley*, Edmund Goulding
1949　*Crossfire*, Edward Dmytryk
　　　Border Incident, Anthony Mann
　　　Thieves' Highway, Jules Dassin
　　　The Set-Up, Robert Wise
1950　*The Breaking Point*, Michael Curtiz
　　　The Lawless, Joseph Losey
1951　*The Big Carnival*, Billy Wilder
1954　*The Wild One*, László Benedek

Filmography

This filmography is a reworking of Borde and Chaumeton's 1955 original, plus those titles referred to in their 1979 postface and in Duhamel's 1955 preface. For foreign-language films, the authors' minimal cataloguing has been followed. The cinematographers of all American and British film noirs have been included, since these figures helped define the look of the genre. Readers wishing further detail on the titles below may want to consult the Internet Movie Database at http://www.imdb.com.

Abbreviations

Prod: Producer
Dir: Director
Scr: Scriptwriter
Ph: Photographer

Studio abbreviations

ABPC: Associated British Picture Corporation
BIPC: British International Pictures Corporation
BLFC: British Lion Film Corporation
BNF: British National Films
Col: Columbia Pictures Corporation
Fox: 20th Century-Fox Film Corporation
MGM: Metro-Goldwyn-Mayer
Mono: Monogram Pictures
Par: Paramount Pictures
Rep: Republic Pictures Corporation
RKO: RKO-Radio Pictures
UA: United Artists Corporation
Univ: Universal Pictures
WB: Warner Brothers Pictures, Inc.

A toi de faire, Archibald
(France) 1952. Dir: Marcel Cravenne. [Short]

A toi de jouer, Callaghan
(France) 1954. Dir: Willy Rozier. Scr: Xavier Vallier, from a Peter Cheyney novel.

Across the Pacific
WB 1942. Prod: Jack Saper, Jerry Wald. Dir: John Huston, Vincent Sherman (uncredited). Scr: Richard Macauley, from a Robert Carson story. Ph: Arthur Edeson. Cast: Humphrey Bogart, Mary Astor, Sydney Greenstreet, Monte Blue.

Act of Violence
MGM 1948. Prod: William H. Wright. Dir: Fred Zinnemann. Scr: Robert L. Richards, from a Collier Young story. Ph: Robert Surtees. Cast: Van Heflin, Robert Ryan, Janet Leigh, Mary Astor.

Adventures of Robin Hood, The
WB 1938. Prod: Hal B. Wallis. Dir: Michael Curtiz, William Keighley. Scr: Norman Reilly Raine. Cast: Errol Flynn, Basil Rathbone, Olivia de Havilland.

Affair in Trinidad
Col 1952. Prod / Dir: Vincent Sherman. Scr: Virginia Van Upp, Berne Giler, Oscar Saul, James Gunn. Ph: Joseph Walker. Cast: Rita Hayworth, Glenn Ford, Alexander Scourby.

After the Thin Man
MGM 1936. Prod: Hunt Stromberg. Dir: W.S. Van Dyke. Scr: Frances Goodrich, from the Dashiell Hammett story. Cast: William Powell, Myrna Loy, James Stewart.

Age d'or, L'
(France) 1930. Dir: Luis Buñuel. Scr: Luis Buñuel, Salvador Dalí.

Air Force
WB 1943. Prod: Hal B. Wallis. Dir: Howard Hawks. Scr: Dudley Nichols, William Faulkner (uncredited). Cast: John Garfield, Arthur Kennedy, Faye Emerson.

Along Came Jones
RKO 1945. Prod: Gary Cooper. Dir: Stuart Heisler. Scr: Nunnally Johnson, from an Alan Le May novel. Cast: Gary Cooper, Loretta Young, Dan Duryea.

All About Eve
Fox 1950. Prod: Darryl F. Zanuck. Dir / Scr: Joseph L. Mankiewicz. Cast: Bette Davis, Anne Baxter, George Sanders, Celeste Holm, Gary Merrill, Thelma Ritter, Marilyn Monroe.

All Quiet on the Western Front
Univ 1930. Prod: Carl Laemmle Jr. Dir: Lewis Milestone. Scr: George Abbott, from the E. M. Remarque novel. Cast: Lew Ayres, Louis Wolheim.

All the King's Men
Col 1949. Prod / Dir: Robert Rossen. Scr: Robert Rossen, from the Robert Penn Warren novel. Cast: Broderick Crawford, John Ireland, Mercedes McCambridge, Joanne Dru, John Derek.

Amants maudits, Les
(France) 1951. Dir: Willy Rozier. Scr: Xavier Vallier.

Amazing Dr. Clitterhouse, The
WB 1938. Prod / Dir: Anatole Litvak. Scr: John Wexley, John Huston, from the Barré Lyndon play. Cast: Edward G. Robinson, Claire Trevor, Humphrey Bogart.

American in Paris, An
MGM 1951. Prod: Arthur Freed. Dir: Vicente Minnelli. Scr: Alan Jay Lerner. Cast: Gene Kelly, Leslie Caron, Oscar Levant.

And Then There Were None
Fox 1945. Prod / Dir: René Clair. Scr: Dudley Nichols, from the Agatha Christie novel. Cast: Barry Fitzgerald, Walter Huston, Louis Hayward, Judith Anderson, Roland Young, June Duprez.

Angel Face
Fox 1952. Prod / Dir: Otto Preminger. Scr: Oscar Millard, Frank S. Nugent, Ben Hecht (uncredited), from a Chester Erskine story. Ph: Harry Stradling Sr. Cast: Jean Simmons, Robert Mitchum, Herbert Marshall, Mona Freeman, Leon Ames.

Angels with Dirty Faces
WB 1938. Prod: Samuel Bischoff. Dir: Michael Curtiz. Scr: John Wexley, Warren Duff, Ben Hecht, Charles MacArthur (last two uncredited). Cast: James Cagney, Pat O'Brien.

Anna
(Italy) 1951. Dir: Alberto Lattuada. Scr: G. Berto, D. Risi, I. Perilli, F. Brusati, R. Sonego.

Another Man's Poison
UA / Eros Films (UK) 1952. Prod: D. Fairbanks Jr., D.M. Angel. Dir: Irving Rapper. Scr: Val Guest, from the Leslie Sands play *Deadlock*. Ph: Robert Krasker. Cast: Bette Davis, Gary Merrill, Anthony Steele.

Antoine et Antoinette
(France) 1947. Dir: Jacques Becker. Scr: Françoise Giroud, Jacques Becker, Maurice Griffe.

Aroused
Cambist Films 1966. Prod / Dir: Anton Holden. Scr: Anton Holden, Ray Jacobs. Cast: Janine Lenon, Fleurette Carter, Joana Mills.

Arsenic and Old Lace
WB 1944. Prod / Dir: Frank Capra. Scr: J.J. & P.G. Epstein, from the Joseph Kesselring play. Cast: Cary Grant, Priscilla Lane, Raymond Massey, Peter Lorre, Jack Carson.

Asphalt Jungle, The
MGM 1950. Prod / Dir: John Huston. Scr: John Huston, Ben Maddow, from the W.R. Burnett novel. Ph: Harold Rosson. Cast: Sterling Hayden, Louis Calhern, Jean Hagen, Sam Jaffe, James Whitmore, Marilyn Monroe.

Assassinat du Duc de Guise, L'
(France) 1907. Dir: H. Lavedan.

Au p'tit Zouave
(France) 1949. Dir: Gilles Grangier. Scr: Albert Valentin.

Auberge rouge, L'
(France) 1951. Dir: Claude Autant-Lara. Scr: Claude Autant-Lara, Jean Aurenche, Pierre Bost.

Au-delà des grilles
(France / Italy) 1949. Dir: René Clément. Scr: Cesare Zavattini, Suso Cecchi d'Amico, Luigi Guarini, Jean Aurenche, Pierre Bost.

Autour d'une enquête / Voruntersuchung
(France / Germany) 1931. Dir: Robert Siodmak (German version), Henri Chomette (French version). Scr: Henri Chomette, Robert Liebmann, Raoul Ploquin.

Awful Truth, The
Col 1937. Prod / Dir: Leo McCarey. Scr: Viña Richman. Cast: Cary Grant, Irene Dunne, Ralph Bellamy.

Badlands
WB 1973. Prod / Dir / Scr: Terrence Malick. Ph: Tak Fujimoto, Steven Larner, Brian Probyn. Cast: Martin Sheen, Sissy Spacek, Ramon Bieri, Warren Oates.

Bandera, La
(France) 1935. Dir: Jules Duvivier. Scr: Jules Duvivier, Charles Spaak, from the Pierre Mac Orlan novel.

Band Wagon, The
MGM 1953. Prod: Arthur Freed. Dir: Vincente Minnelli. Scr: Betty Comden, Adolph Green. Ph: Harry Jackson. Cast: Fred Astaire, Cyd Charisse, Jack Buchanan, Nanette Fabray, Oscar Levant.

Battleship Potemkin
(USSR). 1925. Dir: Sergei Eisenstein. Scr: Nina Agadzhanova-Shutko.

Beat the Devil
UA 1953. Prod / Dir: John Huston, Scr: Truman Capote, John Huston, from the James Helvick novel. Ph: Oswald Morris. Cast: Humphrey Bogart, Jennifer Jones, Gina Lollobrigida, Peter Lorre, Robert Morley.

Behave Yourself
RKO 1951. Prod: Jerry Wald, Norman Krasna. Dir / Scr: George Beck. Ph: James Wong Howe. Cast: Farley Granger, Shelley Winters, William Demarest.

Best Years of Our Lives, The
MGM 1946. Prod: Samuel Goldwyn. Dir: William Wyler. Scr: Robert E. Sherwood, from a MacKinlay Kantor novel. Ph: Gregg Toland. Cast: Fredric March, Myrna Loy, Teresa Wright, Dana Andrews, Harold Russell, Cathy O'Donnell.

Bête humaine, La
(France) 1938. Dir: Jean Renoir. Scr: Jean Renoir, from the Emile Zola novel.

Beyond the Forest
WB 1949. Prod: Henry Blanke. Dir: King Vidor. Scr: L. Coffee, from a Stuart Engstrand novel. Cast: Bette David, Joseph Cotten, David Brian, Ruth Roman.

Big Carnival, The
Par 1951. Prod / Dir: Billy Wilder. Scr: Billy Wilder, Lesser Samuels, Walter Newman. Ph: Charles Lang. Cast: Kirk Douglas, Jan Sterling, Richard Benedict, Porter Hall, Bob Arthur.

Big Clock, The
Par 1948. Prod: Richard Malbaum. Dir: John Farrow. Scr: Jonathan Latimer, from the Kenneth Fearing novel. Ph: Daniel L. Fapp, John F. Seitz. Cast: Ray Milland, Charles Laughton, Maureen O'Sullivan, George MacReady.

Big Heat, The
Col 1953. Prod: Robert Arthur. Dir: Fritz Lang. Scr: Sydney Boehm, from the William P. McGivern novel. Ph: Charles Lang. Cast: Glenn Ford, Gloria Grahame, Jocelyn Brando, Alexander Scourby, Jeanette Nolan, Lee Marvin.

Big House, The
MGM 1930. Prod: (uncredited). Dir: George Hill. Scr: Joseph Farnham, Martin Flavin, Frances Marion, Lennox Robinson. Cast: Chester Morris, Wallace Beery, Lewis Stone, Robert Montgomery.

Big Sleep, The
WB 1946. Prod: Jack L. Warner, Howard Hughes. Dir: Howard Hawks. Scr: William Faulkner, Jules Furthman, Leigh Brackett, from the Raymond Chandler novel. Ph: Sid Hickox. Cast: Humphrey Bogart, Lauren Bacall, John Ridgely, Martha Vickers, Dorothy Malone.

Bílá Tma
(Czechoslovakia) 1948. Dir: Frantisek Cap.

Bivio, Il
(Italy) 1951. Dir: Ferdinando Cerchio. Scr: Leonardo Benvenuti, Giuseppe Mangione.

Black Angel
Univ 1946. Prod: Tom McKnight, Roy William Neill. Dir: Roy William Neill. Scr: Roy Chanslor, from the Cornell Woolrich novel. Ph: Paul Ivano. Cast: Dan Duryea, June Vincent, Peter Lorre, Broderick Crawford.

Black Hand, The
MGM 1949. Prod: William H. Wright. Dir: Richard Thorpe. Scr: Luther Davis. Ph: Paul C. Vogel. Cast: Gene Kelly, J. Carroll Naish, Marc Lawrence, Teresa Celli.

Black Tuesday
UA 1954. Prod: Robert Goldstein. Dir: Hugo Fregonese. Scr: Sydney Boehm. Ph: Stanley Cortez. Cast: Edward G. Robinson, Peter Graves, Sylvia Findley.

Blind Alley
Col 1939. Prod: Fred Kohlmar. Dir: Charles Vidor. Scr: P. MacDonald, M. Blankfort, A. Duffy, L. Meltzer, from the James Warwick play. Cast: Chester Morris, Ralph Bellamy, Ann Dvorak.

Blue Dahlia, The
Par 1946. Prod: John Houseman, George Marshall. Dir: George Marshall. Scr: Raymond Chandler. Ph: Lionel Lindon. Cast: Alan Ladd, Veronica Lake, Doris Dowling, Howard da Silva, William Bendix.

Blue Lamp, The
Eagle-Lion / Ealing Studios (UK) 1950. Prod: Michael Balcon. Dir: Basil Dearden. Scr: T.E.B. Clarke, Alexander Mackendrick. Ph: Gordon Dines. Cast: Jack Warner, Dirk Bogarde.

Body and Soul
MGM 1947. Prod: Bob Roberts. Dir: Robert Rossen. Scr: Abraham Polonsky. Ph: James Wong Howe. Cast: John Garfield, Lilli Palmer, Hazel Brooks, Anne Revere.

Bonnes à tuer
(France) 1954. Dir: Henri Decoin. Scr: Henri Decoin, J. de Baroncelli, J.-C. Eger, from a Pat MacGerr novel.

Boomerang!
Fox 1947. Prod: Louis de Rochemont. Dir: Elia Kazan. Scr: Richard Murphy, from an Anthony Abbott article. Ph: Norbert Brodine. Cast: Dana Andrews, Jane Wyatt, Lee J. Cobb, Arthur Kennedy.

Border Incident
MGM 1949. Prod: Nicholas Nayfack. Dir: Anthony Mann. Scr: J.C. Higgins, G. Zuckerman. Ph: Jack Alton. Cast: Ricardo Montalban, George Murphy, Howard da Silva, James Mitchell.

Born to Kill
RKO 1947. Prod: Sid Rogell. Dir: Robert Wise. Scr: Eve Green, Richard Macauley, from the James Gunn novel *Deadlier Than the Male*. Ph: Robert de Grasse. Cast: Lawrence Tierney, Claire Trevor, Audrey Long, Elisha Cook Jr.

Brasher Doubloon, The
Fox 1947. Prod: Robert Bassler. Dir: John Brahm. Scr: Dorothy Bennet, Leonard Praskins, from the Raymond Chandler novel *The High Window*. Ph: Lloyd Ahern. Cast: George Montgomery, Nancy Guild, Conrad Janis.

Breaking Point, The
WB 1950. Prod: Jerry Wald. Dir: Michael Curtiz. Scr: Ranald MacDougall, from the Ernest Hemingway novel *To Have and Have Not*. Ph: Ted McCord. Cast: John Garfield, Patricia Neal, Phyllis Thaxter, Wallace Ford.

Brelan d'as
(France) 1952. Dir: Henri Verneuil. Scr: Jacques Companéez, from stories by S.A. Steeman, Georges Simenon, Peter Cheyney.

Brighton Rock
ABPC 1947. Prod: Roy Boulting. Dir: John Boulting. Scr: Terence Rattigan, Graham Greene, from the latter's novel. Ph: Harry Waxman. Cast: Richard Attenborough, Carol March, Hermione Baddeley.

Brute Force
Univ 1947. Prod: Mark Hellinger. Dir: Jules Dassin. Scr: Richard Brooks, from a Robert Patterson story. Ph: William Daniels. Cast: Burt Lancaster, Hume Cronyn, Charles Bickford, Yvonne de Carlo, Ann Blyth, Ella Raines.

Bullets or Ballots
WB 1936. Prod: Luois F. Edelman. Dir: William Keighley. Scr: Seton I. Miller. Cast: Edward G. Robinson, Joan Blondell, Barton MacLane, Humphrey Bogart.

Bullitt
WB 1968. Prod: Phil D'Antoni. Dir: Peter Yates. Scr: Alan Trustman, Harry Kleiner, from the Robert L. Pike novel *Mute Witness*. Ph: William A. Fraker. Cast: Steve McQueen, Robert Vaughn, Jacqueline Bissett, Don Gordon, Robert Duvall.

Ça va barder
(France) 1954. Dir: John Berry. Scr: John Berry, Henri-François Rey.

Caccia tragica
(Italy) 1947. Dir: Giuseppe de Santis. Scr: Giuseppe de Santis, Michelangelo Antonioni, Carlo Lizzani, Corrado Álvaro, Umberto Barbaro, Gianni Puccini.

Call Northside 777
Fox 1948. Prod: Otto Lang. Dir: Henry Hathaway. Scr: Jerome Cady, Jay Dratler, from articles by James P. MacGuire. Ph: Joe MacDonald. Cast: James Stewart, Richard Conte, Lee J. Cobb, Helen Walker.

Calling Bulldog Drummond
MGM 1951. Prod: Hayes Goetz. Dir: Victor Saville. Scr: Howard E. Rogers, Gerard Fairlie, Arthur Wimperis. Ph: F.A. Young. Cast: Walter Pidgeon, Margaret Leighton, Robert Beatty, Peggy Evans.

Camille
MGM 1937. Prod: Bernard H. Hyman. Dir: George Cukor. Scr: Zoe Akins, Frances Marion, James Hilton, from an Alexandre Dumas fils novel. Cast: Greta Garbo, Robert Taylor.

Cammino della speranza, Il
(Italy) 1950. Dir: Pietro Germi. Scr: P. Germi, F. Fellini, T. Pinelli, N. Di Maria.

Canon City
Eagle-Lion 1948. Prod: Robert T. Kane, Bryan Foy. Dir / Scr; Crane Wilbur. Ph: John Alton. Cast: Scott Brady, Jeff Corey, Whit Bissell.

Capture, The
RKO 1950. Prod: Niven Busch. Dir: John Sturges. Scr: Niven Busch. Ph: Edward Cronjager, Cast: Lew Ayres, Teresa Wright, Victor Jory, Barry Kelley.

Cause for Alarm
MGM 1951. Prod: Tom Lewis. Dir: Tay Garnett. Scr: Mel Dinelli, Tom Lewis. Ph: Joseph Ruttenberg. Cast: Loretta Young, Barry Sullivan, Bruce Cowling.

Cet homme est dangereux
(France) 1953. Dir: Jean Lacha. Scr: Jacques Berland, Marcel Duhamel, from a Peter Cheyney novel.

Champion
UA 1949. Prod: Stanley Kramer. Dir: Mark Robson. Scr: Carl Foreman, from the Ring Lardner story. Ph: Frank Planer. Cast: Kirk Douglas, Ruth Roman, Arthur Kennedy, Paul Stewart, Marilyn Maxwell.

Charlie Chan in Egypt
Fox 1935. Prod: Edward T. Lowe. Dir: Louis King. Scr: Robert Ellis, Helen Logan. Cast: Warner Oland, Pat Paterson, Rita Cansino [aka Hayworth].

Charlie Chan's Secret
Fox 1936. Prod: John Stone. Dir: Gordon Wiles. Scr: Robert Ellis, Helen Logan. Cast: Warner Oland, Rosina Lawrence, Charles Quigley.

Chase, The
UA 1946. Prod: Seymour Nebenzahl. Dir: Arthur Ripley. Scr: Philip Yordan, from the Cornell Woolrich novel *The Black Path of Fear*. Ph: Frank Planer. Cast: Robert Cummings, Peter Lorre, Steve Cochran, Michèle Morgan.

Chicago Deadline
Par 1949. Prod: Robert Fellows. Dir: Lewis Allen, Scr: Warren Duff, from a Tiffany Thayer novel. Ph: John F. Seitz. Cast: Alan Ladd, Donna Reed, Arthur Kennedy, June Havoc.

Chicago Digest
(France) 1951. Dir: Paul Paviot. Scr: Louis Sapin, Albert Vidalie. [Short]

Chienne, La
(France) 1931. Dir: Jean Renoir. Scr: Pierre Lestringuez, from the Georges de la Fouchardière novel.

Chinatown Nights
Par 1929. Prod: David O. Selznick. Dir: William Wellman. Scr: O.H.P. Garrett, W.B. Jutte, B.G. Kohn. Cast: Wallace Beery, Florence Vidor, Warner Oland.

Citizen Kane
RKO 1941. Prod / Dir: Orson Welles. Scr: Herman J. Mankiewicz, Orson Welles. Cast: Orson Welles, Joseph Cotten, Dorothy Comingore, Agnes Moorehead.

City That Never Sleeps, The
Rep 1953. Prod: Herbert J. Yates. Dir: John H. Auer. Scr: Steve Fisher. Ph: John L. Russell. Cast: Gig Young, Mala Powers, Edward Arnold, William Talman.

Clouded Yellow
Col / Rank (UK) 1951. Prod: Betty E. Box. Dir: Ralph Thomas. Scr: Janet Green. Ph: Geoffrey Unsworth. Cast: Jean Simmons, Trevor Howard, Kenneth More.

Club 73
[Unidentified. Given its French title, *Le Club des trois,* possibly *The Unholy Three.* MGM 1925. Dir: Tod Browning].

Cobra Woman
Univ 1944. Prod: George Waggner. Dir: Robert Siodmak. Scr: Gene Lewis, R. Brooks. Cast: Maria Montez, John Hall, Sabu, Lon Chaney Jr.

Colorado Territory
WB 1949. Prod: Anthony Veiller. Dir: Raoul Walsh. Scr: J. Twist, E.H. North. Cast: Joel McCrea, Virginia Mayo, Dorothy Malone.

Come Back, Little Sheba
Par 1952. Prod: Hal B. Wallis. Dir: Daniel Mann. Scr: Ketty Frings, from the William Inge play. Ph: James Wong Howe. Cast: Burt Lancaster, Shirley Booth, Terry Moore, Richard Jaeckel.

Come Fill the Cup
WB 1951. Prod: Henry Blanke. Dir: Gordon Douglas. Scr: I. Goff, B. Roberts. Ph: Robert Burks. Cast: James Cagney, Phyllis Thaxter, Raymond Massey, Gig Young, James Gleason.

Confidential Agent
WB 1945. Prod: Robert Buckner. Dir: Herman Shumlin. Scr: Robert Buckner, from a Graham Greene story. Ph: James Wong Howe. Cast: Charles Boyer, Lauren Bacall, Victor Francen, Peter Lorre, Katina Praxinou, Wanda Hendrix.

Conflict
WB 1945. Prod: William Jacobs. Dir: Curtis Bernhardt. Scr: Arthur T. Horman, Dwight Taylor, from a Robert Siodmak & Alfred Neumann story. Ph: Merritt Gerstad. Cast: Humphrey Bogart, Alexis Smith, Sydney Greenstreet, Rose Hobart.

Congrès des belles-mères, Le
(France) 1954. Dir / Scr: Emile Couzinet.

Conversation, The
Par 1974. Prod / Dir / Scr: Francis Ford Coppola. Ph: Bill Butler. Cast: Gene Hackman, John Cazale, Allen Garfield, Frederic Forrest, Cindy Williams.

Coogan's Bluff
Univ 1969. Prod: Don Siegel. Dir: Don Siegel. Scr: Herman Miller, Dean Riesner, Howard Rodman, from a Herman Miller story. Ph: Bud Thackery. Cast: Clint Eastwood, Lee J. Cobb, Susan Clark, Tisha Sterling, Don Stroud.

Corbeau, Le
(France) 1943. Dir: H.-G. Clouzot. Scr: Louis Chavance.

Cornered
RKO 1945. Prod: Adrian Scott. Dir: Edward Dmytryk. Scr: John Paxton, John Wexley, Ben Hecht (uncredited). Ph: Harry J. Wild. Cast: Dick Powell, Micheleine Cheirel, Walter Slezak.

Coroner Creek
Col 1948. Prod: Harry Joe Brown. Dir: Ray Enright. Scr: K. Gamet, from a Luke Short novel. Cast: Randolph Scott, Marguerite Chapman, George MacReady.

Crime of Dr. Crespi, The
Rep 1935. Prod / Dir: John H. Auer. Scr: J.H. Auer, Lewis Graham, Edward Oldstead Cast: Erich von Stroheim, Paul Guilfoyle, Geraldine Kaye.

Crime School
WB 1938. Dir: Lewis Seiler. Scr: Crane Wilbur, Vincent Sherman. Cast: Humphrey Bogart, Gale Page.

Crimson Pirate, The
WB 1952. Prod: Hrold Hecht. Dir: Robert Siodmak. Scr: Roland Kibbee. Cast: Burt Lancaster, Eva Bartok.

Criss Cross
Univ 1949. Prod: Michel Kraike. Dir: Robert Siodmak. Scr: Daniel Fuchs, from a Don Tracy novel. Ph: Frank Planer. Cast: Burt Lancaster, Yvonne DeCarlo, Dan Duryea, Stephen McNally.

Crooked Way, The
UA 1949. Prod: Benedict Bogeaus. Dir: Robert Florey. Scr: Richard Landau. Ph: John Alton. Cast: John Payne, Sonny Tufts, Ellen Drew, Rhys Williams.

Crossfire
RKO 1947. Prod: Adrian Scott. Dir: Edward Dmytryk. Scr: John Paxton, from the Richard Brooks novel *The Brick Foxhole*. Ph: J. Roy Hunt. Cast: Robert Ryan, Robert Mitchum, Gloria Grahame, George Cooper, Robert Young, Sam Levene, Paul Kelly, Jacqueline White.

Cry of the City
Fox 1948. Prod: Sol C. Siegel. Dir: Robert Siodmak. Scr: Richard Murphy, Ben Hecht (uncredited), from the Henry E. Helseth novel *The Chair for Martin Rome*. Ph: Lloyd Ahern. Cast: Victor Mature, Richard Conte, Shelley Winters, Debra Paget.

Cuckoo Clock, The
MGM 1950. Dir: Tex Avery. [Cartoon]

Dames du Bois de Boulogne, Les
(France) 1945. Dir: Robert Bresson. Scr: Robert Bresson, from a Diderot story.

Damned Don't Cry, The
WB 1950. Prod: Jerry Wald. Dir: Vincent Sherman. Scr: Harold Medford, Jerome Weidman, from a Gertrude Walker story. Ph: Ted McCord. Cast: Joan Crawford, David Brian, Steve Cochran, Kent Smith.

Dark City
Par 1950. Prod: Hal B. Wallis. Dir: William Dieterle. Scr: John M. Lucas, Ketti Frings, Larry Marcus, from the latter's story. Ph: Victor Milner. Cast: Charlton Heston, Lizabeth Scott, Viveca Lindfors, Jack Webb.

Dark Corner, The
Fox 1946. Prod: Fred Kohlmar. Dir: Henry Hathaway. Scr: Jay Dratler, Bernard Schoenfeld, from a Leo Rosten story. Ph: Joe MacDonald. Cast: Mark Stevens, Lucille Ball, Clifton Webb, William Bendix, Cathy Downs.

Dark Mirror, The
Univ 1946. Prod: Nunnally Johnson. Dir: Robert Siodmak. Scr: Nunnally Johnson, from a Vladimir Pozner novel. Ph: Milton Krasner. Cast: Olivia de Havilland, Lew Ayres, Thomas Mitchell, Richard Long.

Dark Passage
WB 1947. Prod: Jerry Wald. Dir: Delmer Daves. Scr: Delmer Daves, from the David Goodis novel. Ph: Sid Hickox. Cast: Humphrey Bogart, Lauren Bacall, Bruce Bennett, Tom d'Andrea, Agnes Moorehead.

Dark Past, The
Col 1948. Prod: Buddy Adler. Dir: Rudolph Maté. Scr: P. MacDonald, M. Blankfort, A. Duffy, from the James Warwick play *Blind Alley*. Ph: Joseph Walker. Cast: William Holden, Lee J. Cobb, Nina Foch, Adele Jergens.

Dark Victory
WB 1939. Prod: Hal B. Wallis. Dir: Edmund Goulding. Scr: Casey Robinson. Cast: Bette Davis, George Brent, Humphrey Bogart.

David and Bathsheba
Fox 1951. Prod: Darryl F. Zanuck. Dir: Henry King. Scr: Philip Dunne. Cast: Gregory Peck, Susan Hayward, Raymond Massey.

David Copperfield
MGM 1935. Prod: David O. Selznick. Dir: George Cukor. Scr: Hugh Walpole, Howard Estabrooke. Cast: W.C. Fields, Lionel Barrymore, Maureen O'Sullivan, Frank Lawton.

Day the Earth Stood Still, The
Fox 1951. Prod: Julian Blaustein. Dir: Robert Wise. Scr: Edmund H. North, from a Harry Bates story. Cast: Michael Rennie, Patricia Neal, Hugh Marlowe, Sam Jaffe.

Dead End
WB 1937. Prod: Samuel Goldwyn. Dir: William Wyler. Scr: Lillian Hellman, from the Sidney Kingsley play. Cast: Humphrey Bogart, Joel McCrea, Silvia Sidney, Claire Trevor.

Dead of Night
Ealing Studios (UK) 1945. Prod: Michael Balcon. Dir: Alberto Cavalcanti, Charles Crichton, Basil Dearden, Robert Hamer. Scr: John Baines, Angus MacPhail, T.E.B. Clarke. Cast: Mervyn Johns, Googie Withers, Miles Malleson, Michael Redgrave.

Dead Reckoning
Col 1947. Prod: Sidney Biddell. Dir: John Cromwell. Scr: Steve Fisher, O.H.P. Garrett, Allen Rivkin. Ph: Leo Tover. Cast: Humphrey Bogart, Lizabeth Scott, William Prince, Morris Carnowski.

Death of a Salesman
Col 1951. Prod: Stanley Kramer. Dir: László Benedek. Scr: Stanley Roberts, from the Arthur Miller play. Cast: Fredric March, Mildred Dunnock, Kevin McCarthy.

Death Wish
Par 1974. Prod: Dino de Laurentiis. Dir: Michael Winner. Scr: Wendell Mayes, from a Brian Garfield novel. Ph: Arthur J. Ornitz. Cast: Charles Bronson, Hope Lange, Vincent Gardenia.

Decoy
Mono 1946. Prod: Jack Bernhard, Bernard Brandt. Dir: Jack Bernhard. Ph: L.W. O'Connell. Cast: Jean Gillie, Edward Norris, Robert Armstrong.

Dédée d'Anvers
(France) 1948. Dir: Yves Allégret. Scr: Jacques Sigurd, from the Ashelbé novel.

Dernier Tournant, Le
(France) 1939. Dir: Pierre Chenal. Scr: Charles Spaak, Henri Torres, from the James M. Cain novel *The Postman Always Rings Twice.*

Destination Tokyo
WB 1943. Prod: Jerry Wald. Dir: Delmer Daves. Scr: Delmer Daves, Albert Maltz, from a Steve Fisher story. Cast: Cary Grant, John Garfield, Alan Hale.

Detective, The
Fox 1968. Prod: Aaron Rosenberg. Dir: Gordon Douglas. Scr: Abby Mann. Ph: Joseph F. Biroc. Cast: Frank Sinatra, Lee Remick, Ralph Meeker, Jack Klugman.

Detective Story
Par 1951. Prod / Dir: William Wyler. Scr: Philip Yordan, Robert Wilder, from the Sidney Kingsley play. Ph: Lee Garmes. Cast: Kirk Douglas, Eleanor Parker, William Bendix, Lee Grant, George MacReady.

Deux Sous de violettes
(France) 1951. Dir: Jean Anouilh. Scr: Monelle Valentin.

Devil-Doll, The
MGM 1936. Prod: Edward J. Mannix. Dir: Tod Browning. Scr:
Tod Browning, Garrett Fort, Guy Endore, Erich von Stroheim,
from the A.A. Merritt novel *Burn, Witch Burn*. Cast: Lionel
Barrymore, Margaret O'Sullivan, Frank Lawton.

Diaboliques, Les
(France) 1954. Dir: H.-G. Clouzot. Scr: H.-G. Clouzot, Jérôme
Géronimi, René Masson, F. Grendel, from the Boileau and
Narcejac novel.

Dial 1119
MGM 1950. Prod: Richard Goldstone. Dir: Gerald Mayer. Scr:
H. King, D. McGuire, J. Monks Jr. Ph: Paul C. Vogel. Cast:
Marshall Thompson, Sam Levene, Virginia Field, Andrea King.

Dillinger
Mono 1945. Prod: King Bros. Dir: Max Nosseck. Scr: Philip
Yordan. Ph: Jackson Rose. Cast: Lawrence Tierney, Anne Jeffreys,
Edmund Lowe, Mark Lawrence, Elisha Cook Jr.

Diplomatic Courier
Fox 1952. Prod: Casey Robinson. Dir: Henry Hathaway. Scr:
Casey Robinson, Liam O'Brien, from a Peter Cheyney novel.
Ph: Lucien Ballard. Cast: Tyrone Power, Patricia Neal, Stephen
McNally, Hildegarde Neff, Karl Malden.

Dirty Harry
WB 1971. Prod / Dir: Don Siegel. Scr: Harry Fink, R.M. Fink,
Dean Riesner, John Milius, from a Harry Fink & R.M. Fink story.
Ph: Bruce Surtees. Cast: Clint Eastwood, Harry Guardino, Reni
Santoni, Andy Robinson.

Dr. Jekyll and Mr. Hyde
MGM 1941. Prod / Dir: Victor Fleming. Scr: John Lee Mahin,
from the Robert Louis Stevenson novel. Ph: Joseph Ruttenberg.
Cast: Spencer Tracy, Ingrid Bergman, Lana Turner, Ian Hunter,
Donald Crisp.

Domenica d'agosto
(Italy) 1950. Dir: Luciano Emmer. Scr: Sergio Amidei, Cesare Zavattini.

Don Is Dead, The
Univ 1973. Prod: Hal B. Wallis. Dir: Richard Fleischer. Scr: Marvin H. Albert, from his novel. Ph: Richard H. Cline. Cast: Anthony Quinn, Robert Forster, Frederic Forrest, Al Lettieri.

Don't Bother to Knock
Fox 1952. Prod: Julian Blaustein. Dir: Roy Ward Baker. Scr: Dan Taradash, from the Charlotte Armstrong novel *Mischief*. Ph: Lucien Ballard. Richard Widmark, Marilyn Monroe, Anne Bancroft, Elisha Cook Jr.

Double Indemnity
Par 1944. Prod: Buddy G. DeSylva. Dir: Billy Wilder. Scr: Billy Wilder, Raymond Chandler, from the James M. Cain novel. Ph: John F. Seitz. Cast: Barbara Stanwyck, Fred MacMurray, Edward G. Robinson.

Dr. No
UA 1962. Prod: Albert R. Broccoli, Harry Salzman. Dir: Terence Young. Scr: Richard Maibaum, Johanna Harwood, from the Ian Fleming novel. Ph: Ted Moore. Cast: Sean Connery, Ursula Andress, Joseph Wiseman, Jack Lord, Bernard Lee, Lois Maxwell, Anthony Dawson.

Dragonwyck
Fox 1946. Prod: Darryl F. Zanuck. Dir: Joseph L. Mankiewicz. Scr: Joseph L. Mankiewicz, from the Anya Seyton novel. Ph: Arthur Miller. Cast: Gene Tierney, Walter Huston, Vincent Price, Glenn Langan, Anne Revere.

Dreigroschenoper, Die
(Germany) 1931. Dir: G.W. Pabst. Scr: Ernst Vajda, Leo Lania, Bela Balázs, from the Bertolt Brecht / John Gay play.

Du rififi chez les hommes
(France) 1954. Dir: Jules Dassin. Scr: René Wheeler, Jules Dassin, Auguste Le Breton, from the latter's novel.

Dupont-Barbès / Malou de Montmartre.
(France) 1951. Dir: Henri Lepage. Scr: A.P. Antoine.

Each Dawn I Die
WB 1939. Prod: Jack L. Warner. Dir: William Keighley. Scr: Warren Duff, N.R. Raine. Cast: James Cagney, George Raft, Jane Bryan, George Bancroft.

El
(Mexico) 1953. Dir: Luis Buñuel. Scr: Luis Buñuel, Luis Alcoriza, from the Mercedes Pinto novel.

Enforcer, The
WB 1951. Prod: Milton Sperling. Dir: Bretaigne Windust, Raoul Walsh (uncredited). Scr: Martin Rackin. Ph: Robert Burks. Cast: Humphrey Bogart, Zero Mostel, Everett Sloane, Ted de Corsia, Michael Tolan.

Ennemi public no. 1
(France) 1953. Dir: Henri Verneuil. Scr: Michel Audiard, Jean Manse.

Eskimo
MGM 1933. Prod: W.S. Van Dyke, Hunt Stromberg. Dir: W.S. Van Dyke. Scr: John Lee Mahin. Cast: Edward Dearing, Peter Freuchen, Mala.

Eternel Retour, L'
(France) 1943. Dir: Jean Delannoy. Scr: Jean Cocteau.

Experiment Perilous
RKO 1944. Prod: Warren Duff. Dir: Jacques Tourneur. Scr: Warren Duff, from the Margaret Carpenter novel. Ph: Tony Gaudio. Cast: George Brent, Hedy Lamarr, Paul Lukas, Albert Dekker.

Fabiola
(Italy) 1949. Dir / Scr: Alessandro Blasetti. Scr: V. Brancati, J.-G. Auriol.

Face Behind the Mask, The
Col 1941. Prod: Wallace MacDonald. Dir: Robert Florey. Scr: Paul Jarrico, Allen Vincent. Ph: Franz Planer. Cast: Peter Lorre, Evelyn Keyes, Don Beddoe.

Fallen Angel
Fox 1945. Prod / Dir: Otto Preminger. Scr: Harry Kleiner, from the Marty Holland novel, Ph: Joseph LaShelle. Cast: Alice Faye, Dana Andrews, Linda Darnell, Charles Bickford.

Fear
Mono 1946. Prod: Lindsley Parsons. Dir: Alfred Zeisler. Scr: Alfred Zeisler, Dennis Cooper. Ph: Jackson Rose. Cast: Francis Pierlot, Peter Cookson, Warren William, Anne Gwynne.

Fear in the Night
Par 1947. Prod: W.H. Pine, W.C. Thomas. Dir: Maxwell Shane. Scr: Maxwell Shane, from a Cornell Woolrich story. Ph: Jack Greenhalgh. Cast: Paul Kelly, De Forrest Kelley, Ann Doran.

Femmes s'en balancent, Les
(France) 1953. Dir: Bernard Borderie. Scr: Bernard Borderie, from a Peter Cheyney novel.

File on Thelma Jordan, The
Par 1949. Prod: Hal B. Wallis. Dir: Robert Siodmak. Scr: Ketty Frings, from a Marty Holland story. Ph: George Barnes. Cast: Barbara Stanwyck, Wendell Corey, Paul Kelly, Joan Tetzel.

Flamingo Road
WB 1949. Prod: Jerry Wald. Dir: Michael Curtiz. Scr: Robert Wilder, Edmund H. North, from the Robert Wilder play. Cast: Joan Crawford, Zachary Scott, Sydney Greenstreet, David Brian.

Flesh and Fantasy
Univ 1943. Prod: Charles Boyer, Julien Duvivier. Dir: Julien Duvivier. Scr: Ernest Pascal, Samuel Hoffenstein, Ellis Saint-Joseph: Ph: Stanley Cortez, Paul Ivano. Cast: Charles Boyer, Edward G. Robinson, Barbara Stanwyck, Robert Cummings.

For Love of Ivy
Cinerama 1968. Prod: Edgar J. Scherick, Jay Weston. Dir: Daniel Mann. Scr: Robert Alan Arthur, Sidney Poitier. Ph: Joseph F. Coffey. Cast: Sidney Poitier, Abbey Lincoln, Beau Bridges.

Force of Evil
MGM 1948. Prod: John Garfield, Abraham Polonsky. Dir: Abraham Polonsky. Scr: Abraham Polonsky, Ira Wolfert, from the latter's novel *Tucker's People*. Ph: George Barnes. Cast: John Garfield, Beatrice Pearson, Roy Roberts, Sid Tomack, Thomas Gomez, Paul Fix.

Foreign Correspondent
UA 1940. Prod: Walter Wanger. Dir: Alfred Hitchcock. Scr: Charles Bennett, Joan Harrison, Ph: Rudolph Maté. Cast: Joel McCrea, Laraine Day, Herbert Marshall, Georges Sanders, Albert Bassermann, Robert Benchley.

Forever Amber
Fox 1947. Prod: William Perlberg. Dir: Otto Preminger. Scr: Ring Lardner Jr., Philip Dunne, from the Kathleen Winsor novel. Cast: Linda Darnell, Cornell Wilde, George Sanders, Richard Greene.

Fourteen Hours
Fox 1951. Prod: Sol C. Siegel. Dir: Henry Hathaway. Scr: John Paxton, from a Joel Sayre article. Ph: Joe MacDonald. Cast: Richard Basehart, Paul Douglas, Barbara Bel Geddes, Agnes Moorehead.

French Cancan
(France) 1955. Dir: Jean Renoir. Scr: André-Paul Antoine, Jean Renoir.

French Connection, The
Fox 1971. Prod: Phil D'Antoni. Dir: William Friedkin. Scr: Ernest Tidyman, from the Robin Moore novel. Ph: Owen Roizman. Cast: Gene Hackman, Fernando Rey, Roy Scheider, Tony Lo Bianco, Marcel Bozzuffi.

Fröken Julie
(Sweden) 1951. Dir: Alf Sjöberg. Scr: Alf Sjöberg, from the Strindberg play.

Fuller Brush Girl, The
Col 1950. Prod: Jack Fier. Dir: Lloyd Bacon. Scr: Frank Tashlin, Francis McDowell. Cast: Lucille Ball, Eddie Albert, Carl Benton Reid.

Fury
MGM 1936. Prod: Joseph L. Mankiewicz. Dir: Fritz Lang. Scr: Fritz Lang, Bartlett Comack, from a Norman Krasna story. Cast: Spencer Tracy, Silvia Sidney, Walter Abel.

Gaslight
BNF 1940. Prod: John Corfield. Dir: Thorold Dickinson. Scr: A.R. Rawlinson, Bridget Boland, Patrick Hamilton, from the latter's play *Angel Street*. Cast: Anton Walbrook, Diane Wynyard.

Gaslight
MGM 1944. Prod: Arthur Hornblow Jr. Dir: George Cukor. Scr: John Van Druten, Walter Reish, John Balderston, from the Patrick Hamilton play *Angel Street*. Ph: Joseph Ruttenberg. Cast: Ingrid Bergman, Charles Boyer, Joseph Cotten, Angela Lansbury.

Gatan
(Sweden) 1948. Dir: Gostä Werner. Scr: Marten Edlund.

Gilda
Col 1946. Prod: Virginia Van Upp. Dir: Charles Vidor. Scr: Marion Parsonnet, from the E.A. Ellington novel. Ph: Rudolph Maté. Rita Hayworth, Glenn Ford, George MacReady, Stephen Geray.

Girl Hunters, The
Colorama (UK) 1963. Prod: Robert Fellows, Charles Reynolds. Dir: Roy Rowland. Scr: Robert Fellows, Roy Rowland, Mickey Spillane. Ph: Kenneth Talbot. Cast: Mickey Spillane, Lloyd Nolan, Shirley Eaton.

Glass Key, The
Par 1942. Prod: Fred Kohlmar. Dir: Stuart Heisler. Scr: Jonathan Latimer, from the Dashiell Hammett novel. Ph: Theodor Sparkuhl. Cast: Alan Ladd, Brian Donlevy, Veronica Lake, Bonita Granville, William Bendix, Joseph Calleia.

G-Men
WB 1935. Prod: Hal B. Wallis, Jack L. Warner. Dir: William Keighley. Scr: Seton I. Miller. Ph: Sol Polito. Cast: James Cagney, Lloyd Nolan, Margaret Lindsay, Ann Dvorak.

Godfather, The
Par 1972. Prod: Al Ruddy. Dir: Francis Ford Coppola. Scr: Francis Ford Coppola, Mario Puzo, from the latter's novel. Ph: Gordon Willis. Cast: Marlon Brando, Al Pacino, James Caan, Sterling Hayden, Robert Duvall, Diane Keaton.

Grand Jeu, Le
(France) 1934. Dir: Jacques Feyder. Scr: J. Feyder, Charles Spaak.

Grapes of Wrath
Fox 1940. Prod: Darryl F. Zanuck. Dir: John Ford. Scr: Nunnally Johnson, from the John Steinbeck novel. Cast: Henry Fonda, Jane Darwell, John Carradine.

Great Gambini, The
Par 1937. Prod: B.P. Schulberg. Dir: Charles Vidor. Scr: F.J. Jackson, F. Partos, H.I. Young. Cast: Akim Tamiroff, John Trent, Marian Marsh.

Great Turning Point, The
(USSR) 1946. Dir: Friedrich Ermler. Scr: Boris Chirskov.

Guadalcanal
[Unidentified documentary. Possibly *Guadalcanal Diary*. Fox 1943. Dir: Lewis Seiler.]

Gueule d'amour
(France) 1937. Dir: Jean Grémillon. Scr: Jean Grémillom, Charles Spaak.

Gun Crazy
UA 1950. Prod: King Bros. Dir: Joseph H. Lewis. Scr: MacKinlay Kantor, Millard Kaufman (as front for Dalton Trumbo), from a MacKinlay Kantor story. Ph: Russell Harlan. Cast: Peggy Cummins, John Dall, Berry Kroeger, Morris Carnovsky, Anabel Shaw.

Gunn
Par 1967. Prod: Owen Crump. Dir: Blake Edwards. Scr: Blake Edwards, William Peter Blatty. Ph: Philip Lathrop. Cast: Craig Stevens, Laura Devon, Edward Asner, Sherry Jackson.

Hanged Man, The
Univ 1964. Prod: Ray Wagner. Dir: Don Siegel. Scr: Jack Laird, Stanford Whitmore, from the Dorothy B. Hughes novel *Ride the Pink Horse*. Ph: Bud Thackery. Cast: Robert Culp, Edmond O'Brien, Vera Miles, Norman Fell.

Hangover Square
Fox 1945. Prod: Robert Bassler. Dir: John Brahm. Scr: Barré Lyndon, from the Patrick Hamilton novel. Ph: Joseph LaShelle. Cast: Laird Cregar, Linda Darnell, George Sanders.

Harper
WB 1966. Prod: Jerry Gershwin, Elliott Kastner. Dir: Jack Smight. Scr: William Goldman, from the Ross Macdonald novel *The Moving Target*. Ph: Conrad Hall. Cast: Paul Newman, Janet Leigh, Robert Wagner, Lauren Bacall, Julie Harris, Arthur Hill.

He Walked By Night
Eagle-Lion 1948. Prod: Robert T. Kane. Dir: Alfred Werker. Scr: J.C. Higgins, from a Crane Wilbur story. Ph: John Alton. Cast: Richard Basehart, Scott Brady, Roy Roberts, Whit Bissell.

High Wall
MGM 1947. Prod: Robert Lord. Dir: Curtis Bernhardt. Scr: Sydney Boehm, Lester Cole. Ph: Paul Vogel. Cast: Robert Taylor, Audrey Totter, Herbert Marshall, Dorothy Patrick.

Highway 301
WB 1950. Prod: Bryan Foy. Dir / Scr: Andrew L. Stone. Ph: Carl Guthrie. Cast: Steve Cochran, Virginia Grey, Gaby André.

Hollow Triumph
Eagle-Lion 1948. Prod: Paul Henreid. Dir: Steven Sekely. Scr: Daniel Fuchs, from the Murray Forbes novel. Ph: John Alton. Cast: Paul Henreid, Joan Bennett, Edward Franz.

Home of the Brave
UA 1949. Prod: Stanley Kramer. Dir: Mark Robson. Scr: Carl Foreman, from an Arthur Laurents play. Ph: Robert De Grasse. Cast: James Edwards, Frank Lovejoy, Lloyd Bridges, Steve Brodie, Jeff Corey, Douglas Dick.

Homme de Londres, L'
(France) 1943. Dir: Henri Decoin. Scr: Henri Decoin, from a Georges Simenon novel.

Homme qui cherche la vérité, L'
(France) 1940. Dir: Alexandre Esway. Scr: Pierre Wolfe.

Hoodlum Empire
Rep 1952. Prod: Herbert J. Yates. Dir: Joseph Kane. Scr: Bruce Manning, from a Bob Considine news story. Ph: Reggie Lanning. Cast: Brian Donlevy, Claire Trevor, Forrest Tucker, Vera Ralston, Luther Adler.

House of Strangers
Fox 1949. Prod: Sol C. Siegel. Dir: Joseph L. Mankiewicz. Scr: Philip Yordan, Joseph L. Mankiewicz (uncredited), from the Jerome Weidman novel *I'll Never Go There Anymore*. Ph: Milton Krasner. Cast: Edward G. Robinson, Susan Hayward, Richard Conte.

House of Wax
WB 1953. Prod: Bryan Foy. Dir: André de Toth. Scr: Crane Wilbur, from a Charles Belden story. Cast: Vincent Price, Roy Roberts, Carolyn Jones, Phyllis Kirk, Frank Lovejoy.

House on 92ⁿᵈ Street, The
Fox 1945. Prod: Louis de Rochemont. Dir: Henry Hathaway. Scr: Barré Lyndon, Jack Moffitt, John Monks Jr., from a Charles G. Booth story. Ph: Norbert Brodine. Cast: William Eythe, Lloyd Nolan, Signe Hasso, Gene Lockhart.

I Am a Fugitive from a Chain Gang
WB 1932. Prod: Hal B. Wallis. Dir: Mervyn LeRoy. Scr: Sheridan Gibney, Brown Holmes, Howard J. Green, from the Robert E. Burns autobiography. Ph: Sol Polito. Cast: Paul Muni, Glenda Farrell, Helen Vinson, Noel Francis, Everett Brown.

I Love Trouble
Col 1948. Prod / Dir: S. Sylvan Simon. Scr: Roy Huggins, from his novel *The Double Take*. Ph: Charles Lawton Jr. Cast: Franchot Tone, Janet Blair, Janis Carter, Adele Jergens, Glenda Farrell.

I Walk Alone
Par 1947. Prod: Hal B. Wallis. Dir: Byron Haskin. Scr: Robert Smith, John Bright, from a Theodore Reeves play. Ph: Leo Tover. Cast: Burt Lancaster, Lizabeth Scott, Kirk Douglas, Wendell Corey, Kristine Miller.

I Want You
RKO 1951. Prod: Samuel Goldwyn. Dir: Mark Robson. Scr: Irwin Shaw, from an Ed Newhouse story. Ph: Harry Stradling Sr. Cast: Dana Andrews, Dorothy McGuire, Farley Granger, Peggy Dow.

I'll Get You for This
Fox / Romulus Films (UK) 1950. Prod: Joseph Kaufman. Dir: Joseph M. Newman. Scr: George Callahan, William Rose, from a James Hadley Chase novel. Ph: Otto Heller. Cast: George Raft, Coleen Gray, Enzo Staiola.

Identité judiciaire
(France) 1950. Dir: Hervé Bromberger. Scr: J. Rémy, H. Jeanson.

In a Lonely Place
Col 1950. Prod: Robert Lord, Henry S. Kesler. Dir: Nicholas Ray. Scr: Andrew Solt, from the Dorothy B. Hughes novel. Ph: Burnett Guffey. Cast: Humphrey Bogart, Gloria Grahame, Frank Lovejoy, Carl Benton Reid, Art Smith.

In the Heat of the Night
UA 1967. Prod: Walter Mirisch. Dir: Norman Jewison. Scr: Stirling Silliphant, from the John Ball novel. Ph: Haskell Wexler. Cast: Sidney Poitier, Rod Steiger, Lee Grant, Warren Oates.

In the Sands of Central Asia
(USSR) 1943. Dir / Scr: Alexander Zguridi.

Inconnus dans la maison, Les
(France) 1942. Dir: Henri Decoin. Scr: H.-G. Clouzot, from a Georges Simenon novel.

Inhumaine, L'
(France) 1924. Dir: Marcel L'Herbier. Scr: Pierre Mac Orlan.

Invisible Stripes
WB 1939. Prod: Hal B. Wallis, Jack L. Warner. Dir: Lloyd Bacon. Scr: Warren Duff, Jonathan Finn, from the Warden Lewis Lawes book. Ph: Ernie Haller. Cast: George Raft, Humphrey Bogart, William Holden.

It Always Rains on Sundays
Eagle-Lion / Ealing Studios (UK) 1948. Prod: Michael Balcon. Dir: Robert Hamer. Scr: Henry Cornelius, Robert Hamer, Angus MacPhail, from an Arthur Labern novel. Ph: Douglas Slocombe. Cast: Googie Withers, Edward Chapman, Susan Shaw.

It Happened in the Donbas
(USSR) 1945. Dir: Leonid Lukov. Scr: Boris Gorbatov, Mikhail Bleiman, Sergei Antonov.

It's in the Bag
Col 1945. Prod: Jack H. Skirball. Dir: Richard Wallace. Scr: Jay Dratler, Alma Reville, Morrie Ryskind. Cast: Fred Allen, Jack Benny, Don Ameche.

Ivy
Univ 1947. Prod: William Cameron Menzies. Dir: Sam Wood. Scr: Charles Bennett, from Marie Belloc Lowndes' novel *The Story of Ivy*. Ph: Russell Metty. Cast: Joan Fontaine, Patric Knowles, Herbert Marshall, Sir Cedric Hardwicke, Richard Ney.

Jamaica Inn
Par / Mayflower Pictures (UK) 1939. Prod: Erich Pommer, Charles Laughton. Dir: Alfred Hitchcock. Scr: Sidney Gilliatt, Joan Harrison, J.B. Priestley, Alma Reville, from the Daphne du Maurier novel. Cast: Charles Laughton, Horace Hodges, Hay Petrie, Frederick Piper, Leslie Banks, Marie Ney, Maureen O'Hara.

Jeopardy
MGM 1953. Prod: Sol B. Fielding. Dir: John Sturges. Scr: Mel Dinelli, Maurice Zimm. Ph: Victor Milner. Cast: Barbara Stanwyck, Barry Sullivan, Ralph Meeker.

Jezebel
WB 1938. Prod / Dir: William Wyler. Scr: John Huston, A. Finkel, C. Ripley, R. Buckner, from the Owen Davis play. Cast: Bette Davis, Henry Fonda, George Brent.

Joan of Arc
RKO 1948. Prod: Walter Wanger. Dir: Victor Fleming. Scr: Andrew Solt, Maxwell Anderson, from the latter's play. Cast: Ingrid Bergman, José Ferrer, Francis L. Sullivan.

Johnny Allegro
Col 1949. Prod: Irving Starr. Dir: Ted Tetzlaff. Scr: Karen De Wolf, Guy Endore, from a James Edward Grant story. Ph: Joseph F. Biroc. Cast: George Raft, Nina Foch, George MacReady, Will Geer.

Johnny O'Clock
Col 1947. Prod: Edward G. Nealis. Dir: Robert Rossen. Scr: Robert Rossen, from a Milton Holmes story. Ph: Burnett Guffrey. Cast: Dick Powell, Evelyn Keyes, Lee J. Cobb, Ellen Drew, Nina Foch, Thomas Gomez.

Jour se lève, Le
(France) 1939. Dir: Marcel Carné. Scr: Jacques Viot, Jacques Prévert.

Journey into Fear
RKO 1942. Prod: Orson Welles. Dir: Norman Foster, Orson Welles (uncredited). Scr: Joseph Cotten, Orson Welles, Ben Hecht (uncredited), from the Eric Ambler novel. Ph: Karl Struss. Cast: Joseph Cotten, Dolores Del Rio, Orson Welles, Everett Sloane, Ruth Warwick, Agnes Moorehead.

Juliette ou la Clé des songes
(France) 1950. Dir: Marcel Carné. Scr: Jacques Viot, Marcel Carné, Georges Neveu, from the latter's play.

Kabinett des Doktor Caligari, Das
(Germany) 1919. Dir: Robert Wiene. Scr: Carl Mayer.

Kansas City Confidential
UA 1952. Prod: Edward Small. Dir: Phil Karlson. Scr: George Bruce, Harry Essex, Harold Greene. Ph: George E. Diskant. Cast: John Payne, Coleen Gray, Preston Foster, Neville Brand.

Key Largo
WB 1948. Prod: Jerry Wald. Dir: John Huston. Scr: Richard Brooks, John Huston, from the Maxwell Anderson play. Ph: Karl Freund. Cast: Humphrey Bogart, Edward G. Robinson, Lauren Bacall, Lionel Barrymore, Claire Trevor.

Killers, The
Univ 1946. Prod: Mark Hellinger. Dir: Robert Siodmak. Scr: Anthony Veiller, Richard Brooks, John Huston (last two uncredited, from the Ernest Hemingway story. Ph: Woody Bredell, Cast: Burt Lancaster, Ava Gardner, Edmond O'Brien, Albert Dekker, William Conrad, Sam Levene, Jeff Corey, Charles McGraw, Phil Brown.

Killers, The
Univ 1964. Prod: Don Siegel. Dir: Don Siegel. Scr: Gene L. Coon, from the Ernest Hemingway story. Ph: Richard L. Rawlings. Cast: Lee Marvin, John Cassavetes, Angie Dickinson, Ronald Reagan, Clu Gulager.

King Solomon's Mines
MGM 1950. Prod: Sam Zimbalist. Dir: Compton Bennett, Andrew Marton. Scr: H. Deutsch, from the H. Rider Haggard novel. Cast: Stewart Granger, Deborah Kerr, Richard Carlson, Hugo Haas.

King-size Canary
MGM 1947. Dir: Tex Avery. [Cartoon]

King's Row
WB 1942. Prod: David Lewis, Hal B. Wallis. Dir: Sam Wood. Scr: Casey Robinson, from a Henry Bellamann novel. Ph: James Wong Howe. Scr: Ann Sheridan, Robert Cummings, Ronald Reagan.

Kiss Me Deadly
UA 1955. Prod / Dir: Robert Aldrich. Scr: A.I. Bezzerides, from a Mickey Spillane novel. Ph: Ernest Laszlo. Cast: Ralph Meeker, Albert Dekker, Cloris Leachman, Paul Stewart, Juano Hernandez, Wesley Addy, Gaby Rodgers.

Kiss of Death
Fox 1947. Prod: Fred Kohlmar. Dir: Henry Hathaway. Scr: Ben Hecht, Charles Lederer, from an Eleazar Lipsky story. Ph: Norbert Brodine. Cast: Victor Mature, Brian Donlevy, Richard Widmark, Coleen Gray.

Kiss the Blood Off My Hands
Univ 1948. Prod: Richard Vernon. Dir: Norman Foster. Scr: Leonardo Bercovici, Ben Maddow, Walter Bernstein, from the Gerald Butler novel. Ph: Russell Metty. Cast: Burt Lancaster, Joan Fontaine, Robert Newton.

Kiss Tomorrow Goodbye
WB 1950. Prod: William Cagney. Dir: Gordon Douglas. Scr: Harry Brown, from the Horace McCoy novel. Ph: Peverell Marley. Cast: James Cagney, Barbara Payton, Helena Carter, Ward Bond.

Lady from Shanghai, The
Col 1948. Prod / Dir: Orson Welles. Scr: Orson Welles, William Castle, Charles Lederer, Fletcher Markle (last three uncredited), from the Sherwood King novel *If I Die Before I Wake*. Ph: Charles Lawton Jr., Rudolph Maté, Joseph Walker (last two uncredited). Cast: Orson Welles, Rita Hayworth, Everett Sloane, Glenn Anders.

Lady in Cement
Fox 1968. Prod: Aaron Rosenberg. Dir: Gordon Douglas. Scr: Jack Guss, Marvin H. Albert. Ph: Joseph F. Biroc. Cast: Frank Sinatra, Raquel Welch, Richard Conte, Martin Gabel.

Lady in the Lake, The
MGM 1946. Prod: George Haight. Dir: Robert Montgomery. Scr: Steve Fisher, from the Raymond Chandler novel. Ph: Paul C. Vogel. Cast: Robert Montgomery, Audrey Totter, Lloyd Nolan, Tom Tully, Leon Ames, Jane Meadows.

Lady Vanishes, The
Gainsborough Pictures (UK) 1938. Prod: Edward Black. Dir: Alfred Hitchcock. Scr: Sidney Gilliat, Frank Launder, from an Ethel Lina White novel. Cast: Margaret Lockwood, Michael Redgrave, Paul Lukas, Dame May Whitty.

Lady Without a Passport
MGM 1950. Prod: Samuel Marx. Dir: Joseph H. Lewis. Scr: Howard Dimsdale, C. Hume, from an L. Taylor story. Cast: Hedy Lamarr, John Hodiak, George MacReady, James Craig.

Last Warning, The
Univ 1929. Prod: Carl Laemlle. Dir: Paul Leni. Scr: A.A. Cohn, J.G. Hawks, R.F. Hill, T. Reed. Cast: Laura La Plante, Montagu Love, Roy D'Arcy.

Laura
Fox 1944. Prod: Otto Preminger. Dir: Otto Preminger, Rouben Mamoulian (uncredited). Scr: Jay Dratler, Samuel Hoffenstein, Betty Reinhardt, Ring Lardner Jr. (uncredited), from the Vera Caspary novel. Ph: Joseph LaShelle, Lucien Ballard (uncredited). Cast: Gene Tierney, Dana Andrews, Clifton Webb, Vincent Price, Judith Anderson.

Lawless, The
Par 1950. Prod: William Pine, William Thomas. Dir: Joseph Losey. Scr: Daniel Mainwaring (as Geoffrey Homes). Ph: J. Roy Hunt. Cast: MacDonald Carey, Gail Russell, Johnny Sands.

Leave Her to Heaven
Fox 1945. Prod: William A. Bacher. Dir: John M. Stahl. Scr: Jo Swerling, from the Ben Ames Williams novel. Ph: Leon Shamroy. Cast: Gene Tierney, Cornell Wilde, Jeanne Crain, Vincent Price.

Lemon Drop Kid, The
Par 1951. Prod: Robert L. Welch. Dir: Sidney Lanfield. Scr: Ed Hartmann, R. O'Brien, Frank Tashlin, from a Damon Runyon story. Cast: Bob Hope, Marilyn Maxwell.

Let There Be Light
United States Army Pictorial Services 1945. Dir / Scr: John Huston. Ph: Stanley Cortez, John Doran, Lloyd Fromm, Joseph Jackman, George Smith (all uncredited). [Documentary]

Little Women
RKO 1933. Prod: Merian C. Cooper. Dir: George Cukor. Scr: Sarah Y. Mason, from the Louisa May Alcott novel. Cast: Katharine Hepburn, Paul Lukas, Edna May Oliver, Frances Dee, Jean Parker.

Locket, The
RKO 1946. Prod: Bert Granet. Dir: John Brahm. Scr: Sheridan Gibney. Ph: Nicholas Musuraca. Cast: Laraine Day, Robert Mitchum, Brian Aherne, Gene Raymond.

Lodger, The
Fox 1944. Prod: Robert Bassler. Dir: John Brahm. Scr: Barré Lyndon, from a Marie Belloc Lowndes novel. Ph: Lucien Ballard. Cast: Merle Oberon, Laird Cregar, George Sanders.

Long Goodbye, The
UA 1973. Prod: Jerry Bick. Dir: Robert Altman. Scr: Leigh Brackett, from the Raymond Chandler novel. Ph: Vilmos Zsigmond. Cast: Elliott Gould, Sterling Hayden, Mark Rydell, Nina Van Pallandt.

Lost Weekend, The
Par 1945. Prod: Charles Brackett. Dir: Billy Wilder. Scr: Charles Brackett, Billy Wilder, from the Charles Jackson novel. Ph: John F. Seitz. Cast: Ray Milland, Jane Wyman, Howard da Silva, Doris Dowling, Phillip Terry.

Loups chassent la nuit, Les
(France) 1951. Dir: Bernard Borderie. Scr: Bernard Borderie, Francis Thuret.

Love Affair
RKO 1939. Prod / Dir: Leo McCarey. Scr: Delmer Daves, Donald Ogden Stewart. Cast: Charles Boyer, Irene Dunne.

Love Letters
Par 1945. Prod: Hal B. Wallis. Dir: William Dieterle. Scr: Ayn Rand. Ph: Lee Garmes. Cast: Jennifer Jones, Joseph Cotten, Anita Louise.

M
(Germany) 1931. Dir: Fritz Lang. Scr: Thea von Harbou.

M
Col 1951. Prod: Semour Nebenzahl. Dir: Joseph Losey. Scr: Norman Reilly Raine, Leo Katcher, Waldo Salt. Ph: Ernest Laszlo. Cast: David Wayne, Howard da Silva, Luther Adler, Martin Gabel.

Macao
RKO 1952. Prod: Alex Gottlieb. Dir: Josef von Sternberg (additional dir: Nicholas Ray). Scr: Bernard C. Schoenfeld, Stanley Rubin. Ph: Harry J. Wild. Cast: Robert Mitchum, Jane Russell, Gloria Grahame, William Bendix, Thomas Gomez.

Macbeth
Rep 1948. Prod / Dir / Scr: Orson Welles. Ph: John L. Russell. Cast: Orson Welles, Jeanette Nolan, Dan O'Herlihy.

Magnificent Ambersons, The
RKO 1942. Prod / Dir / Scr: Orson Welles. Cast: Joseph Cotten, Dolores Del Rio, Tim Holt.

Magnum Force
WB 1973. Prod: Robert Daley. Dir: Ted Post. Scr: John Milius, Michael Cimino. Ph: Frank Stanley. Cast: Clint Eastwood, Hal Holbrook, Mitch Ryan, David Soul, Tim Matheson.

Maltese Falcon, The
WB 1941. Prod: Hal B. Wallis. Dir: John Huston. Scr: John Huston, from the Dashiell Hammett novel. Ph: Athur Edeson. Cast: Humphrey Bogart, Mary Astor, Gladys George, Peter Lorre, Sydney Greenstreet, Ward Bond, Barton MacLane, Elisha Cook Jr., Jerome Cowan.

Man Hunt
Fox 1941. Prod: Kenneth Macgowan. Dir: Fritz Lang. Scr: Dudley Nichols, from the Geoffrey Household novel *Rogue Male*. Ph: Arthur Miller. Cast: Walter Pidgeon, Joan Bennett, George Sanders, John Carradine.

Manèges
(France) 1949. Dir: Yves Allégret. Scr: Jacques Sigurd.

Manhandled
Par 1949. Prod: William Pine, William Thomas. Dir: Lewis R. Foster, Scr: Lewis R. Foster, Whitman Chambers, from an L..S. Goldsmith story. Ph: Ernest Laszlo. Cast: Dorothy Lamour, Dan Duryea, Sterling Hayden.

Marie Antoinette
MGM 1938. Prod: Hunt Stromberg. Dir: W.S. Van Dyke. Scr: Donald Ogden Stewart, Ernest Vajda, Claudine West, fron the Stefan Zweig biography. Cast: Norma Shearer, Tyrone Power, Robert Morley, John Barrymore.

Marie du port, La
(France) 1949. Dir: Marcel Carné. Scr: Louis Chavance, Marcel Carné, from the Georges Simenon novel.

Marked Woman
WB 1937. Prod: Hal B. Wallis. Dir: Lloyd Bacon. Scr: Robert Rossen, Abem Finkel. Cast: Bette Davis, Humphrey Bogart, Lola Lane, Eduardo Clannelli.

Martin Roumagnac
(France) 1945. Dir: Georges Lacombe. Scr: P.H. Wolf.

Mask of Dimitrios, The
WB 1944. Prod: Henry Blanke. Dir: Jean Negulesco. Scr: Frank Gruber, from the Eric Ambler novel. Ph: Arthur Edeson. Cast: Peter Lorre, Sydney Greenstreet, Zachary Scott, Faye Emerson, Victor Francen.

Massacre en dentelles
(France) 1951. Dir: André Hunebelle. Scr: Michel Audiard.

Méfiez-vous des blondes
(France) 1950. Dir: André Hunebelle. Scr: Michel Audiard.

Men, The
UA 1950. Prod: Stanley Kramer. Dir: Fred Zinnemann. Scr: Carl Foreman. Ph: Robert De Grasse. Cast: Marlon Brando, Teresa Wright, Everett Sloane, Jack Webb.

Merrily We Live
MGM 1938. Prod: Hal Roach. Dir: Norman Z. MacLeod. Scr: Jack Jevne, Eddie Moran. Cast: Constance Bennett, Brian Aherne.

Mildred Pierce
WB 1945. Prod: Jerry Wald. Dir: Michael Curtiz. Scr: Ronald MacDougall, Catherine Turney, from the James M. Cain novel. Ph: Ernest Haller. Cast: Joan Crawford, Jack Carson, Zachary Scott, Eve Arden, Ann Blyth, Bruce Bennett, Lee Patrick.

Mine Own Executioner
Fox / London Film Productions (UK) 1947. Prod / Dir: Anthony Kimmins. Scr: Nigel Balchin, from his novel. Ph: Wilkie Cooper. Cast: Burgess Meredith, Dulcie Gray, Kieron Moore.

Ministry of Fear
Par 1944. Prod: Seton I. Miller. Dir: Fritz Lang. Scr: Seton I. Miller, from the Graham Greene novel. Ph: Henry Sharp. Cast: Ray Milland, Marjorie Reynlds, Carl Esmond.

Minne, l'ingénue libertine, L'
(France) 1950. Dir: Jacqueline Audry. Scr: Pierre Laroche, from the Colette novel.

Mirage
Univ 1965. Prod: Harry Keller. Dir: Edward Dmytryk. Scr: Howard Fast, Peter Stone. Ph: Joseph MacDonald. Cast: Gregory Peck, Diane Baker, Walter Matthau.

Miroir, Le
(France) 1946. Dir: Raymond Lamy. Scr: Carlo Rim, Paul Olivier.

Mission à Tanger
(France) 1949. Dir: André Hunebelle. Scr: Michel Audiard.

Mob, The
Col 1951. Prod: Jerry Bresler. Dir: Robert Parrish. Scr: William Bowers, from the Ferguson Findley novel *Waterfront*. Ph: Joseph Walker. Cast: Broderick Crawford, Ernest Borgnine, Betty Buehler, Richard Kiley.

Mollenard
(France) 1938. Dir: Robert Siodmak. Scr: Oscar Paul Gilbert, Charles Spaak.

Môme vert-de-gris, La
(France) 1952. Dir: Bernard Borderie. Scr: J. Berland, from a Peter Cheyney novel.

Monsieur Verdoux
UA 1947. Prod / Dir: Charles Chaplin. Scr: Charles Chaplin, from an Orson Welles idea. Ph: Roland Totheroh. Cast: Charles Chaplin, Mady Correll, Martha Raye, Isobell Elsom.

Moonrise
Rep 1948. Prod: Charles Haas. Dir: Frank Borzage. Scr: Charles Haas, from a Theodore Strauss novel. Ph: John L. Russell. Cast: Dane Clark, Gail Russell, Ethel Barrymore.

Most Dangerous Game, The
RKO 1932. Prod: Merian C. Cooper. Dir: Ernest B. Schoedsack, Irving Pichel. Scr: James Creelman, from a Richard Connell story. Cast: Joel McCrea, Fay Wray, Robert Armstrong, Leslie Banks.

Moulin Rouge
UA 1953. Prod / Dir: John Huston. Scr: Anthony Veiller, John Huston, from the Pierre La Mure book. Cast: José Ferrer, Colette Marchand.

Mr. District Attorney
Rep 1941. Prod: Leonard Fields. Dir: William Morgan. Scr: Malcolm Stuart Boylan, Karl Brown, Phillips H. Lord, from the latter's radio series. Ph: Reggie Lanning. Cast: Peter Lorre, Helen Brown, Dennis O'Keefe, Joan Blair.

Mr. Lucky
RKO 1943. Prod: David Hempstead. Dir: H.C. Potter. Scr: Milton Holmes, Adrian Scott. Cast: Cary Grant, Laraine Day, Charles Bickford.

Murder, He Says
Par 1945. Prod: E.D. Leshin. Dir: George Marshall. Scr: Lou Breslow, from a Jack Moffitt story. Ph: Theodor Sparkuhl. Cast: Fred MacMurray, Helen Walker, Marjorie Main.

Murder, My Sweet
RKO 1944. Prod: Adrian Scott. Dir: Edward Dmytryk. Scr: John Paxton, from the Raymond Chandler novel *Farewell, My Lovely*. Ph: Harry J. Wild. Cast: Dick Powell, Claire Trevor, Ann Shirley, Otto Kruger, Mike Mazurki.

Mutiny
UA 1952. Prod: King Bros. Dir: Edward Dmytryk. Scr: Philip Yordan, Sidney Harmon. Cast: Mark Stevens, Angela Lansbury, Patric Knowles.

My Favorite Brunette
Par 1947. Prod: Daniel Dare. Dir: Elliott Nugent. Scr: Edmund Beloin, Jack Rose. Cast: Bob Hope, Dorothy Lamour, Peter Lorre, Lon Chaney Jr.

My Man Godfrey
Univ 1936. Prod / Dir: Gregory La Cava. Scr: Morrie Ryskind, Eric Hatch. Cast: Carole Lombard, William Powell.

Mystery Street
MGM 1950. Prod: Frank E. Taylor. Dir: John Sturges. Scr: Sydney Boehm, Richard Brooks, from a Leonard Spigelgass story. Ph: John Alton. Cast: Ricardo Montalban, Sally Forest, Bruce Bennett, Jan Sterling.

Naked City
Univ 1948. Prod: Mark Hellinger. Dir: Jules Dassin. Scr: Albert Maltz, Melvin Wald, from the latter's novel. Ph: William Daniels. Cast: Barry Fitzgerald, Howard Duff, Dorothy Hart, Don Taylor, Ted de Corsia.

Narrow Margin, The
RKO 1952. Prod: Stanley Rubin. Dir: Richard Fleischer. Scr: Earl Felton, Martin Goldsmith, Jack Leonard. Ph: George E. Diskant. Cast: Charles McGraw, Marie Windsor, Jacqueline White.

Niagara
Fox 1952. Prod: Charles Brackett. Dir: Henry Hathaway. Scr: Charles Brackett, Walter Reisch, Richard Breen. Cast: Marilyn Monroe, Joseph Cotten, Jean Peters, Casey Adama, Dennis O'Dea.

Night and the City
Fox 1950. Prod: Samuel G. Engel. Dir: Jules Dassin. Scr: Jo Eisinger, from a Gerald Kersch novel. Ph: Max Greene. Cast: Richard Widmark, Gene Tierney, Googie Withers, Hugh Marlowe, Francis Sullivan.

Night Club Scandal
Par 1937. Prod / Dir: Ralph Murphy. Scr: Lillie Hayward, from a Daniel Nathan Rubin play. Cast: John Barrymore, Lynne Overman, Charles Bickford.

Night Must Fall
MGM 1937. Prod: Hunt Stromberg. Dir: Richard Thorpe. Scr: John Van Druten, from an Emlyn Williams play. Cast: Robert Montgomery, Rosalind Russell, Dame May Whitty.

Nightmare Alley
Fox 1947. Prod: George Jessel. Dir: Edmund Goulding. Scr: Jules Furthman, from the William Lindsay Gresham novel. Ph: Lee Garmes. Cast: Tyrone Power, Joan Blondell, Coleen Gray, Helen Walker.

No Orchids for Miss Blandish
USA Film Alliance / Renown Pictures Corp (UK) 1948. Prod: George Minter. Dir: St John Legh Clowes. Scr: St John Legh Clowes, from the James Hadley Chase novel. Ph: Gerald Gibbs. Cast: Jack La Rue, Hugh McDermott, Linden Travers.

No Way Out
Fox 1950. Prod: Darryl F. Zanuck. Dir: Joseph L. Mankiewicz. Scr: Joseph L. Mankiewicz, Lesser Samuels. Ph: Milton Krasner. Cast: Richard Widmark, Linda Darnell, Sidney Poitier, Stephen McNally.

Nocturne
RKO 1946. Prod: Joan Harrison, Jack J. Gross. Dir: Edwin L. Marin. Scr: Jonathan Latimer, Joan Harrison. Ph: Harry J. Wild. Cast: George Raft, Lynn Bari, Virginia Huston, Joseph Pevney.

None But the Lonely Heart
RKO 1944. Prod: David Hempstead. Dir: Clifford Odets. Scr: Clifford Odets, from the Richard Llewellyn novel. Cast: Cary Grant, Ethel Barrymore, June Duprez, Barry Fitzgerald.

Nosferatu, eine Symphonie des Grauens
(Germany) 1922. Dir: F.W. Murnau. Scr: Henrik Galeen, from the Bram Stoker novel *Dracula*.

Notorious
RKO 1946. Prod: Alfred Hitchcock. Dir: Alfred Hitchcock. Scr: Ben Hecht, from a Hitchcock treatment. Ph: Ted Tetzlaff. Cast: Ingrid Bergman, Cary Grant, Claude Rains, Louis Calhern, Leopoldine Konstantin, Reinhold Schünzel.

Nuit fantastique, La
(France) 1942. Dir: Marcel L'Herbier. Scr: Louis Chavance, Maurice Henry,

Obsession
(France) 1954. Dir: Jean Delannoy. Scr: R. Laudenbach, A. Blondin, Jean Delannoy, from a William Irish novel.

Obsession
Eagle-Lion / Independent Sovereign Films (UK) 1949. Prod: Nat A. Bronsten. Dir: Edward Dmytryk. Scr: Alex Coppell, from his novel *A Man About a Dog*. Ph: C.M. Pennington-Richards. Cast: Robert Newton, Sally Gray, Phil Brown, Naunton Wayne.

Of Mice and Men
UA 1939. Prod: Hal Roach. Dir: Lewis Milestone. Scr: Eugene Sollow, from the John Steinbeck novel. Cast: Burgess Meredith, Lon Chaney Jr., Betty Field, Charles Bickford.

Olivia
(France) 1950. Dir: Jacqueline Audry. Scr: Pierre Laroche.

Olvidados, Los
(Mexico) 1950. Dir: Luis Buñuel. Scr: Luis Buñuel, Luis Alcoriza.

On Dangerous Ground
RKO 1951. Prod: John Houseman. Dir: Nicholas Ray. Scr: Nicholas Ray, A.I. Bezzerides, from the Gerald Butler novel *Mad with Much Heart*. Ph: George E. Diskant. Cast: Ida Lupino, Robert Ryan, Ward Bond, Charles Kemper.

On the Waterfront
Col 1954. Prod: Sam Spiegel. Dir: Elia Kazan. Scr: Budd Schulberg, from Malcolm Johnson's newspaper articles. Ph: Boris Kaufman. Cast: Marlon Brando, Eva Marie Saint, Karl Malden, Lee J. Cobb, Rod Steiger.

One Way Passage
WB 1932. Prod: Hal B. Wallis, Robert Lord. Dir: Tay Garnett. Scr: Joseph Jackson, Wilson Mizner, from a Robert Lord story. Cast: William Powell, Kay Francis, Frank McHugh.

One Way Street
Univ 1950. Prod: Leonard Goldstein. Dir: Hugo Fregonese. Scr: Lawrence Kimble. Ph: Maury Gertsman. Cast: James Mason, Marta Toren, Dan Duryea, William Conrad.

Only Angels Have Wings
Col 1939. Prod / Dir: Howard Hawks. Scr: Jules Furthman, Howard Hawks. Cast: Cary Grant, Jean Arthur, Richard Barthelmess.

Ossessione
(Italy) 1942. Dir: Luchino Visconti. Scr: Mario Alicati, Antonio Pietrangeli, Gianni Puccini, Giuseppe de Santis, Luchino Visconti, from the James M. Cain novel *The Postman Always Rings Twice*.

Our Town
UA 1940. Prod: Sol Lesser. Dir: Sam Wood. Scr: Frank Craven, Harry Chandler, Thornton Wilder, from the latter's play. Cast: Thomas Mitchell, Martha Scott, William Holden.

Out of the Past
RKO 1947. Prod: Warren Duff, Robert Sparks. Dir: Jacques Tourneur. Scr: Geoffrey Homes, from his novel *Build My Gallows High*. Ph: Nicholas Musuraca. Cast: Robert Mitchum, Jane Greer, Kirk Douglas, Rhonda Fleming, Steve Brodie.

Outlaw, The
UA 1941. Prod / Dir: Howard Hughes. Scr: Jules Furthman. Cast: Jane Russell, Jack Buetel, Thomas Mitchell, Walter Huston.

P.J.
Univ 1968. Prod: Edward Montagne. Dir: John Guillermin. Scr: Philip H. Reisman Jr., from an Edward Montagne story. Ph: Loyal Griggs. Cast: George Peppard, Gail Hunnicutt, Raymond Burr.

Panic in the Streets
Fox 1950. Prod: Sol C. Siegel. Dir: Elia Kazan. Scr: Richard Murphy, Daniel Fuchs. Ph: Joe MacDonald. Cast: Richard Widmark, Paul Douglas, Barbara Bel Geddes, Jack Palance.

Paradine Case, The
Selznick International 1947. Prod: David O. Selznick. Dir: Alfred Hitchcock. Scr: David O. Selznick, Alma Reville, from the Robert Hichens novel. Ph: Lee Garmes. Cast: Gregory Peck, Ann Todd, Charles Laughton, Ethel Barrymore. Charles Coburn, Louis Jourdan, Alida Valli.

Pas de coup dur pour Johnny
(France) 1954. Dir: Emile Roussel. Scr: Jacques Berland.

Pas de whisky pour Callaghan
(France) 1955. Dir: Willy Rozier. Scr: Xavier Vallier, from a Peter Cheyney novel.

Passion de Jeanne d'Arc, La
(France) 1928. Dir: Carl Dreyer. Scr: Carl Dreyer, Antonin Artaud.

Peking Express
Par 1951. Prod: Hal B. Wallis. Dir: William Dieterle. Scr: H. Harvey, J. Meredith Lucas, J. Furthman. Cast: Joseph Cotten, Corinne Calvet, Edmund Gwen, Marvin Miller.

Pépé le Moko
(France) 1937. Dir: Julien Duvivier. Scr: Ashelbé, Julien Duvivier, Henri Jeanson.

Pépées font la loi, Les
(France) 1955. Dir: Raoul André. Scr: Raymond Caillava.

Personal Property
MGM 1937. Prod: John W. Considine Jr. Dir: W.S. Van Dyke. Scr: Hugh Mills, Ernest Vajda. Cast: Robert Taylor, Jean Harlow.

Peter Ibbetson
Par 1935. Prod: Louis D. Lighton. Dir: Henry Hathaway. Scr: Waldemar Young, Constance Collier, Vincent Lawrence, from the George du Maurier novel. Cast: Gary Cooper, Ann Harding, John Halliday, Ida Lupino.

Phantom Lady
Univ 1944. Prod: Joan Harrison. Dir: Robert Siodmak. Scr: Bernard C. Schoenfeld, from the William Irish novel. Ph: Woody Bredell. Cast: Franchot Tone, Ella Raines, Alan Curtis, Thomas Gomez, Elisha Cook Jr.

Pickup
Col 1951. Prod / Dir: Hugo Haas. Scr: Hugo Haas, Arnold Philips, from the Joseph Kopta novel *Watchman 47*. Ph: Paul Ivano. Cast: Hugo Haas, Allan Nixon, Beverly Michaels.

Pièges
(France) 1939. Dir: Robert Siodmak. Scr: Ernest Neuville, Jacques Companéez.

Point Blank
MGM 1967. Prod: Judd Bernard, Robert Chartoff. Dir: John Boorman. Scr: Alexander Jacobs, David & Rafe Newhouse, from the Richard Stark novel *The Hunter*. Ph: Philip H. Lathrop. Cast: Lee Marvin, Angie Dickinson, Keenan Wynn, John Vernon, Sharon Acker, Carroll O'Connor.

Port of New York
Eagle-Lion 1949. Prod: Aubrey Schenck. Dir: László Benedek. Scr: Eugene Ling, from an Arthur Ross & Bert Murray story. Phot: George E. Diskant. Cast: Scott Brady, Richard Rober, K.T. Stevens, Yul Brynner, Lynn Carter.

Possessed
WB 1947. Prod: Jerry Wald. Dir: Curtis Bernhardt. Scr: Silvia Richards, Ranald MacDougall, Lawrence Menkin, from a Rita Weiman story. Ph: Sid Hickox. Cast: Joan Crawford, Van Heflin, Raymond Massey, Geraldine Brooks.

Postman Always Rings Twice, The
MGM 1946. Prod: Carey Wilson. Dir: Tay Garnett. Scr: Harry Ruskin, Niven Busch, from the James M. Cain novel. Ph: Sidney Wagner. Cast: John Garfield, Lana Turner, Cecil Kellaway, Hume Cronyn, Leon Ames, Audrey Totter, Alan Reed.

Processo contro ignoto
(Italy) 1954. Dir: Guido Brignone. Scr: Loffredo, Guido Brignone.

Prowler, The
UA 1951. Prod: S.P. Eagle. Dir: Joseph Losey. Scr: Hugo Butler. Ph: Arthur Miller. Cast: Van Heflin, Evelyn Keyes, J. Maxwell.

Puritain, Le
(France) 1938. Dir: Jef Musso. Scr: Jef Musso, from a Liam O'Flaherty novel.

Pursued
WB 1947. Prod: Milton Sperling. Dir: Raoul Walsh. Scr: Niven Busch. Cast: Robert Mitchum, Teresa Wright.

Quai des brumes, Le
(France) 1938. Dir: Marcel Carné. Scr: Jacques Prévert, from the Pierre Mac Orlan novel.

Quai des Orfèvres
(France) 1947. Dir: H.-G. Clouzot. Scr: H.-G. Clouzot, from the S.H. Steeman novel.

Quo Vadis
MGM 1951. Prod: Sam Zimbalist. Dir: Mervyn LeRoy. Scr: John Lee Mahin, S.N. Berman, Sonya Levien. Cast: Robert Taylor, Deborah Kerr, Leo Genn, Peter Ustinov.

Racket, The
RKO 1951. Prod: Edmund Grainger. Dir: John Cromwell. Scr: William Wister Haines, W.R. Burnett, from a Bartlett Cormack play. Ph: George E. Diskant. Cast: Robert Ryan, Robert Mitchum, Lizabeth Scott, William Talman.

Rage in Heaven
MGM 1941. Prod: Gottfried Reinhardt. Dir: W.S. Van Dyke, Richard Thorpe (uncredited). Scr: Christopher Isherwood, Robert Thoeren. Cast: Robert Montgomery, Ingrid Bergman, George Sanders.

Raw Deal
Eagle-Lion 1948. Prod: Edward Small. Dir: Anthony Mann. Scr: Leopold Atlas, John C. Higgins. Ph: John Alton. Cast: Dennis O'Keefe, Claire Trevor, John Ireland, Marsha Hunt, Raymond Burr.

Rawhide
Fox 1951. Prod: Samuel G. Engel. Dir: Henry Hathaway. Scr: Dudley Nichols. Cast: Tyrone Power, Susan Hayward, Hugh Marlowe, George Tobias, Dean Jagger.

Razzia sur la chnouf
(France) 1955. Dir: Henri Decoin. Scr: Henri Decoin, Maurice Griffe, Auguste Le Breton, from the latter's novel.

Rebecca
UA 1940. Prod: David O. Selznick. Dir: Alfred Hitchcock. Scr: Robert E. Sherwood, Joan Harrison, from the Daphne du Maurier novel. Ph: George Barnes. Cast: Laurence Olivier, Joan Fontaine, George Sanders.

Red House, The
UA 1947. Prod: Sol Lesser. Dir: Delmer Daves. Scr: Delmer Daves, Albert Maltz (uncredited), from the G.A. Chamberlain novel. Ph: Bert Glennon. Cast: Edward G. Robinson, Lon McCallister, Rory Calhoun, Allene Roberts, Judith Anderson.

Red Light
UA 1949. Prod / Dir: Roy Del Ruth. Scr: George Callahan, Charles Grayson. Ph: Bert Glennon. Cast: George Raft, Virginia Mayo, Gene Lockhart, Raymond Burr.

Remorques
(France) 1939. Dir: Jean Grémillon. Scr: Jacques Prévert, from the Roger Vercel novel.

Ride the Pink Horse
Univ 1947. Prod: Joan Harrison. Dir: Robert Montgomery. Scr: Ben Hecht, Charles Lederer, from the Dorothy B. Hughes novel. Ph: Russell Metty. Cast: Robert Montgomery, Wanda Hendrix, Thomas Gomez, Fred Clark, Art Smith.

Riffraff
MGM 1936. Prod: Irving Thalberg (uncredited). Dir: J. Walter Ruben. Scr: H.W. Hanemann, Anita Loos. Cast: Jean Harlow, Spencer Tracy, Una Merkel, Joseph Calleia.

Ring, The
British International Pictures 1927. Prod: John Maxwell. Dir: Alfred Hitchcock. Scr: Frank Mills, Alma Reville. Cast: Carl Brisson, Lillian Hall-Davies, Ian Hunter.

Rizo amaro
(Italy) 1949. Dir: Giuseppe de Santis. Scr: G. De Santis, C. Alvaro, C. Lizzani, C. Musso, I. Perilli, G. Puccini.

Roman Holiday
Par 1953. Prod / Dir: William Wyler. Scr: John Dighton, Ian McLellan Hunter (front for Dalton Trumbo). Cast: Gregory Peck, Audrey Hepburn, Eddie Albert.

Rope of Sand
Par 1949. Prod: Hal B. Wallis, Dir: William Dieterle. Scr: Walter Doniger, John Paxton. Ph: Charles Lang. Cast: Burt Lancaster, Paul Henreid, Claude Rains, Peter Lorre, Corinne Calvet, Sam Jaffe.

Rope
WB / Transatlantic Pictures (UK) 1948. Prod: Sidney Bernstein, Alfred Hitchock. Dir: Alfred Hitchcock. Scr: Arthur Laurents, Hume Cronyn, from the Patrick Hamilton play. Ph: Joseph Valentine, William V. Skall. Cast: James Stewart, Farley Granger, John Dall, Joan Chandler.

Royal Scandal, A
Fox 1945. Prod: Ernst Lubitsch. Dir: Ernst Lubitsch, Otto Preminger. Scr: Edwin Justus Mayer, Bruno Frank. Cast: Tallulah Bankhead, William Eythe, Charles Coburn.

Sabotage
Gaumont British 1936. Prod: Michael Balcon. Dir: Alfred Hitchcock. Scr: Charles Bennett, from the Joseph Conrad novel *The Secret Agent*. Cast: Silvia Sidney, Oscar Homolka, Desmond Tester, John Loder.

Saboteur
Univ 1942. Prod: Frank Lloyd, Jack H. Skirball. Dir: Alfred Hitchcock. Scr: Peter Viertel, Joan Harrison, Dorothy Parker, from a Hitchcock treatment. Ph: Joseph Valentine. Cast: Robert Cummings, Priscilla Lane, Otto Kruger.

Salaire de la peur, Le
(France) 1953. Dir: H.-G. Clouzot. Scr: H.-G. Clouzot, from the Georges Arnaud novel.

Salauds vont en enfer, Les
(France) 1955. Dir: Robert Hossein. Scr: René Wheeler, Robert Hossein.

San Francisco
MGM 1936. Prod: John Emerson, Bernard H. Hyman. Dir: W.S. Van Dyke. Scr: Anita Loos, from a Robert Hopkins story. Cast: Clark Gable, Spencer Tracy, Jeanette MacDonald.

Sang des bêtes, Le
(France) 1949. Dir / Scr: Georges Franju. [Short]

Scandal Sheet
Col 1952. Prod: Edward Small. Dir: Phil Karlson. Scr: Ted Sherdeman, Eugene Ling, James Poe from the Samuel Fuller novel *The Dark Page*. Ph: Burnett Guffrey. Cast: Broderick Crawford, Rosemary DeCamp, John Derek, Henry O'Neill.

Scarface
UA 1932. Prod: Howard Hughes, Howard Hawks. Dir: Howard Hawks. Scr: Ben Hecht, from the Ermitage Trail novel. Cast: Paul Muni, George Raft, Ann Dvorak, Vince Barnett, Karen Morley.

Scarlet Street
Univ 1945. Prod / Dir: Fritz Lang. Scr: Dudley Nichols, from the Georges de la Fouchardière novel *La Chienne*. Ph: Milton Krasner. Cast: Edward G. Robinson, Joan Bennett, Dan Duryea.

Second Woman, The
UA 1950. Prod: Mort Briskin, Robert Smith. Dir: James V. Kern. Scr: Mort Briskin, Robert Smith. Ph: Hal Mohr. Cast: Robert Young, Betsy Drake, John Sutton.

Secret Beyond the Door, The
Univ 1948. Prod / Dir: Fritz Lang. Scr: Silvia Richards, from a Rufus King novel. Ph: Stanley Cortez. Cast: Joan Bennett, Michael Redgrave, Anne Revere, Barbara O'Neil.

Senza pietà
(Italy) 1948. Dir: Alberto Lattuada. Scr: F. Fellini, A. Lattuada, T. Pinelli.

Sergeant York
WB 1941. Prod: Howard Hawks, Jesse L. Lasky, Hal B. Wallis. Dir: Howard Hawks. Scr: Abem Finkel, Harry Chandler, Howard Koch, John Huston. Cast: Gary Cooper, Walter Brennan.

Série noire
(France) 1955. Dir: Pierre Foucaud. Scr: René Gaspard-Huit.

Serpico
Par 1973. Prod: Martin Bregman. Dir: Sidney Lumet. Scr: Waldo Salt, Norman Wexler, from the Peter Maas book. Ph: Arthur J. Ornitz. Cast: Al Pacino, John Randolph, Jack Kehoe, Biff McGuire.

Set-Up, The
RKO 1949. Prod: Richard Goldstone. Dir: Robert Wise. Scr: Art Cohn, from a Joseph Moncure March poem. Ph: Milton Krasner. Cast: Robert Ryan, Audrey Totter, George Tobias, Alan Baxter.

Shadow of a Doubt
Univ 1943. Prod: Jack H. Skirball. Dir: Alfred Hitchcock. Scr: Thornton Wilder, Alma Reville, Salley Benson, from a Gordon McDonnell story. Ph: Joseph Valentine. Scr: Joseph Cotten, Teresa Wright, MacDonald Carey, Patricia Collinge, Henry Travers, Hume Cronyn.

Shanghai Express
Par 1932. Prod: Adolph Zukor. Dir: Josef von Sternberg. Scr: Jules Furthman. Cast: Marlene Dietrich, Clive Brook, Anna May Wong, Warner Oland.

Shanghai Gesture, The
UA 1941. Prod: Arnold Pressburger. Dir: Josef von Sternberg. Scr: Josef von Sternberg, Karl Vollmöller, Geza Herczeg, Jules Furthman, from the John Colton play. Ph: Paul Ivano. Cast: Gene Tierney, Ona Munson, Walter Huston, Victor Mature, Phyllis Brooks, Marcel Dalio.

She Defends Her Country
(USSR) 1943. Dir: Friedrich Ermler. Scr: Mikhail Bleiman, I. Blondin.

She Knew All the Answers
Col 1941. Prod: Charles R. Rogers. Dir: Richard Wallace. Scr: Kenneth Earl, Curtis Kenyon, Harry Segall. Cast: Luis Alberni, Eve Arden, Roscoe Ates, Don Beddoe.

Shoot First
UA 1953. Prod: Raymond Stross. Dir: Robert Parrish. Scr: Eric Ambler, from the Geoffrey Household novel *A Rough Shoot*. Ph: Stanley Parey. Cast: Joel McCrea, Laurence Naismith, Evelyn Keyes, Marius Goring.

Side Street
MGM 1950. Prod: Sam Zimbalist. Dir: Anthony Mann. Scr: Sydney Boehm. Ph: Joseph Ruttenberg. Cast: Farley Granger, Cathy O'Donnell, James Craig, Paul Kelly, Jean Hagen.

Sign of the Ram, The
Col 1947. Prod: Irving Cummings Jr. Dir: John Sturges. Scr: Charles Bennett, from a Margaret Ferguson novel. Cast: Susan Peters, Alexander Knox, Phyllis Thaxter, Allene Roberts.

Singin' in the Rain
MGM 1952. Prod: Arthur Freed. Dir: Gene Kelly, Stanley Donen. Scr: Betty Comden, Adolph Green, from their own story. Cast: Gene Kelly, Debbie Reynolds, Donald O'Connor, Jean Hagen, Cyd Charisse.

Singoalla
(France / Sweden) 1949. Dir: Christian-Jaque. Scr: Pierre Véry, Christian-Jaque.

Sinner Take All
MGM 1937. Prod: Lucien Hubbard, Samuel Marx. Dir: Errol Taggart. Scr: Leonard Lee, Walter Wise. Cast: Bruce Cabot, Margaret Lindsay, Joseph Calleia.

Slap Happy Lion
MGM 1947. Dir: Tex Avery. [Cartoon]

Sleep, My Love
UA 1948. Prod: Charles Buddy Rogers, Ralph Cohn. Dir: Douglas Sirk. Scr: St Clair McKelway, Leo Rosten. Ph: Joseph Valentine. Cast: Claudette Colbert, Robert Cummings, Don Ameche, Hazel Brooks.

Snake Pit, The
Fox 1948. Prod: Anatole Litvak, Robert Bassler. Dir: Anatole Litvak. Scr: Frank Partos, Millen Brand, from the Mary Jane Ward novel. Ph: Leo Tover. Cast: Olivia de Havilland, Mark Stevens, Leo Genn, Celeste Holm.

Sniper, The
Col 1952. Prod: Stanley Kramer. Dir: Edward Dmytryk. Scr: Harry Brown from an Edward and Edna Anhalt story. Ph: Burnett Guffey. Cast: Arthur Franz, Adolphe Menjou, Marie Windsor, Gerald Mohr, Frank Faylen.

So Evil My Love
Par 1948. Prod: Hal B. Wallis. Dir: Lewis Allen. Scr: Leonard Spiegelgass, Ronald Millar, from a Joseph Shearing novel. Ph: Max Greene. Cast: Ray Milland, Ann Todd, Geraldine Fitzgerald, Leo G. Carroll.

Somewhere in the Night
Fox 1946. Prod: Anderson Lawler. Dir: Joseph L. Mankiewicz. Scr: Joseph L. Mankiewicz, Howard Dimsdale, Lee Strasberg, from the Marvin Borowsky novel *The Lonely Journey*. Ph: Norbert Brodine. Cast: John Hodiak, Nancy Guild, Lloyd Nolan, Richard Conte, Josephine Hutchinson.

Song of the Thin Man
MGM 1947. Prod: Nat Perrin. Dir: Edward Buzzell. Scr: Steve Fisher, Nat Perrin, Stanley Roberts. Ph: Charles Rosher. Cast: William Powell, Myrna Loy, Keenan Wynn, Dean Stockwell.

Sorry, Wrong Number
Par 1948. Prod: Hal B. Wallis, Anatole Litvak. Dir: Anatole Litvak. Scr: Lucille Fletcher, from her radio play. Ph: Sol Polito. Cast: Barbara Stanwyck, Burt Lancaster, Ann Richards, Wendell Corey, Harold Vermilyea.

Sound of Fury, The
UA 1950. Prod: Robert Stillman. Dir: Cy Endfield. Scr: Jo Pagano, Cy Endfield (uncredited). Ph: Guy Roe. Cast: Frank Lovejoy, Lloyd Bridges, Kathleen Ryan, Richard Carlson.

Sous le ciel de Paris
(France) 1951. Dir: Julien Duvivier. Scr: J. Duvivier, René Lefèvre.

Southerner, The
Loew 1945. Prod: Robert Hakim. Dir: Jean Renoir. Scr: Hugo Butler, from the G.S. Perry novel *Hold Autumn in Your Hands*. Cast: Zachary Scott, Betty Field, Beulah Bindi, J. Carroll Naish.

Soylent Green
MGM 1973. Prod: Walter Seltzer, Russell Thacher. Dir: Richard Fleischer. Scr: Stanley R. Greenberg, Harry Harrison, from the latter's novel *Make Room! Make Room!* Ph: Richard H. Kline. Cast: Charlton Heston, Leigh Taylor-Young, Chuck Connors, Joseph Cotten, Edward G. Robinson.

Spellbound
UA 1945. Prod: David O. Selznick. Dir: Alfred Hitchcock. Scr: Ben Hecht, from the Francis Beeding novel *The House of Dr. Edwardes*. Ph: George Barnes. Cast: Ingrid Bergman, Gregory Peck, Jean Acker, Rhonda Fleming, Donald Curtis, John Emery, Leo G. Carroll, Norman Lloyd.

Spiral Staircase, The
RKO 1946. Prod: Dore Schary. Dir: Robert Siodmak. Scr: Mel Dinnelli, from the Ethel Lina White novel *Some Must Watch*. Ph: Nicholas Musuraca. Cast: Dorothy McGuire, George Brent, Ethyl Barrymore, Rhonda Fleming.

Stage Fright
WB / ABPC 1950. Prod / Dir: Alfred Hitchcock. Scr: Whitfield
Cook, Alma Reville, James Bridie. Ph: Wilkie Cooper. Cast:
Marlene Dietrich, Jane Wyman, Michael Wilding, Richard Todd,
Alastair Sim, Dame Sybil Thorndike.

Stagecoach
UA 1939. Prod: Walter Wanger. Dir: John Ford. Scr: Dudley
Nichols, from an Ernest Haycox story. Cast: John Wayne, Claire
Trevor, Andy Devine, John Carradine, Thomas Mitchell, George
Bancroft.

Stalingrad
(USSR) 1943. Dir: Leonid Varlamov. [Documentary]

Steel Helmet, The
Lippert Pictures 1951. Prod / Dir / Scr: Samuel Fuller. Cast: Gene
Evans, Robert Hutton, Steve Brodie.

Stone Killer, The
Col 1973. Prod / Dir: Michael Winner. Scr: Gerald Wilson, from
the John Gardner novel *A Complete State of Death*. Ph: Richard
Moore. Cast: Charles Bronson, Martin Balsam, Jack Colvin, Paul
Koslo.

Strange Love of Martha Ivers, The
Par 1946. Prod: Hal B. Wallis. Dir: Lewis Milestone. Scr: Robert
Rossen, from a Jack Patrick story. Ph: Victor Milner. Cast: Bar-
bara Stanwyck, Van Heflin, Lizabeth Scott, Kirk Douglas, Judith
Anderson.

Stranger, The
RKO 1946. Prod: S.P. Eagle. Dir: Orson Welles. Scr: Victor Trivas,
Decla Dunning, Anthony Veiller, Orson Welles, John Huston
(last two uncredited). Phot: Russell Metty. Cast: Orson Welles,
Edward G. Robinson, Loretta Young, Richard Long.

Strangers on a Train
WB 1951. Prod / Dir: Alfred Hitchcock. Scr: Raymond Chandler, Czenzi Ormonde, from the Patricia Highsmith novel. Ph: Robert Burks. Cast: Robert Walker, Farley Granger, Ruth Roman, Leo G. Carroll, Patricia Hitchcock.

Street With No Name, The
Fox 1948. Prod: Samuel G. Engel. Dir: William Keighley. Scr: Harry Kleiner. Ph: Joe MacDonald. Cast: Mark Stevens, Richard Widmark, Lloyd Nolan, Barbara Lawrence.

Streetcar Named Desire, A
WB 1951. Prod / Dir: Elia Kazan. Scr: O. Saul, from the Tennessee Williams play. Cast: Marlon Brando, Vivien Leigh, Kim Hunter, Karl Malden.

Sudden Fear
RKO 1952. Prod: Joseph Kaufman. Dir: David Miller. Scr: Lenore J. Coffee, Robert Smith, from the Edna Sherry novel. Ph: Charles Lang. Cast: Joan Crawford, Jack Palance, Gloria Grahame, Bruce Bennett.

Sullivan's Travels
Par 1941. Prod: Paul Jones. Dir / Scr: Preston Sturges. Cast: Joel McCrea, Veronica Lake.

Sunset Boulevard
Par 1950. Prod: Charles Brackett. Dir: Billy Wilder. Scr: Charles Brackett, Billy Wilder, D.M. Marshman. Ph: John F. Seitz. Cast: Gloria Swanson, William Holden, Nancy Olson, Erich von Stroheim.

Suspect, The
Univ 1944. Prod: Islin Auster. Dir: Robert Siodmak. Scr: Bertram Millhauser, Arthur T. Horman, from the James Ronald novel *This Way Out*. Ph: Paul Ivano. Cast: Charles Laughton, Ella Raines, Molly Lamont, Stanley Ridges.

Suspense
Mono 1946. Prod: King Bros. Dir: Frank Tuttle. Scr: Philip Yordan.
Ph: Karl Struss. Cast: Belita, Barry Sullivan, Bonita Granville,
Albert Dekker.

Suspicion
RKO 1941. Prod / Dir: Alfred Hitchcock. Scr: Samson Raphaelson,
Joan Harrison, Alma Reville, from the Francis Iles novel *Before
the Fact*. Ph: Harry Stradling. Cast: Cary Grant, Joan Fontaine,
Nigel Bruce, Sir Cedric Hardwicke, Dame May Whitty.

They Gave Him a Gun
MGM 1937. Prod: Harry Rapf. Dir: W.S. Van Dyke. Scr: Cyril
Hume, Richard Maibaum, Maurice Rapf. Cast: Spencer Tracy,
Franchot Tone, Gladys George.

They Live by Night
RKO 1949. Prod: John Houseman. Dir: Nicholas Ray. Scr: Charles
Schnee, Nicholas Ray, from the Edward Anderson novel *Thieves
Like Us*. Ph: George E. Diskant. Cast: Farley Granger, Cathy
O'Donnell, Howard da Silva, Jay C. Flippen.

They Made Me a Fugitive
WB / Alliance Film Corporation (UK) 1947. Prod: Nat A.
Bronstein, James A. Carter. Dir: Alberto Cavalcanti. Scr: Noel
Langley, from the Jackson Budd novel *A Convict Has Escaped*.
Ph: Otto Heller. Cast: Sally Gray, Trevor Howard, Griffith Jones,
René Ray.

They Won't Forget
WB 1937. Prod / Dir: Mervyn LeRoy. Scr: Alan Kandel, Robert
Rossen. Cast: Claude Rains, Gloria Dickson, Edward Norris.

Thief, The
UA 1952. Prod: Harry M. Popkin, Clarence Greene. Dir: Russell
Rouse. Scr: Russell Rouse, Clarence Greene. Ph: Sam Leavitt. Cast:
Ray Milland, Martin Gabel, Harry Bronson, Rita Vale, Rita Gam.

Thieves' Highway
Fox 1949. Prod: Robert Bassler. Dir: Jules Dassin. Scr: A.I. Bezzerides, from his novel *Thieves' Market*. Ph: Norbert Brodine. Cast: Richard Conte, Valentina Cortese, Lee J. Cobb, Barbara Lawrence, Jackie Oakie.

Thin Man, The
MGM 1934. Prod: Hunt Stromberg. Dir: W.S. Van Dyke. Scr: Albert Hackett, Frances Goodrich, from the Dashiell Hammett novel. Cast: William Powell, Myrna Loy, Maureen O'Sullivan.

Thing, The
RKO 1951. Prod: Howard Hawks. Dir: Christian Nyby. Scr: Charles Lederer, from a John W. Campbell Jr. Story. Cast: Margaret Sheridan, Kenneth Tobey, Robert Cornthwaite.

Third Man, The
BIPC 1949. Prod: Alexander Korda, David O. Selznik. Dir: Carol Reed. Scr: Graham Greene, Alexander Korda, Carol Reed, Orson Welles (last two uncredited). Ph: Robert Krasker. Cast: Joseph Cotten, Orson Welles, Alida Valli, Trevor Howard.

Thirteenth Chair, The
MGM 1937. Prod / Dir: George B. Seitz. Scr: Marion Parsonnet. Cast: Dame May Whitty, Madge Evans, Lewis Stone.

Thirty-nine Steps, The
Gaumont British 1935. Prod: Michael Balcon. Dir: Alfred Hitchcock. Scr: Charles Bennett, Alma Reville, from the John Buchan novel. Cast: Madeleine Carroll, Robert Donat, Lucie Mannheim, Godfrey Tearle, Peggy Ashcroft.

This Gun for Hire
Par 1942. Prod: Richard Blumenthal. Dir: Frank Tuttle. Scr: Albert Maltz, W.R. Burnett, from the Graham Greene novel *A Gun for Sale*. Ph: John F. Seitz. Cast: Alan Ladd, Veronica Lake, Tully Marshall, Laird Cregar, Robert Preston.

Three Encounters
(USSR) 1948. Dir: Sergei Yutkevich, Vsevolod Pudovkin, Alexander Ptushko. Scr: Sergei Yermolinsky, Nikolai Pogodin, Mikhail Bleiman.

T-Men
Eagle-Lion 1947. Prod: Aubrey Schenck. Dir: Anthony Mann. Scr: James Higgins, from a Virginia Kellogg story. Ph: John Alton. Cast: Dennis O'Keefe, Mary Meade, Alfred Ryver.

To Have and Have Not
WB 1944. Prod / Dir: Howard Hawks. Scr: Jules Furthman, William Faulkner, from the Ernest Hemingway novel. Ph: Sid Hickox. Cast: Humphrey Bogart, Lauren Bacall, Walter Brennan, Dolores Moran, Hoagy Carmichael.

To the Ends of the Earth
Col 1948. Prod: Sidney Buchman. Dir: Robert Stevenson. Scr: Jay Richard Kennedy. Ph: Burnett Guffey. Cast: Dick Powell, Signe Hasso, Harry J. Anslinger, Maylia.

Tobacco Road
Fox 1941. Prod: Jack Kirkland, Harry H. Oshrin. Dir: John Ford. Scr: Nunnally Johnson, from the Erskine Caldwell novel. Cast: Charley Grapewin, Marjorie Rambeau. Elizabeth Petterson, Slim Summerville, Ward Bond.

Tokyo File 212
RKO 1951. Prod: George Breakston, Dorrell McGowan. Dir: Dorrell & Stuart McGowan. Scr: Dorrell & Stuart McGowan, George Breakston. Ph: Herman Schopp. Cast: Florence Marly, Robert Peyton, Katsuhiko Haida.

Too Late for Tears
UA 1949. Prod: Hunt Stromberg. Dir: Byron Haskin. Scr: Roy Huggins. Ph: William Mellor. Cast: Lizabeth Scott, Don DeFore, Dan Duryea, Arthur Kennedy, Kristine Miller.

Touchez pas au grisbi
(France) 1953. Dir: Jacques Becker. Scr: Jacques Becker, Maurice Griffe, Albert Simonin, from the latter's novel.

Trapped
Eagle-Lion 1949. Prod: Bryan Foy. Dir: Richard Fleischer. Scr: Earl Felton, George Zuckerman. Ph: Guy Roe. Cast: Lloyd Bridges, John Hoyt, Barbara Payton, James Todd.

Tumultes / Stürme der Leidenschaft
(France / Germany) 1932. Dir: Robert Siodmak. Scr: R. Liebmann, Hans Muller.

Turning Point, The
Par 1952. Prod: Irving Asher. Dir: William Dieterle, Fridrikh Ermler. Scr: Warren Duff, from a Horace McCoy story. Ph: Lionel Lindon. Cast: William Holden, Edmond O'Brien, Alexis Smith, Tom Tully.

Two Mrs. Carrolls, The
WB 1947. Prod: Mark Hellinger. Dir: Peter Godfrey. Scr: Robert Smith. Cast: Humphrey Bogart, Barbara Stanwyck, Alexis Smith, Nigel Bruce.

Un flic
(France) 1947. Dir: Maurice de Canonge. Scr: Jacques Campaneez, Michel Duran.

Un grand patron
(France) 1951. Dir: Yves Ciampi. Scr: Pierre Véry, Yves Ciampi.

Under Capricorn
WB / Transatlantic Pictures (UK) 1949. Prod: Sidney Bernstein, Alfred Hitchcock. Dir: Alfred Hitchcock. Scr: James Bridie, Hume Cronyn, from the Helen Simpson novel. Ph: Jack Cardiff. Cast: Ingrid Bergman, Joseph Cotten, Michael Wilding, Margaret Leighton.

Undercover Man, The
Col 1949. Prod: Robert Rossen. Dir: Joseph H. Lewis. Scr: Sydney Boehm, Jack Rubin, Melvin Wald. Ph: Burnett Guffey. Cast: Glenn Ford, Nina Foch, Barry Kelley, James Whitmore.

Undercurrent
MGM 1946. Prod: Pandro S. Berman. Dir: Vincente Minnelli. Scr: Ed Chodorov, George Oppenheimer, Marguerite Roberts, from a Thelma Strabel story. Ph: Karl Freund. Cast: Katharine Hepburn, Robert Taylor, Robert Mitchum, Edmund Gwenn.

Underworld
Par 1927. Prod: Hector Turnbull. Dir: Josef von Sternberg. Scr: Robert N. Lee, Charles Furthman, from a Ben Hecht story. Cast: George Bancroft, Clive Brook, Evelyn Brent, Larry Semon, Fred Kohler.

Une balle suffit
(France) 1954. Dir / Scr: Jean Sacha.

Une si jolie petite plage
(France 1949). Dir: Yves Allégret. Scr: Jacques Sigurd.

Unfaithfully Yours
Fox 1948. Prod / Dir / Scr: Preston Sturges. Cast: Rex Harrison, Linda Darnell.

Union Station
Par 1950. Prod: Jules Schermer. Dir: Rudolph Maté. Scr: Sydney Boehm, from a Theodore Walsh novel. Ph: Daniel L. Fapp. Cast: William Holden, Nancy Olson, Barry Fitzgerald, Jan Sterling, Lyle Bettger.

Unseen, The
Par 1945. Prod: John Houseman. Dir: Lewis Allen. Scr: Hagar Wilde, Raymond Chandler, Ken Englund, from an Ethel Lina White novel. Ph: John F. Seitz. Cast: Joel McCrea, Gail Russell, Herbert Marshall.

Upturned Glass, The
Univ / Rank (UK) 1947. Prod: Sydney Box, James Mason. Dir: Lawrence Huntington. Scr: Pamela Kellino, from a John P. Monaghan story. Cast: James Mason, Rosamund Johns, Pamela Kellino.

Vampires, Les
(France) 1915. Dir: Louis Feuillade.

Vérité sur Bébé Donge, La
(France) 1952. Dir: Henri Decoin. Scr: Maurice Aubergé, from the Georges Simenon novel.

Votre dévoué Blake
(France) 1954. Dir: Jean Laviron. Scr: J. Vilfrid, J. Epstein.

Walk a Crooked Mile
Col 1948. Prod: Grant Whytock. Dir: Gordon Douglas. Scr: George Bruce, from a Bertram Millhauser story. Ph: George Robinson. Cast: Dennis O'Keefe, Louis Hayward, Louise Allbritton, Raymond Burr.

We Were Strangers
Col 1949. Prod: S.P. Eagle. Dir: John Huston. Scr: Peter Viertel, John Huston, from the Robert Sylvester novel *Rough Sketch*. Ph: Russell Metty. Cast: John Garfield, Jennifer Jones, Pedro Armendariz, Ramon Novarro, Gilbert Roland.

Web, The
Univ 1947. Prod: Jerry Bressler. Dir: Michael Gordon. Scr: William Bowers, Bertram Millhauser, from a Harry Kurnitz story. Ph: Irving Glassberg. Cast: Edmond O'Brien, Ella Raines, William Bendix, Vincent Price.

Well, The
UA 1951. Prod: Clarence Greene, Leo Popkin. Dir: Leo Popkin, Russell Rouse. Scr: Russell Rouse, Clarence Greene. Ph: Ernest Laszlo. Cast: Gwendolyn Laster, Richard Rober, Maidie Norman.

Werewolf of London, The
Univ 1935. Prod: Stanley Bergerman. Dir: Stuart Walker. Scr: Robert Harris. Cast: Henry Hull, Warner Oland, Valerie Hobson.

Westerner, The
UA 1940. Prod: Samuel Goldwyn. Dir: William Wyler. Scr: Jo Swerling, Niven Busch, from a Stuart Lake story. Cast: Gary Cooper, Walter Brennan, Dana Andrews.

Where the Sidewalk Ends
Fox 1950. Prod / Dir: Otto Preminger. Scr: Ben Hecht, Victor Trivas, Frank P. Rosenberg, Robert E. Kent, from the William L. Stuart novel *Night Cry*. Ph: Joseph LaShelle. Cast: Dana Andrews, Gene Tierney, Gary Merrill, Tom Tully, Bert Freed, Karl Malden.

Whirlpool
Fox 1949. Prod / Dir: Otto Preminger. Scr: Ben Hecht, Andrew Solt, from a Guy Endore novel. Ph: Arthur Miller. Cast: Gene Tierney, Richard Conte, José Ferrer, Charles Bickford.

White Heat
WB 1949. Prod: Louis F. Edelman. Dir: Raoul Walsh. Scr: Ivan Goff, Ben Roberts, from a Virginia Kellogg story. Ph: Sid Hickox. Cast: James Cagney, Virginia Mayo, Edmond O'Brien, Margaret Wycherly, Steve Cochran.

White Shadows of the South Seas
MGM 1928. Prod: Hunt Stromberg, David O. Selznick, Irving Thalberg. Dir: W.S. Van Dyke, Robert Flaherty (uncredited). Scr: Jack Cunningham, Ray Doyle, John Colton, Robert Flaherty. Cast: Monte Blue, Raquel Torres, Robert Anderson.

Wild One, The
Col 1954. Prod: Stanley Kramer. Dir: László Benedek. Scr: John Paxton, Ben Maddow, from the Frank Rooney novel *The Cyclists' Raid*. Ph: Hal Mohr. Cast: Marlon Brando, Mary Murphy, Robert Keith, Lee Marvin, Ray Teal.

Window, The
RKO 1949. Prod: Frederic Ullman Jr., Dore Schary. Dir: Ted Tetzlaff. Scr: Mel Dinelli, from a Cornell Woolrich story. Ph: William Steiner. Cast: Bobby Driscoll, Paul Stewart, Ruth Roman, Barbara Hale, Arthur Kennedy.

Witness to Murder
UA 1954. Prod: Chester Erskine. Dir: Roy Rowland. Scr: Chester Erskine, Nunnally Johnson (uncredited). Ph: John Alton. Cast: Barbara Stanwyck, George Sanders, Gary Merrill, Jesse White.

Wives Under Suspicion
Univ 1938. Prod: Edmund Grainger. Dir: James Whale. Scr: Myles Connolly, from a Ladislas Fodor story. Cast: Warren William, Gail Patrick, Constance Moore.

Woman in Hiding
Univ 1950. Prod: Michel Kraike. Dir: Michael Gordon. Scr: Oscar Saul, Roy Huggins, from the James Webb novel *Fugitive from Terror*. Ph: William Daniels. Cast: Ida Lupino, Stephen McNally, Peggy Dow, John Litel, Howard Duff.

Woman in the Window, The
RKO 1944. Prod: Nunnally Johnson. Dir: Fritz Lang. Scr: Nunnally Johnson, from a J.H. Wallis novel. Ph: Milton Krasner. Cast: Edward G. Robinson, Joan Bennett, Dan Duryea, Raymond Massey, Edmund Breon.

Woman on the Beach, The
RKO 1947. Prod: Jack J. Gross, W. Price. Dir: Jean Renoir. Scr: Frank Davis, Jean Renoir, from the Mitchell Wilson novel *None So Blind*. Cast: Joan Bennett, Robert Ryan, Charles Bickford, Nan Leslie.

Woman on the Run
Univ 1950. Prod: Howard Welsch. Dir: Norman Foster. Scr: Alan Campbell, Norman Foster, from a Sylvia Tate story. Ph: Hal Mohr. Cast: Ann Sheridan, Dennis O'Keefe, Robert Keith, Ross Elliott.

You Can't Get Away With Murder
WB 1939. Prod: Hal B. Wallis, Jack L. Warner, Samuel Bischoff. Dir: Lewis Seiler. Scr: Robert Buckner, Kenneth Gamet, Don Ryan, from a Warden Lewis E. Lawes play. Cast: Humphrey Bogart, Billy Halop, Gale Page, John Litel.

You Only Live Once
UA 1937. Prod: Walter Wanger. Dir: Fritz Lang. Scr: Graham Baker, Gene Towne. Cast: Henry Fonda, Silvia Sidney, Barton MacLane, Jean Dixon.

Zaza
Par 1939. Prod: Albert Lewin. Dir: George Cukor. Scr: Zoe Akins.
Cast: Claudette Colbert, Herbert Marshall, Bert Lahr.

Ziegfeld Follies
MGM 1946. Prod: Arthur Freed. Dir: Vincente Minnelli (and 5
others). Scr: John Murray Anderson (and 31 others). Cast: Fred
Astaire, Lucille Ball, Lucille Bremer.

Index

This index includes references to titles of films, books, periodicals, articles, songs, poems, and art works as well as to names of directors, writers, actors, cinematographers, and others. Not indexed are authorities cited in notes.